KT-561-403

Contents

Acknowledgements

Stars in My Universe

The Inspiration: Deborah Harry; **The Support Network:** Eric Doeringer, Lorraine, Ron and Marc Holzman, Brendan Hora, Donald Suggs, Brad Lamm, Norman Korpi, Dina Suggs, Nora Burns and Timothy Murphy; **The Mentors:** Craig and Ruthie Gilmore, Evelyn McDonnell, Christopher Bagley, Vickie Starr, Michael Musto, Paul Burston, David A. Keeps, John Palomino (1964–97), Cyndi Stivers and everyone at *Time Out New York*; **The Agents:** Neeti Madan and Sarah Lazin; **The Publisher:** André Deutsch; **The Editor:** Roland Hall; and finally, **Special Thanks To:** Rob Roth, Guy Furrow, Michael Schmidt, Justin Vivian Bond, Romy Ashby, ChiChi Valenti, Lester Bangs, Roberta Bayley, Raquel Bruno, Victor Bockris, Louis A. Bustamante, John Holmstrom, Howdy Do, Barry L. Kramer, David LaChapelle, Glenn O'Brien, John Roecker, Stephen Saban, Fred Schruers, Chris Stein, Mark D.R. Stern, and all the other writers, thinkers, advocates, artists and glitterati who generously contributed to this book.

DEBORAH HARRY

THE BIOGRAPHY

CATHAY CHE

ANDRE
DEUTSCH

This updated edition first published in 2014.
First published in Great Britain in 1999 by

byAndré Deutsch
an imprint of the
Carlton Publishing Group
20 Mortimer Street
London W1T 3JW

1 3 5 7 9 10 8 6 4 2

Printed and bound by CPI Group (UK) Ltd, Croydon, CR0 4YY

Prologue

APRIL 18, 1998

FraggleRock, NYC

Roughly two blocks west of the infamous birthplace of New York's punk scene, CBGB's, a sweaty crowd of young revelers – most of them sporting multi-colored hair and the late-90s grunge uniform of baby tees, shrunken jeans, tattoos and at least one facial piercing – are about to witness the reincarnation of a downtown legend.

The night is called FraggleRock – a monthly music event, about two years old. The traveling party is packed this evening into the anonymous Acme Underground basement. A band comprised of a vocalist with luminous bleached blonde hair and dark roots, and four musicians dressed in black pants, white shirts and skinny ties, take the stage. People who have been waiting for the show to start for more than two hours now, are giddy with anticipation. There is a recorded sound of a phone ringing twice, and the tune is instantly recognizable, even before the rush of the familiar whine – I'm in a phone booth, it's the one across the haaall. The song, 'Hanging On The Telephone', instantly infects the audience with the musical confection that is Blondie.

Well, almost Blondie. Tonight's version is all female – a group of tribute players comprised of assorted members of local girl bands. First there's the Lunachicks' lead singer

Theo Kogan as Deborah Harry; Lunachicks' guitarist Gina as Chris Stein and Luscious Jackson's drummer Kate Schellenbach as Clem Burke; Itchy Kitty Studio's Lydiaemily as keyboard player Jimmy Destri, BETTY's bass player Alyson Palmer and Motochronic's guitarist, Allegra, standing in second-string Blondie members Nigel Harrison, Gary Valentine and Frank Infante.

As the band continues to rock the house, the crowd, a 70:30 percent split in favor of women, bounces around playfully and sings along. The vibe is friendly, with none of the edge of the usual live rock venue – no one is pummeling heads to get closer to the stage, no one is fall-down drunk, and certainly, no one wants to brawl. Comments from the crowd reflect what appears to be a genuine 'feel-good' moment. 'Blondie helped me survive my adolescence,' says a man, clearly a minority in the room as someone over 30. 'But I had to listen to them in secret – my Christian parents would have made me burn the album.' His friend chimes in, 'I love Blondie because I hated disco.' He laughs. 'Even though they did "Heart of Glass", I think they thought [disco] was a joke too. They were always interested in what was new. Blondie is the music that helped say goodbye to the 70s and ring in the 80s.'

A trio of women, ranging in age from 23 to 28, had this to say: 'I think the first album I ever brought was *Parallel Lines* and I still know every word to every song,' says the 28 year old. The youngest in the group adds, 'Even people my age think of Blondie as heroes. And then, the Lunachicks are like my favorite band of right now, so to see Theo and Gina doing Blondie – well, it's pretty much the best night of my life so far.' The third friend interjects forcefully, lest we forget the obvious, 'I loved Blondie because Debbie Harry was so fuckin' cool! I wanted to look like her, I wanted to sing like her and I wanted to live in New York like her.' The 23 year old jokes, giving her pal a nudge, 'Well, at least you got one out of three, babe.'

As the set continues, careening between such Blondie chart-toppers as 'Rapture' and lesser-known singles such as the drop-dead cool 'You Look Good In Blue', there are two people standing anonymously towards the back to whom this spectacle is particularly amusing – Blondie's founders, Deborah Harry and Chris Stein. Flattered by the tribute, Harry and Stein were too curious to stay away. No longer a couple, but still best friends, Harry and Stein are instantly recognizable, even though both now have silver-streaked hair.

After the show, they are escorted into the dressing room to hang out with the tribute players. While their presence went undetected by most people in the crowd, the impersonating musicians were in on the secret. Even for these seasoned professionals, having their idols in the house wreaked havoc on their nerves.

'When I knew we were doing the Blondie Tribute at FraggleRock, I called mutual friends, begging them, Please get Debbie to come!' confesses Theo Kogan. An 11-year veteran of the band the Lunachicks and a downtown punk goddess in her own right, Kogan is often referred to as 'the Debbie Harry of the 90s'. By her own admission, she's a huge Deborah Harry fan. 'But once I knew she was coming and bringing Chris, I was terrified.'

Kate Schellenbach, a native New Yorker, says her love of Blondie propelled her into hanging out at CBGB's at the age of 14. It was on the scene that she first met her Luscious Jackson band mates, along with friends the Beastie Boys, who would help them record their first album. Schellenbach confirms with a laugh, 'Yeah, I think we were all a little star struck that night.'

'The Blondie Tribute was a mad, maniacal mayhem of pure devotion,' says Alyson Palmer, of the once Washington, DC based band BETTY. Palmer credits Blondie with turning her on to the music scene in NYC and inspiring the band to relocate. 'It would have been fantastic just to play Blondie's music – the whole band was so into it anyway. But knowing Debbie was in the house was just magical.'

FraggleRock's founder, Brooke Webster, was thrilled too, although she says it wasn't the first time Harry had dropped by. 'The thing about Debbie and Chris that is so cool is they are very accessible and still enjoy going out to see live music. They keep in touch with what's happening downtown. Debbie had been to FraggleRock a couple of times before – I think she came once with RuPaul [American drag queen TV hostess], but I didn't know she was bringing Chris.' She smiles reflectively. 'Wow. It was especially great for the band. They were so freaked out beforehand, but they really rocked it.'

After the show, Webster arranged for the players to hang out with Harry and Stein privately in the dressing room. Harry, who literally glowed with pride, commented, 'That was fun! They did a great job. And when you see someone else doing your music, you can appreciate it, like, Hey, that was a pretty good song.' The musicians slowly filed in, wiping the sweat from their brows, all circling the room a little timidly, a reaction to being in the same room as their teenage icons.

Palmer later remembers, 'You know, over the years, I've met Debbie and I've performed at benefits with Debbie, but when I came off stage that night, I literally couldn't talk to her,' she says, shaking her head. 'I remember her smiling and radiating warmth like we'd done the right thing, and I'm sure she said positive stuff, but I didn't hear a thing.'

Kogan recalls, 'By the time I got down to the dressing room, Debbie was already there. The first thing she said to me was, You're very brave. VERY brave.' Kogan, who has met Harry a number of times through mutual friends, says anxiously, 'I'm thinking, is that a compliment or does she hate me now? Then we took some pictures and in some of them, she's strangling me!' But Kogan had nothing to worry about. Harry, who had seen Kogan perform with the Lunachicks before, referred to her that night as 'my teen dream'.

After a few minutes of chatter and photographs, some uninvited guests crashed the scene and Harry and Stein were quickly escorted away into the night. Before Harry left however, she said to Kogan, 'Now we have to do a duet!' Kogan laughs, 'I didn't think she was serious, but of course I said, Just name the time and the place.' Kogan got the shock of her life when four weeks later, Harry called her up and asked her to sing back up on two tracks for the Blondie album, *No Exit*.

Schellenbach also got a surprise phone call from Harry about two months after the tribute. 'She called me out of the blue to ask me to play drums for Blondie at an unannounced show. She was like, "Hi Kate, this is Deborah Harry". And I was like, Okay, this is a joke, who could it be? But it was too ridiculous to be fake!' She chuckles, 'She was like, "I hope you don't mind me calling you. We're doing this show and Clem isn't coming. Do you think you could do it?"'

The show at Tramps in New York on 17 July was spectacular, earning the reunited Blondie (minus drummer Clem Burke) a rave review in the *Village Voice*. Schellenbach counts this night as one of the highlights of her career. 'I never got to see Blondie play when I was a fan of theirs in high school, so what could be better than to play with them fifteen years later?'

Schellenbach muses, 'Afterwards, I said to Debbie, you know this is a dream come true, and she was like, "Yeah, it's a dream come true for me too – I'm a big fan of your band." And I was like, "Oh, right. Whatever."' But Harry meant it. When Schellenbach and Luscious Jackson asked Harry to guest star on their album *Electric Honey*, she enthusiastically agreed. Harry's reason? 'Luscious Jackson is a really great band – one of my all time favourites.'

If this warm, accessible, generous Deborah Harry bears little resemblance to Blondie's icy new wave princess – who, before Madonna, was the most famous and most photographed woman of the early 80s – you may have to reconcile yourself with the fact that you don't know who Deborah Harry is any more. Maybe you never knew her. But the woman she was and the woman she is now, are very much alive and living in New York.

Foreword

By Evelyn McDonnell

There are two ways of looking at it:

Deborah Harry brought a pin-up, starlet sensibility to rock and roll,

Or

Deborah Harry brought a punk sensibility to the pin-up/starlet.

Or both.

Deborah Harry wasn't the first rock singer to take her glamour cue from Hollywood. All the girl groups of the 60s did, whether it was the Supremes in their floor-length sequinned gowns (how Audrey Hepburn), the Shangri-Las in their pedal pushers (very Doris Day), or the Ronettes in their tight dresses (Jayne Mansfield anyone?). True, later that decade, folksingers offered women a simple, functional alternative to bustiers and girdles – blue jeans, peasant skirts – and Janis Joplin showed us how to dress wild.

As with Harry, unapologetic sexual desire was part of the Janis package. Joplin created a new sort of sex symbol: raw, brash, Wild West, a woman who could fight you as well as fuck you. Harry tapped into an established icon, into the kind of image that switches off men's brains and turns on their dicks: the sex kitten of 50s girlie mags, the Playboy bunny (a job she once held), the blonde wet dream – Marilyn Monroe. It was a very calculated, purposefully retro move. Harry dyed her brown hair peroxide blonde, and her boyfriend and bandmate Chris Stein sent provocative photos of her to rock 'n' roll fanzines, which published them as centerfolds. It was a move that pissed off many people in New York's percolating 70s punk scene, most infamously Patti Smith, who was busy creating her own new sort of imagery: artsy, androgynous, Joan of Arc in *poete maudite* clothes. After all, Harry had a facial structure that could have made Marlene Dietrich weep. Was it fair for her to be blonde and scantily clad too?

Peroxide is dangerous stuff, a potent chemical weapon. It doesn't just mess with the head it's on; it messes with other people's. If you're not willing to take the plunge, try a blonde wig for a day. People – well, mostly guys – will treat you completely differently. Heads will turn, lips will purse, catcalls will follow. The drag queen, Mistress Formika, once told me she got a whole new insight on the human race, and the daily hassles of being a woman, when she went blonde. That's how Blondie got their name: from all the guys shouting it at Harry, as if she was no longer a person, just a hair color. Blondes don't always have more fun.

But sometimes they do. Women are given so few forms of power in our culture, I say, to quote Janis, 'Get it while you can'. The men who reduce blondes to brainless objects are only trying to bring them to their own level: brain-blinded by blonde. And brainless is something Deborah Harry has never been. That's where, and how, she turned the tables on starletry. To quote film theory, she was never merely the object of the gaze – its passive, powerless victim. Harry always stared right back at the camera, those luminous eyes full, not of submissive desire or even smouldering passion, but radiating fearless, hungry intelligence and a 'fuck you' smirk. There's not a trick this woman didn't think of first. As a matter of fact, she may be too kinky for you.

As this book reveals, Harry was pretty sexually active as a teenager, especially considering the time (the early 60s). Blondie's first single was a love song to a sex offender. As her friends and associates point out, Harry's always quick with the dirty joke or the *double entendre*. She's into science fiction, H. R. Giger, dresses made out of razor blades. Maybe the secret to Harry's goddess-like iconicity is that she made the pin-up star the sexual subject, us mere mortals her objects.

Harry wasn't trying to look exactly like Marilyn – and she wasn't aiming to die sad and on drugs. She left her roots dark; she wore fetishistic, ripped, and yes, androgynous clothes. She was angry, confrontational, bristling with attitude. She was a punk. Yes, she was being ironic, she was deconstructing an image, she was striking a pose. But it's more than that: she wasn't just reacting to something received; she was actively creating.

And still is. When Blondie's fame grew out of control, and was no longer any fun, Harry decided it was more important for her to challenge her fans – and herself – than appease them. Sensationalists and sentimentalists say it was the time she spent nursing Stein out of illness that destroyed Harry's career, but her 15 minutes of fame were already ticking to a close. A decade – an era – was ending; people were henceforth not going to be so patient with a woman who didn't grovel before the camera. But Harry has flourished as an artist out of the spotlight: in movies, as a solo act, performing in her beloved New York nightclubs, singing with the Jazz Passengers. *No Exit*, the 1999 Blondie reunion album, reveals that her voice has grown deeper, perhaps even more sensual. When she sings the hit 'Maria' – a perfect Blondie pop paean – time recycles, and one remembers that the image would have been nothing without the songs.

Maybe, the image wasn't even necessary. 'X–Offender', 'Rip Her to Shreds', '(I'm Always Touched by Your) Presence, Dear', 'Hanging on the Phone', 'I'm Gonna Love You Too', 'One Way or Another', 'Dreaming', 'Heart of Glass', 'Rapture', 'The Tide Is High' – two decades later, the songs are still that good. Harry wrote from the perspectives of people she imagined including, but not limited to, the Blondie character. She told stories; she was a clever but not pretentious lyricist. And she had one of the best bands in rock 'n' roll with her. Over the years, Blondie experimented with musical styles – rap, disco, rock-steady – without losing their knack for pop songcraft, their respect for the Top 40.

A quarter of a century after Blondie's CBGB's heyday, a woman leaves her band and her stage name behind. In the video for her first single as a solo performer, Geri Halliwell – the artist formerly known as Ginger Spice – looks strikingly like Deborah Harry: a knockout. The ex-Spice Girl has the verve, the energy, the looks, and the blonde ambition. Only she's got it all wrong. She's singing about being an image, a fantasy, an object – all the things Harry ripped to shreds. Many, many artists have followed in Blondie's footsteps. Some have even eclipsed Harry in both fame and success ('I'm more famous than successful,' Harry once told me). But none have left as enduring a musical legacy. And none have had Harry's originality, her anger, her attitude.

'Blondie is a group', a late 70s ad campaign for New York's most commercially successful punk group practically pleaded – a futile effort to give Chris Stein, Clem Burke, Jimmy Destri and Gary Valentine their due. Then who's Deborah Harry? This book reveals the story of an actress playing the role of Blondie, the platinum singer for a rock band, a wannabe starlet whose roots are showing because she can't afford a new dye job. Reinventing herself was a very smart idea because when Blondie died, Harry was able to go on living. Who knows, the best may be yet to come.

CHAPTER ONE

The Deborah Harry Interview

PART 1

Interviewing Deborah Harry is hard work. It's not that she's difficult or inarticulate, in fact, she's quite the opposite. The problem certainly isn't a lack of material either. Harry has had an amazing life, full of tremendous highs and lows, with an extremely colorful supporting cast of friends and collaborators. In fact, even her detractors are pretty intriguing – for example, how many people can claim that they were told to get the fuck out of rock 'n'roll by the legendary Patti Smith?

No, the reason that one of the most unconventional and enigmatic pop icons of all time is hard to interview, is that her least favorite subject of discussion is herself. With a celebrity, this is an unexpected challenge. This reluctance stems, in part, from having to respond to the same dozen preposterous questions and statements for the past twenty years. Ask her, 'How does it feel to be a sex symbol?', probably her least favorite of all questions, and you can literally see the lights go down behind her eyes. Autopilot! Ms Harry has left the building.

Good manners play a role as well. For example, ask Harry a question about her relationship with her mother, and she may turn around and ask you about yours. Harry's intelligence drives her to be curious about new subjects, which means that she is always interested in hearing about other people. So you find yourself giving information about yourself to get information about her. To make matters even more awkward, she's genuinely interested in you, which is very flattering, but of no interest to anyone reading this book.

But the most shocking of all realizations is that Deborah Harry isn't wholly convinced that her life's accomplishments and artistic achievements, as yet, are worthy of a volume such as this. In fact, when she was approached about cooperating with this book, she took a look at the outline and pronounced, 'I'm sure it'll be a fascinating book. If only my life was that interesting that'd be really great.'

Always one to crack a joke at her own expense, Harry remains somewhat detached from her own fame. It's not *naiveté* or a lack of self-esteem as much as a healthy sense of perspective and an instinct for self-preservation. After all, for Harry, success has ebbed and flowed over the years, and at this point, everything good and everything bad has been said about her a hundred times.

What she's most comfortable being lauded for is her contribution to Blondie's ground-breaking sound and her other artistic collaborations in music and acting. As clichéd as this may sound, what has always been important to Harry is creative self-expression. Although this is what all artists say, Harry can back it up – she's been at the top of the game and she's turned her back on the fame. Even with the Blondie Reunion in full swing, she's a reluctant pop star.

Harry learned early on that success didn't solve any of her problems. In fact, success compounded them and made them worse. For example, the more money she made, the more money she seemed to owe – to her record label, to her

2

various managers and former managers, to her band mates and former band mates, and finally, to the taxman. Next, new friends and old friends who were falling on hard times came asking for financial help, which she accommodated as best she could.

But then, no amount of success, beauty or fame could help Harry when her partner and Blondie co-founder, Chris Stein, was struck with a rare and mysterious life-threatening skin disease in 1982. Stein recovered by 1985, but in retrospect Harry and Stein could see that the illness was related to the pressures of being in Blondie – the stress, the life on the road, the excesses of rock 'n'roll. Harry and Stein got a big wake-up call.

But the hardships haven't managed to sour Harry. She'd even go through it all again, which is perhaps why she never got bitter. She remains a survivor with a superb sense of humor, tremendous character and integrity, and of course, a face so beautiful, any interviewer might lose their train of thought while speaking with her.

The following excerpts are taken from a series of interviews conducted over a period of a year from February 1998 to February 1999 in New York City. The first interview was done for an article in *Time Out New York* magazine, and the revealing insights it provided into Deborah Harry's character formed the basis of this book. Harry intends to pen her own memoir in the future, and as this generous glimpse into Harry's persona suggests, it will be well worth waiting for.

Regretfully, what can't be captured here is all the different textures of Harry's speaking voice, which range from sexy and breathy to nasal with a slight New Jersey accent, to giddy and childish to really, really, tough and slightly menacing. Her laughter also erupts in multiple tones, from silent chuckles to horsey snorts, to measured heh-heh-hehs to a single, sharp Ha!. But it's important to know that when talking about herself, Deborah Harry laughs a lot.

3

Some of the facts of Deborah Harry's background are still unknown, even to her. But the basics are that she was born on 1 July, 1945 (that makes her a Cancer) in Miami, Florida and adopted at the age of three months by gift shop proprietors, Catherine (née Peters) Harry and Richard Harry. She grew up in the suburbs just outside Patterson, New Jersey, a prototype neighborhood embodying all of the conservatism and repressed morality of America in the 50s.

There is no clue in Harry's reasonably happy childhood as to how or why she would grow up and become so remarkably nonconformist. By all accounts, her parents were loving, and she had one little sister named Martha. She always had that beautiful face and she always sang, although she was shy and introspective. She developed her imagination playing make-believe and dressing up, and also claims she had a few psychic experiences as a child and sometimes heard voices.

Do you think you'll ever find out about your background and who your biological parents are?

No. My father is dead from a heart problem at 74 and my mother refused to meet with me.

So you did try to find them. Did your mother know who you were?

No, she just wouldn't go into it. The detective tried to ask her a few things but I think her exact words were, 'Please do not bother me ever again. I do not want to be disturbed.' He didn't even get anything out about who I was.

When did you do this?

About seven or eight years ago.

4

In early interviews, you said you wouldn't try to contact your biological parents out of respect to your adopted parents.

Well, at one time in my life, it would have been a real emotional thing for me and I hesitated. I couldn't deal with it, but as I got a better perspective on who I was and felt more in touch with myself, I thought, You know, there are some things in life you should not put off. I thought I was doing the right thing, and I still feel I did the right thing for me.

An American comedienne named Reno made a movie about tracking down her biological mother, and sort of had a similar experience. Her mother was this upper-middle class woman with a new family who had never told anyone that she had another baby. It's so intense to think of living with a secret like that, but for women in the 40s, pregnancy outside of marriage was a heavy stigma.

Yeah, I'm sure it was hard. I think on my father's side, I have seven or eight half-brothers and sisters. My father was already married and my mother was not married. She got pregnant and then found out he was married and had all these children. She was heartbroken and she went away, had me and put me up for adoption. I don't know much more than that.

I understand you had a pretty happy childhood but that you hated school.

Yes. I still dread the fall and end of summer, back to work and back to school. That's the worst feeling. I didn't mind learning stuff [in school] but I didn't like the pressure and I didn't like that sinking feeling in my stomach, that scary feeling of facing the unknown. Although now, I really like that scary feeling of facing the unknown [laughs].

Yeah, the only fun thing about the end of summer and a new school year was getting new clothes.

Did you and your mother get along in terms of clothes?

Yes, pretty much. She let me pick whatever I wanted.

Well, she was cool. My mother and I never got along in terms of clothing at all. She wanted me to look like I was a preppy WASP from Connecticut – that was good fashion to her, and I sort of loathed it. I thought it was just awful stuff. I wanted things that were, well, I guess I liked more beatnik stuff. I always wanted to wear black and I wanted things that were tough looking. There was a phase where I wanted to wear big flannel shirts and tight pants, and I always wanted to wear my sweaters backwards. I had clear ideas about what I wanted and it really had nothing to do with the times. So my mother and I never agreed.

Sounds like even back then you wanted to put a twist on convention.

Yes, definitely.

As a girl growing up in the suburbs, often you don't have a lot of outlets to express yourself except through your clothes.

Yeah, make-up, hair and clothes.

Were you always rebelling against being a good girl, or were you a good girl who just liked to wear freaky clothes?

My parents were pretty strict, so I didn't really get to act out too much. I did have regular boyfriends and with them, I could be a bad girl, but I wasn't like a bad girl for the neighborhood or a big slut. I was free thinking and I carried out my free thinking with certain people.

Where did you get your free thinking from? If you look at the decade you grew up in – the 50s, and where you grew up, New Jersey – it's a mystery.

Yeah, I don't know. It was there in me and I just had to be like that, there was no other way. As a kid, I just didn't feel comfortable with the status quo and I was searching for [an alternative] identity.

6

Where you in a rush to become a woman or was puberty a burden to you?

I don't know if I have a clear picture of it. I was very turned-on and very sexual. The idea of being normal was going out with boys on dates and having boyfriends. I don't know if I was burdened by puberty *per se*, but I think was probably burdened by everything, I was so disgusted by the idea of falling into the dating, getting engaged and married thing. I grew up in a very traditional setting and that's what girls did, so I was very twisted around.

Did you have any formal vocal training when you were growing up? You have such a great, velvety voice.

Thank you. No. As a kid, I sang in church – I sang in the choir. After that, as a pre-teen, I was really shy and became a closet case – you know, I'd sing in my room with the radio. I listened to the radio a lot. The radio was a big important part of my life, radio more than records really influenced me. As a kid, I didn't buy a lot of records. I never had much money to spend on records, and radio at that point was really good, really varied.

Did you spend much time in Manhattan as a teenager?

No, but I was always dying to move to the city. I'd sneak in on a Saturday and walk around. Bus fare was like 90 cents then. I'd get in around 10am and everyone was still sleeping and everything was closed. I'd never been in a club or anything so it was all in my imagination, but I thought the [Greenwich] Village was particularly fascinating.

So when did you move to the city? As soon as you could?

Yeah, I moved to New York as soon as I finished [college] in 1965. At the time, I wanted to become a painter, but I eventually gravitated towards music.

7

I read somewhere that you rolled in the mud at the original Woodstock?

Yeah, I did actually, I went to the real Woodstock. It was really, really something to have everybody there. Those were such different times, people were able to mobilize under one momentous idea – Peace and Love. It was a simple enough thing. There were shades of difference, but to pull something that big off – it really was something. There really were no hassles, it was unlike anything I've ever been to. And there were no computers then, it just went out over the line and people came.

SEX, DRUGS AND . . . A POLTERGEIST (1970–74)

So what first gave you the confidence to get up on stage?

I think the thing that really drove me was my fear of having a nervous breakdown at forty [laughs]. Oh my God, I'm going to really hate myself if I don't at least try! There is no way to get over being shy or afraid unless you really force yourself. So fear was a big motivation. And a good one. But I had other motivations – I wanted to express myself and I wanted to reach out somehow . . .

You and your band mates in Blondie used CBGB's in the 70s as your playground and your workshop. That was a time and a scene that we love to romanticize. It seems like everyone knew each other and were inspired by each other . . .

And hated each other [laughs].

Were you conscious of how important it was then?

I don't think initially we were convinced of that. We really became more aware of it when it became press worthy. In the initial stages, everybody was just trying it out, then it became encapsulated and documented. We did a lot of stupid things in that scene, but we had fun. I think it's just like now really. New York City has always been a place where people come and try to get exposure. Musicians come here and play. They play cheaply, they play well, they play badly – they experiment with their performance style. It just so happened that we hit it right. The style of the music was different, politics were changing, the media was changing – a lot of things were changing, and we were right there, doing it.

Is the Ramones song 'Something in My Drink' about you?

Gee, I don't know?!

Music writer [and MTV News anchor] Kurt Loder said that Dee Dee Ramone said that he got drugged one night at CBGB's and someone put something in his drink. Then he wrote a song about it.

And Dee Dee thought it was me?! Really?! He thought I put something in his drink?! Well, he never said anything about it to me.

He told Loder he was hitting on you and the next thing he knew, someone had put something in his drink and he got kicked out of the club for passing out.

God, no. Especially having had it happen to me, I would never do that to anyone else. Someone did it to me once at Studio 54 and it was the most awful experience of my life! It was this horrible, endless night of vomiting and hallucination. I don't know what it was, but it made me really sick, just like food poisoning sick. I wouldn't do that to Dee Dee. I love Dee Dee, but I wouldn't do that to anyone.

Tell us about your poltergeist experiences living in that loft on the Bowery when Blondie was first starting out.

Well, I think the building – it was down near Prince Street on the Bowery, had been a factory, like for child labor in the 1800s. The building had no heat in it and it was sort of a

9

cruel environment. It was never fixed up for living. There was one bathroom in the entire place – it was pretty awful. The ground floor had been turned into the liquor store on the Bowery and we all lived upstairs.

You had some wild times there, like when you found that 200-pound bum taking a 300-pound shit in your doorway?

That was horrible! That was on the bicentennial – that was the bicentennial dump. Boy, that stank! We had to clean it up – it was right on the door step and that was nasty! Anyway [about the poltergeist], Chris said he saw a little boy out of the corner of his eye several times. At the time, we didn't have any money and I use to solder these leaded glass belt buckles – like piece work. I use to do it on the top floor, when it was warm enough, and once something came along and pushed my hand. The hair on the back of my neck just went up – whew! I ran down the stairs and I was like, that's enough of that! From then on, I wouldn't go up there alone. We also had a couple of fire things happen there that were very dangerous. There were bad elements there, and that place was clearly a little haunted. Other people who stayed there said some pretty strange things happened to them too.

So it was specific to that place, it wasn't something that followed you around?

No, nothing like that. I think that you have to be party to something like that. Although, since my mother died [last year], I've felt like she was with me, and a few times, I've felt like she was helping me. I don't know, maybe that's just wishful thinking.

What about psychic experiences?

Well, I've always had this thing where I'd know how something was going to happen, like, Oh, this is going to happen like this, and then it would. That kind of thing happens to me quite often. Like I know how things are going to go. It didn't especially give me a sense of calm though, as I was more nervous back then. It's usually small events, not major things. I'd rather be participating on a sensual level than on a metaphysical level anyway. Now I feel like, I'm living, I'm now, I'm organic – let's be that. That's what my resolve is after all these years of debate.

CHAPTER TWO
Downtown Then

There are many layers to Deborah Harry. On the surface, she's a beautiful, world famous pop star, but her aesthetic, her language and her approach to her work reflect her roots in lower Manhattan, a geographic location which gave rise to a credo commonly referred to as 'downtown'. Downtown in the late 60s and 70s was a particularly colorful, creatively rich time, and Harry gravitated to the center of a number of important scenes. She moved to New York in 1965, right out of college, when she was 20 years old. She was just in time to experience the tail end of the beatnik art scene and the psychedelic, hippy culture happening in a neighborhood South of Houston Street (SoHo). As she said herself, she was actually one of the revelers at Woodstock, and in fact, the legendary outdoor rock concert producer, Artie Kornfeld, was the producer of Harry's first band, The Wind in the Willows.

Harry then became part of the glitter rock scene, what we now think of as the scathing response to the peace and love hippy culture. She was a waitress at a restaurant turned legendary hang-out, Max's Kansas City, serving food to the likes of Andy Warhol and Grace Slick. Drifting and hanging out with rock stars, Harry was, in her own words, 'almost a groupie'. She had an affair with the New York Dolls' lead singer, David Johansen. After about nine months at Max's she moved on to another iconic waitress job, working as a Playboy Bunny. She checked out of downtown at the end of the decade to take control of her life and end an addiction to drugs. She moved to upstate New York, then back in with her parents in New Jersey, and did something which no doubt also gave her a definite advantage in re-creating herself – she went to Beauty School.

Slowly integrating herself back into the chaos and the extreme highs and lows of bohemian life, Harry joined a girl trio called the Stilettos, whose glitter-edged performances were combined with flamboyant, gay cabaret-style camp. The lead singer of the group, Elda Gentile, was Warhol superstar survivor, Holly Woodlawn's, roommate, and the group's first gigs were in a pub called the Boburn Tavern, which just happened to be located on the ground floor of their apartment building. It was through the Stilettos that Harry met her partner in love and music, Chris Stein (see Chapter 7 – he tells the whole story), although they soon departed with young lovers' hubris to form a Warholian edged pop band in 1974 called Blondie.

Through Blondie and just being on the burgeoning punk rock scene at CBGB's on the Bowery, Harry met many artists; famous ones like David Byrne, Patti Smith, the Ramones and Television, and others who ultimately expired before their 15 minutes of fame, like Eric Emerson of the Magic Tramps and dominatrix/ designer/entrepreneur, Anya Phillips. Notoriety with Blondie resulted in Harry flirting with disco and the most celebrated bastion of that sound – Studio 54, a scene all to itself. But fame, fashion and magazine covers aside, throughout the last years of the 70s, Harry never forgot her downtown friends. She and Chris Stein continued to participate in things they just thought were really fun and really cool, including two of the most amusing chronicles of the time – *Punk* magazine, and *Glenn*

O'Brien's TV Party, as well as the groundbreaking night spot – The Mudd Club.

One of the best things about Deborah Harry's success, is that it uncovered the various scenes she'd been a part of, and brought a lot of attention to the sometimes tyrannical, but often sublime, cast of characters who helped inspire her.

THE WIND IN THE WILLOWS

The music video for 'Moments Spent' is a little primitive. The pink and blue animated images – astrological signs and the five elements – water, air, earth and fire, mark it unequivocally as a product of the 60s. Then there's the tell-tale music, a sing-song psychedelic folk ditty with lyrics so sincere, evoking 'magic keys', 'music of the wind' and 'my friend' – that it could be a parody of its time instead of its product. But 'Moments Spent', a song written by Paul Klein and Steve De Phillips and a three minute live action, animation and music project produced and directed by Gerald McDermott, is remarkable for two reasons. First, it was made in November of 1967 – a full year before the Beatles' classic 'Yellow Submarine'. In fact, its creators claim it may well be the first ever music video (that matter is currently being investigated in the Library of Congress). But whether that stake is proven or not, 'Moments Spent' has one major thing going for it – it features a beautiful brunette 22-year-old hippy chick singer named Deborah Harry.

Gerald McDermott, the award-winning children's book illustrator, made 'Moments Spent' in collaboration with a folk group called The Wind in the Willows, founded in 1966 by a former civil rights activist named Paul Klein. Klein, now a business consultant with a degree in psychology, living in St Louis, Missouri, explains how the Willows, who were named after the famous Kenneth Grahame novel, started to come together: 'Debbie Harry was best friends in High

School with my former wife, Wendy Simon. Wendy's older sister, Beth Ann was a very gifted artist – sort of a crossover from the 50s beat generation into the 60s. She was a graduate student who studied at Rutgers University, or what was then known as Douglas College for Women, with Andy Warhol, Roy Lichtenstein and that whole bunch of people who became the founders of SoHo.'

According to Klein, Beth Ann was instrumental in first introducing both Harry and himself to SoHo, a fertile bohemian playground for artists in the mid 60s. 'We would go to SoHo to visit Beth Ann and I'd bring my guitar because I always liked to play. There were all these jam sessions going on – some of them would last up to twelve hours at a time, and all kinds of people would hang out and step in, like Chick Corea and Sun Ra and Lou Reed.' At these jam sessions, Klein says he met artist Walter de Maria and a group of people started jamming together in his loft. '[Debbie] was just out of school and this was a very cool scene emerging. We were hanging out a lot and I started to notice this little nasally voice. I thought, if you double track that voice, it would be a very interesting effect. So eventually, Walter, my old friend from school, Steve De Phillips, Debbie and I got together and formed a group that did very silly stuff, although every once in a while, we'd fall back on our rock roots.' Then in 1967, Klein brought in experienced Julliard graduates and musicians Wayne Kirby and Ida Andrews. 'So then we had a group of people who together could play like 20 different instruments on stage and create a lot of effects, and that was the birth of the Willows.'

If it was Beth Ann Simon who first drew Harry and Klein into the SoHo scene, tragically, it was her death in 1967 that Klein says was indirectly responsible for giving the Willows their first break – an encounter with manager Peter Leeds. Leeds would later become the controversial manager of Blondie. But it's a bit of a twisted story. Klein explains, 'Beth Ann was experimenting with all kinds of things and she got into macrobiotics – we all did, but she was the woman who starved herself to death on the Macrobiotic Diet.' An aspiring writer fresh out of college named Robert Christgau, who would later become a distinguished music writer and the Music Editor of the lefty weekly newspaper, the *Village Voice*, ended up doing a story on Beth Ann's death. After the story, Klein and Christgau stayed friends. Klein then suggested that Christgau chronicle the development of The Wind in the Willows as the basis for a story on how a young band gets started in New York. Klein says, 'Bob [Christgau] hanging out and thinking about doing this story on us helped us get some attention, which is how Peter Leeds ended up coming to see us. Leeds looked at us and thought – they've got the harmonies of the Mamas & Papas, they can play all these instruments – I want to sign them.'

Robert Christgau confirms this story, although he adds that part of why he and Klein initially stayed friends is that all of them – he, Harry and Klein – lived on the same block on 7th Street between Avenues C and D. Christgau also clarifies that it was a press agent named Dominic Scicilia, now deceased, who brought Leeds into the picture. 'Dominic Scicilia was one of my first friends in the music business. He was a brilliant guy and very smart. He liked [the Willows] and he got them Leeds.'

Leeds got the Willows a record deal with Capitol Records and their self-titled debut was released in 1968. Klein says, 'And the rest is history, including the mistake of getting involved with Kornfeld who went off to do Woodstock instead of producing the group.' Klein says the first Willows album failed to capture their magic, more of which he says is in evidence on the Willows' second album, which was never released and subsequently disappeared. 'We ended up producing it ourselves. It was done for Capitol – eleven songs. We don't know who has it – maybe it's Kornfeld's personal property.' The album also featured flirtations with the 50s girl group sound, high camp and a song co-written with Harry in 1969 called '19th Child' or 'Buried Treasure'. Ironically, the lyrics to that song contain several references to an incoming high tide, foreshadowing Blondie's later hit cover of 'The Tide Is High'.

Something led us to this spot to dig for buried treasure
The trove it lay, beneath the sand, ten feet from rising
    water
My friend and I dug hastily, we knew the tide was
    coming
We hit upon a solid form when the rising tide came
    spilling. . . .

Klein's only copy of any finished music from the second album is an acetate of the song 'Quite Respectable Older Lady'. Meanwhile, the first Wind in the Willows CD was re-released in 1998 by Drop Out Records in Australia. Klein says he bought a copy of it and it includes a sticker on the case which says boldly 'featuring Debbie Harry'. Klein says a record store clerk in St Louis informed him that it's selling so well, it's in its third printing. 'Of course,' says Klein, 'none of us has seen a penny from it.'

Klein is also slightly baffled by how much Harry's involvement in the Willows has been played down. 'In the footage of Wind in the Willows that VH1 used [in the 1998 *Blondie: Behind The Music* documentary], where Debbie is chasing my toddler son into the ocean, she looks kind of frumpy. But in 'Moments Spent', you can see the all the antecedents of her later style,' says Klein. '[VH1] also said she was just a back-up singer, but that's wrong – she was an equal singer on just about all cuts. Get the CD – you can hear it for yourself.'

In Christgau's estimation, although he says that Paul Klein had quite a presence, he describes the Willows as 'not a bad band, but they weren't anything special', although he concedes they weren't as goofy as they came off looking after their first album was released. He describes Harry from that time in even more lackluster terms: 'She was sort of mousy looking, pretty but not someone you'd really notice. She would just sort of go up and do her little thing but she was not really there.' Christgau, who would later be very impressed by Harry, admits that Klein saw something in her that he didn't. He also gives Klein credit for having two women in the Willows: 'At that time, rock was a very male preserve, so the idea that there were two women in a rock band and one of them didn't sing and played an instrument – that was pretty unusual. I have to give Paul credit for being sufficiently open minded.'

Klein says, 'It's funny because Bob thinks of Debbie from the Willows as a non-persona, but I think, how could you have missed her? The group had a real charm and part of that charm was Debbie – no doubt in my mind.' Klein also remembers that she was shy, but says that was part of her appeal. 'Who were the women singers who were emerging at that time? Women like Grace Slick who were anything but reserved and quiet and soft, but Debbie captivated people's attention even then. Look at "Moments Spent" – all of it is there.'

Klein puts on his psychological hat and says, 'People create their myths and we're all a bit revisionist about our histories. Peter Leeds was her first manager. For better or worse, Peter wanted to make it seem like Debbie's roots were in the CBGB's scene and sort of muddy the waters of her past. It's a great phoenix rising story the way it's been told over the years, which is that she didn't learn anything from the Willows and it had no influence on her. But she was already taking voice lessons at the time and she was exposed to a lot of Dada, tongue in cheek lighthearted cynicism, which I think surfaces later [in Blondie].'

Disheartened by the reception to the first Willows album, the band broke up in 1969. Harry and Klein haven't been in touch, possibly as part of the fallout between Klein and his

18

ex-wife, Harry's friend Wendy Simon. However, Christgau and Harry soon crossed paths again. 'I didn't see her for years and then I ran into her on Second Avenue in 1975. Of course, I remembered her from the Willows. She said, "Come and see me, I'm in a new band."'

CBGB'S

Robert Christgau ended up seeing Debbie Harry's new band, Blondie, at CBGB's, the legendary center of the New York punk scene. He recalls, 'I was dubious at first because I thought she couldn't sing', but says he was pleasantly surprised by Blondie. 'I mean, there were a lot of cute punk bands like Milk 'n' Cookies and The Mumps playing CB's and Blondie was one of them. It would be fair to say that they were not taken very seriously at CB's in the early days, but I would say that from the first, Blondie had something the others didn't.' Christgau's wife, also a writer and a veteran of the New York music scene, Carola Dibbell adds, 'Yeah, but it was hard to know what it was. There was a lot of mess, and somewhere in that there'd be something that would make you want to come again. The other thing was, you'd go to CBGB's and in one night you got Blondie and everyone else.' Christgau finishes the thought, 'That would be a weekend – Friday and Saturday – Talking Heads, Television and Blondie.'

Dibbell has a theory that part of the change in Harry had something to do with her meeting Blondie co-founder Chris Stein, although she doesn't mean to imply that he was the brains of the outfit and Harry was just the beauty. Dibbell says, 'they seemed to come together and then everything happened – it was both romantic and artistic. There was an environment there with the two of them.' Christgau says he suspects the change had to do with her coming back from a down period between the Willows and Blondie:

'Between the Willows and Stilettos/Blondie, I understand she'd been a drug addict and survived something very close to degradation and come out on the other side.'

Harry has openly admitted the years between the Willows and the Stilettos were especially tough ones for her. She self-medicated herself with a variety of drugs including heroin, and actually moved out of the city and back in with her parents to find herself again. But as she says in the previous chapter, a fear of a lifetime of regrets drove her towards the limelight. The stage she found, after meeting Chris Stein in the Stilettos and then forming Blondie with him, was CBGB's.

A lot of ink has been spilled writing about CBGB's – it's impossible to talk about American punk without it. Unlike most of the legendary clubs of that era, CBGB's is still standing and still a live music venue. Although today, try as these new bands might to capture the spirit of punk legends such as Television, the Ramones, Patti Smith, Talking Heads and, of course, Blondie – these days the audiences are filled with yahoos and tourists taking pictures of each other in the club's infamous graffitied bathroom. But in its heyday from 1974 to 1978, it was, as many have described it, a music scene as vital and vibrant as Liverpool in the 60s or Seattle in the 90s.

The bar itself was the brain child of an eccentric entrepreneur named Hilly Kristal. As the legend goes, Kristal had managed the jazz club the Village Vanguard in the 50s and had originally purchased the 315 Bowery space with the intention of turning it into something similar. He opened his new jazz club in 1969, and closed it in 1972. A year later he reopened it as a club with broader musical horizons called Country, Blue Grass, Blues & Other Music From Under Ground, or CBGB & OMFUG. Later, it became known as CBGB's, or as some of the *cognoscenti* refer to it – just CB's.

Music journalist Lisa Robinson started one of the publications that best documented the CB's phenomenon as it was happening – *Rock Scene*, which she now lovingly describes as a 'very underground, cheap, ink came off on your hands type magazine' in early 1975. She remembers it as a golden time. 'Without being pretentious or too serious, because it was also just fun, to all of us, it was the center of the world. We were out every night somewhere we belonged, you could see people play all night long. Television would play four hours at a time – I know that sounds dreary but it wasn't – it was great. It was as important as people now think it is – it really changed things.'

Ironically, as one of the most prolific journalists of that time – an editor for not only *Rock Scene* but *New Musical Express* and *Hit Parader* – Robinson says a big part of why the CBGB's scene was able to develop was because the press, a least at first, didn't know anything about it. Robinson says, 'It was a culturally exciting time in New York. It was before AIDS, before real estate prices went sky high – so "misfits" still gravitated to the city. The 70s were a much freer time and when you're not frightened or repressed in any way, you're open to develop in every way. It was also fun for us because we were young. I'm sure kids are still having fun, but not in the same way because if someone has a band or opens a club now, it gets written up immediately and scenes don't have time to breathe and develop.'

It would seem that CBGB's nurtured almost as many music journalists as it did bands. Also hanging out on the scene with Christgau, Dibbell and Robinson was a reporter from a Long Island newspaper called *Good Times* named Kurt Loder. Loder became a *Rolling Stone* writer and is now familiar as a face on the music sensation of the 80s – MTV. '[Music writer] David Fricke worked [at *Good Times*] too, so we just started going to CBGB's every night until 3am,' Loder remembers. While he agrees that it was a very important playground for bands in development, he also recalls

21

that CB's 'was a pit'. He laughs, 'There was a dog running around, and at one point, I think Hilly was actually living there too.'

Loder also reminds us that not every band from that time was a gem, 'There were also bands like The Blinding Headaches who were so terrible that you never hear about them.' But Loder believes the magic of it was not only did the press fail to see the merits of the rising punk scene, but the music business kept its distance too. 'It was low key, record companies didn't own it, didn't manipulate it – in fact, they hated it because punk records didn't sell. So no one was manufacturing it and selling it to us.' The normally placid and deadpan Loder gets quite animated when talking about these times: 'It was just so direct and fresh to go see these bands. They'd just be walking around and you'd bump into them and they'd talk to you, until it was time to go on. Then they'd just get up on stage and play – it was fabulous.'

If you passed through the doors of CBGB's sometime during its prime, it's likely that you encountered Roberta Bayley, although maybe you never knew her name. 'I worked the door at CBGB's until 1978. 'I got the job because I was going out with Richard Hell who was in Television, and Terry Ork [Television's manager] had been doing the door and one day he just said, Why don't you do it?' According to Bayley, CBGB's had a very casual door policy: 'It was $2 to come in so if you had $2, you were in. It wasn't an exclusive policy but you'd be surprised to what lengths people would go to avoid paying. As it was the only way the bands got paid, I was pleasantly tough about it.'

Bayley's main claim to fame however are her photographs from the time, which have been used to illustrate many articles and books about the scene. It all began for Bayley, who had studied photography in High School, on a whim: 'I didn't have career aspirations, I just wanted to document that scene. Then the bands wanted someone to take pictures of them and there weren't a lot of people around who wanted to do it. I was a part of it and they trusted me, so I ended up doing the Ramones' first cover, Richard Hell's first cover and Johnny Thunders' *Heartbreakers* cover.'

Bayley remembers CBGB's best as 'just the friendly, local place to hang out'. But, she says, she doesn't feel there's been a definitive work about that period. 'A lot of the books have been balanced, but *Please Kill Me: The Uncensored Oral History of Punk* put a lot of emphasis on the drug aspect, which was always there, but it wasn't why we were there. Why were people at CBGB's? It wasn't to get drugs, it was because they were in bands.'

The CBGB's scene, like most creative movements, didn't last very long. The scene dispersed and the lucky ones moved on by 1978 or 1979, but the ties among CBGB's graduating class would remain strong.

PUNK MAGAZINE

Roberta Bayley's pictures of the stars of the CBGB's scene didn't just lounge around in drawers until the punk nostalgia resurgence of the 90s. Starting in 1975, they were first published in what has to be one of the godfathers of all 'zines, and the publication that coined the name of the attitude it defined and celebrated – Punk. The book – *Punk: The Original, A Collection of Material From the First, Best and Greatest Punk 'Zine of All Time*, gives a good idea of what punk was all about. A cover illustration from issue #16 featuring the exploding head of a *Saturday Night Fever* clone makes a pretty clear anti-disco statement. Yet, the Patti Smith graffiti contest, in which readers drew on a provided picture of Smith (issue #5) would suggest that *Punk* refused to take its own icons too seriously as well (either that or they considered Smith to be a little too hippy-ish).

23

Interviews with Sid Vicious in issue #14 and Johnny Rotten in issue #8 imply that *Punk* wasn't interested in drawing a line between what was happening on both sides of the Atlantic. And interviews with AC/DC and the Bay City Rollers in issue #14 suggest *Punk* wasn't a snob on the pop front either. Still, a naked picture of Deborah Harry with a guitar and a centerfold of her as 'Punkmate' of the month in issue #4 makes it clear that *Punk* wasn't stupid and it wasn't sexless. It's also interesting to note that those pictures of Harry were taken by *Punk* contributing photographer, Chris Stein.

John Holmstrom first cooked up the idea for *Punk* with two school chums from Connecticut, including his active *Punk* partner, Eddie 'Legs' McNeil (who 20 years later would co-author the book *Please Kill Me: The Uncensored Oral History of Punk*). Holmstrom, who was responsible for *Punk*'s excellent cartoons and graphic design, is now the publisher of *High Times* magazine. Holmstrom recalls, 'We started *Punk* in October 1975. It just all sort of came together and we moved into this storefront on 10th Avenue and 32nd Street I had found, which we called the *Punk* dump. It was always going to be some comics and some rock music.' Holmstrom says that McNeil came up with the idea for the name, but Holmstrom says he had already heard the term 'punk rock' at the time. To this day, he says McNeil claims he originated the term 'punk'. Holmstrom, who no longer has contact with McNeil continues: 'We interviewed the Ramones first – they were the main band we wanted to talk to. They thought they were going to be in the equivalent of *16 Magazine* and that they were going to break as the next teeny bopper group.'

A cover of *Punk* didn't make the Ramones the next Bay City Rollers, but it did give them a certain notoriety in the CBGB's scene. Enough that other bands began asking to be featured in it too. Chris Stein was among the first to really get *Punk* and what it was trying to do. Holmstrom and Stein were about the same age and had both attended the School of Visual Arts in the early 70s, and they clicked right away. Stein had ideas for Holmstrom that would not only help Blondie but would help *Punk*. 'Chris was one of the smartest guys I'd ever met,' says Holmstrom. 'I mean, I went to talk to other groups and they'd be like, "Hi, write something about me so I can be famous". Chris was like, "What can I do for you?"'

Holmstrom recalls that the first thing Stein did was take pictures of Harry modeling the *Punk* t-shirt. 'Next, he offered to take pictures of Debbie for the centerfold – 'Punkmate of the Month.' Holmstrom says that centerfold really put Blondie on the map and that Stein later told him that the centerfold helped Blondie get their first record contract. Stein's involvement with *Punk* continued. 'Chris was amazing – some of the pictures he took of Debbie for us and for *Creem* were genius. He turned out to be the best photographer we had working for us and Debbie was by far the most beautiful woman we'd ever seen in rock 'n'roll.'

Holmstrom also recalls that Harry and Stein were friendly and just really fun to hang out with. 'One year – 1976 – Eddie [Legs McNeil] and I were leaving the *Punk* dump on New Year's Eve, we had next to no money and we're like, "What are we going to do?" We run into Jimmy [Destri from Blondie] on the street and he says, "Hey, we're going to play Central Park – you guys want to be our road- ies?" So we were like, Okay, so we end up helping them schlepp the equipment up there and set up.' Holmstrom remembers that they were all set up by 10 p.m. and still, no one was there. 'Then suddenly, at midnight, all these people showed up and these people dressed up as giant dancing hands came out into the audience and we were all dancing with them and it was great. That was just what it was like to hang out with Blondie.'

Holmstrom has another story specifically about Harry and Stein, '*Punk* were guests at the First Annual World

Sleaze Convention in Wilmington, Delaware. Some weird person out there who had organized it offered to pay our transportation and put us up. So Eddie and I go down there, and Debbie and Chris insist on coming down in their car – the Blondiemobile. And they bring Anya [Phillips] with them.' Holmstrom says that the honored guest of the convention was The Egg Lady [of John Water's fame]. 'Well, we get there to find out it's just a bunch of transvestites. So Eddie decides we should all meet at this bar, which turns out to be a gay disco! So we're hanging out in this place and miserable and Eddie gets lucky, picks up this girl and goes back to the hotel. So we're sitting there and we decide, we have to get him.' Holmstrom says the group, which also included Television's manager, Marty Thau, came up with the idea to break into the room while McNeil was having sex and throw ice all over him. 'We get back to the hotel, and we go to the ice machine and fill up the buckets. We have these nylons over our heads, we walk in there and throw ice on him and Chris took pictures of the whole thing.'

Roberta Bayley, who was *Punk*'s main photographer, also recalls fun, casual times just hanging out with Harry and Stein, even after Blondie were a hit. 'During the big New York blackout of 1977, I called *Punk* magazine and John Holmstrom was holed up there working and totally broke because you couldn't get any money out of the bank. He had to go down to the deli and beg them for a sandwich.' Bayley offered to meet up with him and the pair traveled uptown to visit Bayley's father who was visiting from out of town. 'Like other people have said [about the blackout], it really did create this positive thing between people ... So the power came back on uptown first and we called Chris and Debbie at their loft on 17th Street to see if the power was back on downtown, and they are like, We have power – come on down! So we get there and Iggy Pop comes over and it's really nice and relaxed. They really did keep their friends downtown even though they were doing other things.' Bayley laughs, 'I mean, when Mick Jagger called and said he wanted to see their new house, they didn't say, Oh no, I'm too busy with my real friends, but they didn't differentiate between their new famous friends and their old ones.'

GLENN O'BRIEN'S TV PARTY

Glenn O'Brien was yet another music journalist who was on the CBGB's scene, but he has one claim that no other there can make – he was the first to write about Deborah Harry and Blondie. At least, in any context that people outside of the punk scene would see – in his influential *Interview* magazine 'Beat' column. 'I probably wrote about them even before *Punk*. I started my column in 1976 and I just thought they were one of the best bands around – great songs, good musicians and Debbie was gorgeous.' O'Brien, who was always into music and also hung around Max's Kansas City before CBGB's, actually remembers seeing the Stilettos as well. 'But I didn't meet them until they were Blondie. I actually remember the exact night – someone introduced us at CBGB's and they knew my writing, which I was thrilled about, and liked their band, so we hit it off. We were all also really big potheads.'

O'Brien himself is quite a legendary character on the scene, known not only for his music writing, quick wit and dapper fashion sense, but his rabid womanizing. 'Anyway, when I started my cable show, *Glenn O'Brien's TV Party* in 1978, Chris was my co-host.' O'Brien says *TV Party* was inspired in part by Hugh Hefner's television show in the early 60s, originally called *Playboy's Penthouse* and later, *Playboy After Dark*. 'The concept of the show was to have a talkshow with entertainment, which was like a party with people hanging out, but also like a political party.'

Apparently it was as amusing as it sounds. 'We had a house band led by Walter Steding, and people like John Lurie, Robert Fripp and David Byrne were on pretty regularly. *TV Party* was where a lot of people first met – that's how Chris and Debbie first met rapper Fab Five Freddy, artist [Jean Michel] Basquiat and the Swiss photographer Edo, who did several of their album covers.'

While *TV Party* only aired in Manhattan on cable access channel J, it did have quite a following. O'Brien: 'To my great pleasure, when [David] Letterman first started his show, he talked about *TV Party*. Paul Shaffer asked, What's the greatest TV show of all time?, and Letterman said, Definitely *Glenn O'Brien's TV Party*.' The show ran weekly from 1978 to 1982, and O'Brien and Stein pretty much paid for it out of their own pockets, although towards the end of the run, they accepted ads from clubs like Danceteria, The Mudd Club, The Pyramid and the Peppermint Lounge.

Unfortunately, it's hard to relive it all now as *TV Party* was pretty low-tech and the sound is particularly poor on many of O'Brien's tapes, but Harry and Stein appear frequently, once or twice Harry would sing a song, some-times she'd direct the show, but mostly they're just hanging out – two arty bohemians among a colorful tribe. It's a little odd considering that, at the time, Blondie was huge in Europe. 'Blondie got mobbed in London at record store signings but it wasn't like that here in New York. New York is still a pretty cool place to be if you're a celebrity. Debbie and Chris also had a very down to earth attitude and that diffuses a lot of that treatment.' O'Brien also says that although there were petty jealousies in the scene, on the whole people felt like Blondie had paid their dues and people respected them for it. 'I don't think people begrudged them their success.'

When Blondie was on tour, sometimes O'Brien stopped *TV Party* and ran reruns, or sometimes Stein would send in Super 8 footage of Blondie on the road and he'd air that. 'But when they were in town, they still hung out, even when they had the number one single.' In the *TV Party* episode dated 4.24.79, Stein and O'Brien comment on 'Heart of Glass' being the number one single in America. But Stein and Harry didn't just appear to be unchanged by fame, in some ways their lives were not altered by Blondie's success: 'I had no money and neither did they. In fact, the week they had the number one record in the country, they borrowed $100 bucks from me,' says O'Brien.

A particularly interesting aspect of *TV Party* was that the show accepted on-air phone calls from random callers. In one of the last episodes of *TV Party*, dated 6.27.82, Harry – a brunette further disguised by dark glasses – and Stein had a hostile, but ultimately hilarious, interaction with several callers. Early on in the show, they played a tape of their new single 'Island of Lost Souls', and Harry sort of mouthed along with the lyrics. Then the calls started to come in:

Caller 1: *It's not so exciting having Miss Harry singing along with a tape.*
Stein: [Explains that it wasn't a performance]
Caller 1: *Don't you think Blondie sold out when they did 'Heart of Glass'?*
Stein: No, it was a mark in history. It brought black and white music together. We weren't thinking about selling out, we were thinking about Kraftwerk and Euro-electric music.
Caller 2: *Can Blondie still sell out gigantic stadiums?*
Stein: We'll know soon enough.
Caller 3: *Debbie, would you like to have a holograph made of yourself?*
Harry: We did already, for the 'Tide Is High' video.
Caller 4: *[the sound of fake crying] What happened to her hair!*
[Harry says nothing]

Caller 5: [Reads a love poem he wrote]
Stein: Oh, that's nice.
Caller 6: Will you dye your hair blonde again?
Everyone ignores remark.
Caller 7: [asks for band advice].
Stein: Read our book. It's all in there – it took us five or
      six years to get going and seven or eight years to
      make money.
Caller 8: Do you have a cat named Scumbag?
Stein & Harry: No.
Caller 9 [frantic]: Who is that woman at the end?
Stein: [pause] Oh, that's Frank.
Caller 9: The woman!
Harry: [in deep voice] Frank.
Caller 9: She looks like Debbie Harry.
Harry: I get that a lot.
Caller 9: But you're prettier.
[Harry looks amused]
Caller 10: Fuck you! Suck my dick!

The pair then go on to discuss their upcoming Hunter
Tour, which, of course, would be Blondie's last for almost 20
years, as a skeletal Stein was about to discover he was
suffering from a potentially fatal skin disease.

ANDY WARHOL

Glenn O'Brien's TV Party wasn't the only New York television show Deborah Harry was a regular on, according to
Vincent Fremont, who worked with Andy Warhol from
1969 until his death and was the producer of his various
television projects: 'Debbie Harry was a semi-regular
contributor to Andy's television projects – *Fashion* (1979–80)
which later became *Andy Warhol's TV* (1980–82) and *Andy
Warhol's 15 Minutes* (1985–7).' Fremont, who still works with

the Andy Warhol Foundation as exclusive agent to Warhol's drawings, paintings and sculptures, recalls, 'The second episode of *Fashion*, which aired on Manhattan Cable channel 10, was an episode called 'Debbie Harry and Friends' made in 1979. Then, she did the last show, the memorial show of *Andy Warhol's 15 Minutes* on MTV in 1987. She and Chris were sitting outside, and they did intros for the segments, most of which were shot before Andy died. Then we showed clips from his memorial and they spoke really passionately about him.' According to Fremont, Harry also did voice overs for *Fashion* and was one of two announcers on *Andy Warhol's TV*. Then she did on-camera introductions for *Andy Warhol's 15 Minutes*.

An episode of *Andy Warhol's 15 Minutes* from 1987 shows Harry, in all of her *Rockbird*-era glory, introducing a segment on an 'up and coming actress', and singing her praises. It's a declaration made, like a lot of Harry's statements, slightly ahead of its time – she was referring to a very young and raw Courtney Love. Harry stayed involved in Warhol's television projects even during Chris Stein's illness. It may in fact be some of the only work she did during that turbulent time.

Fremont believes that Harry participated in the TV projects in part because it was casual and easy for her to do, and in part, out of loyalty to Warhol. Clearly, Deborah Harry and Andy Warhol were very fond of each other and Warhol's ideas had an enormous influence on the presentation of Blondie, but the extent of their actual friendship is hard to determine. Harry is mentioned only a few times in his collected diaries, but Fremont explains that this is possibly because the diaries were edited. His impression was that Warhol liked Harry very much. 'The reason Andy liked her and they got along so well is that she was unpretentious, and actually, so was Andy. She was very comfortable around Andy – she really liked him and got him. Plus, she was very bright, had a great sense of humor and of course, Andy liked blondes.'

Fremont believes that further evidence of Warhol's affection for Harry can be found in his portrait of her: 'Andy made more than just the standard two 40' x 40' portraits of her and he made them slightly bigger than the usual portraits – 42' square. That is very significant.'

As has been repeated a million times, Warhol allegedly called Harry 'my favorite pop star', but no one seems to recall exactly when he said it. Fremont wasn't sure, neither was Warhol photographer, Christopher Makos, who uses the phrase in a caption in his second book, *Makos' Warhol*. 'It was probably in 1978 or 1979,' says Makos looking at the picture, 'Oh, she looks great – she's a real Catherine Deneuve type – those bones.' He admits he's not sure when Andy muttered the phrase, but he's not being difficult, it seems everyone from that time has a problem remembering dates. Makos, in a hilarious, caustic tone, adds, 'You'll have to ask me questions and hope it triggers something. That's why I took pictures my dear – then you don't have to remember, you can just let it go.'

Makos says he first met Harry and started taking pictures of her at CBGB's in 1977 for his first book, *White Trash*: 'I went to down to CBGB's and I focused in on what was fascinating visually and she was it. In a sea of grunge and all these unattractive kids, here was this very sexy little blonde thing. So I met her then and I'd call her up and we were friendly and stuff.'

Makos says he was actually supposed to do the pictures for *Making Tracks: The Rise of Blondie*, Harry's autobiography with Chris Stein and Victor Bockris, 'But it became too difficult and Chris ended up doing the pictures.' When asked about why Warhol liked Harry so much, Makos pauses: 'Well, she was so New York and she had that Warholian triple process blonde – a blonde is a blonde is a blonde. And she had that presence, which she still has.'

Makos, like Fremont, sort of lost touch with Harry in the 90s, but Makos has quite a souvenir of the last time he saw her perform in New York. 'She was singing these moody jazz songs in the basement of Barneys [department store], and well, I was trying to enjoy it but maybe it was just hard to buy that anyone as white as her could go through that kind of suffering. But maybe she did with Chris [when he got sick] and she couldn't sing those light, pop songs anymore. She's very real, very honest and very private in a way.' It's funny that he says this last line considering what he's about to say next. 'But that night, I got the only picture of Debbie Harry's pussy. Yeah, she was sitting crossed-legged on the floor and not wearing any underwear and when I looked at the contact sheets, there it was – Harry pussy!' he laughs, 'Now that's a hanging-out story. Of course, I told her about it and promised I wouldn't publish it.'

Bob Colacello, the editor of *Interview* magazine from 1971 to 1983 and now special correspondent for *Vanity Fair*, has his own ideas about why Warhol was drawn to Harry. 'I think the reason Andy was drawn to her – why we were all drawn to her – is because she had a kind of glamour that wasn't so common in the 70s. There was a real rejection of glamour in the 70s in Hollywood. Most of the glamour was in the fashion business and that's when the designers really came to the forefront as personalities – Valentino, Halston, Calvin Klein, Yves St Laurent – those were the glamorous people, not the movie stars. And some rock stars were glamorous like Mick Jagger and David Bowie and Debbie Harry. She was a cool hip diva in the way that movie stars used to be.'

Colacello, who describes himself as more of an uptown person and the 'right-wing' person at the Factory, says he never set foot in CBGB's. From all accounts, Warhol didn't like it much either. 'Debbie made punk more palatable without making it sweet or saccharine or sentimental, she just made it more human and appealing to people like me.' Harry appeared on the cover of *Interview* magazine only once – in 1979, but Colacello recalls that it was 'one of our hit covers'. After that, Colacello remembers Harry and Stein coming to the Factory for lunches. 'This was the Factory at 860 Broadway – we moved in there in 1975 and stayed until 1983. We would have lunches there about three times a week. Very glamorous, very haphazard but very effective from a business point of view. We might have Halston or Marisa Berenson or Debbie Harry and then we'd invite potential advertisers for *Interview* and some portrait clients for Andy.'

Apparently, Harry could always be counted on in this capacity. 'We had this stable of *Interview* cover girls who we'd call up whenever we had to do interviews, like for *People* magazine or something. They'd want to come by the Factory and see people who had been in the magazine. I could always count on Debbie Harry and Paloma Picasso because while they were both major stars, they never acted like stars. While her image had a diva quality to it, she never behaved like a Marilyn Monroe – she was always on time and just nice and easy to have around. She wasn't that talkative – Chris did most of the talking, but she'd make these cracks that were really funny. She was great to have around and she and Andy had a great rapport.'

Colacello has two distinct memories of hanging out with Harry outside of the Factory. The first concerns a visit that Harry made to the infamous Studio 54: 'I remember owner Steve Rubell wanted to do a party for *Interview* magazine at Studio 54 in 1979 – the last year before they went to jail – when they opened the third floor with the bridge that swept from the back of the club to the front. People on the first and second floors would look up at you on this slowly moving bridge, and I remember standing up there with Andy, Paloma, Debbie, Truman Capote and Lorna Luft – we had about seven or eight people who had been on the cover. And Steve and Ian had made this huge backdrop of

Interview covers and it was really fantastic. Every pappa- razzi in the city was there taking pictures.'

Colacello's other Harry anecdote is a real charmer although it has nothing to do with Andy Warhol and there- fore sheds no new light on their bond. It does however provide a delightful portrait of a strange convergence of society that perhaps only Warhol could inspire, and only Harry could be party to. 'My favorite story about Debbie is when [Warhol's book] *Popism* came out in 1980, we had a party for it, a dinner for about a hundred. It was Saturday night, and as we were leaving, Diana Vreeland [legendary former *Vogue* editor] said, "Bob, see you tomorrow after- noon. We're going to see the movie *Caligula* right?", and I said, "Yes, okay". Harry, who was standing nearby said, "Bob did I overhear Diana Vreeland say you were taking her to see *Caligula* tomorrow?" And I was like, "Yes, believe it or not, she's dying to see it." She then said, "Do you think I could come with you?" and I said, "Sure." So, the next day, Diana's late, as usual, and we get inside the theatre just as the lights are going down and the only seats left are in the second row. So I'm helping Diana, who was then about 85 years old, down the aisle and Debbie goes ahead to secure the seats.' Debbie was wearing her usual Jackie O disguise – a kerchief tied under her chin and dark glasses, but as the lights are going down, she takes it off. So everyone recog- nizes her and they're going – "It's Debbie Harry!" Then they see us with her, and they didn't recognize us, but it must've been such an odd sight, particularly this old lady going to see a triple X-rated movie. So here we are in the second row and Diana whips out her opera glasses and I said to her. "I don't think you really need those," and she says, "Oh but I do. I don't want to miss anything!"

'After the three-hour-plus movie, I asked Debbie if she'd like to have a bite to eat with us. And she said, "Oh I'd love to but I have to go to Brooklyn because my grandmother died two days ago and I have to go to the wake. So thank you very much Bob, and it was good to see you Mrs Vreeland", and she takes off. Afterwards, Diana says to me – "Now did I hear that right Bob? She's telling me she has to go to her grandmother's wake today – what is she doing coming to see *Caligula* if her grandmother just died?" And I said, "Don't ask me – this whole day is so weird – what are you doing coming to see *Caligula*?" When I asked her if she liked it, she said, "This is the cut version. I know a jump cut when I see one. He gets into the bed with the horse and then suddenly there was another scene". So I said, "So what you're really saying Diana is that you're upset because you missed seeing a man have sex with the horse?", and she says, "Well, this is *Caligula* and I expected to see something shocking!"'

THE MUDD CLUB & ANYA PHILLIPS

ChiChi Valenti and Johnny Dynell, proprietors of the infamous downtown club of the 90s, Jackie 60, began their nightlife careers at the club that finally broke down the barriers between the worlds of rock 'n' roll and disco, The Mudd Club. 'Mudd was the quintessential downtown art, fashion, underground nightclub as art gallery,' says Valenti. Although Mudd officially belonged to its financer, Steve Maas, Dynell says the idea for the club, which opened in 1978, came from downtown goddess, designer and close friend of Deborah Harry, Anya Phillips and her cohort, writer and scenester, Diego Cortez. 'Anya and Diego took a punk club with punk sensibilities – [the space] was totally falling apart, but they put velvet ropes outside the front. It was also totally out of the way – nobody had even heard of White Street. And Anya insisted they have a disco ball and a door policy.' Valenti, who worked the door at Mudd, recalls some of Maas' random door fascism, even more cruel than its antithesis, Studio 54: 'Steve would be watching the door from his office through a surveillance camera, and he would call us on the walkie talkie and say, "No black leather", which was absurd, or "American passports only". Then we'd grill him about exceptions. Once he called down and said, "No fat people, unless they are really famous, like Meatloaf, but charge them triple because they take up three times the space, and tell them why."'

The Mudd Club kept growing until it became four floors plus a basement, renowned for its decadence. Valenti says, 'There are more books about Studio 54 than you'd ever want to see, but Mudd is the least documented because it was just a secret you knew about.'

Michael Musto, author of the *Village Voice* column 'La Dolce Musto', recalls that the club was so exclusive, press and celebrities were the least welcome revelers. 'It's a totally alien concept now that even club publicists have publicists. People probably find it hard to believe now that there ever was a Mudd Club, but at the time I wrote about Mudd Club for the *SoHo Weekly News*, people yelled at me and said, "How dare you write about this, you're giving away a great secret and ruining it!" I remember having conflicting feelings, thinking maybe I shouldn't have done it. Now it's not even an issue, but then it was an untouched scene which people wanted to keep underground.' Musto, who is still New York's premier nightlife reporter sighs, 'It was more peer validated than press validated. If you knew about the Mudd Club, you were really cool, and if you were press, you were no better than someone else. And once you were in, you felt like you were a part of something really special. Now there is no underground. Everything is routinely co-opted and turned into a Gap ad.'

It was at Mudd Club that Musto remembers first seeing Deborah Harry perform: 'I saw her live at The Mudd Club and I was blown away. I thought she was phenomenally charismatic and it didn't seem to me to be a put-on, it was so unmannered. She was just a strong, sensual woman and there was very little vulnerability in the music. It was just take no prisoners and fuck you this is who I am, like it or leave it.' Valenti also recalls seeing Debbie at Mudd frequently, but mostly off-stage. 'I just kept seeing her there. One night, I remember her and Walter Steding walking around in mummy bandages, and I think a picture of them like that ended up in that famous "Punk" issue of *People* magazine.'

The appeal for Harry was obvious. Mudd Club was another playground for artists and ideas, and a lot of people were nurtured and inspired by the scene which unfolded there. Valenti says, 'At that time art was in clubs, art was the subtext of clubs, and Mudd was major. Anya invented this new kind of nightlife that began with Mudd and turned into Tier Three, which became Area, which became Jackie. Keith Haring's first job was as the curator of the gallery at Mudd in 1982, Keith and Jean-Michel [Basquiat] first met at Mudd, and at one point, Fred Schnieder [from the B-52's] worked the coat check.'

Harry's participation at Mudd was hampered by Blondie's rise to fame, followed by the illness of Anya Phillips, who developed cancer and died in 1981. Harry and Phillips, a terrible twosome of ferocious females, bonded when they both worked as barmaids in a deadening Wall Street bar called White's Pub in the mid-70s. By all accounts they were best girlfriends, even though more than one person interviewed for this book described Phillips as 'the meanest girl you'd ever met'.

Blondie biographer Victor Bockris, who co-wrote *Making Tracks: The Rise of Blondie* with Harry, confirms that Anya Phillips was an important figure in Harry's life. 'I think the bond between them was that they were two very strong women in this scene that was 90% male dominated. They were two women coming from two different worlds but they both had a strong visual sense, and Debbie was very impressed by Anya's strength and her organisational abilities. The feeling was mutual. Anya was a powerful person and if she gave you her backing it really helped you spiritually.'

Phillips was raised in Asia and was also a close friend of Lou Reed's ex-wife, Sylvia Morales. She contributed to Harry's legacy by designing several of Harry's more outrageous dresses. She worked as a dominatrix and managed her boyfriend, musician James Chance [AKA James White] and The Contortions, alongside her involvement with Mudd. Valenti, who also knew Phillips says, 'Anya died way too soon and she didn't leave much product behind. But you have to know that she was so hard and so gorgeous and so important to Debbie – I'm sure she influenced Debbie a lot. She was so ahead of her time, she even died ahead of her time before her whole generation died.'

Valenti continues, 'Everyone knows Debbie paid for her treatment and was there at the hospital when she was sick. That's why people love Debbie even more. Anya died right before the period we were all entering with AIDS. In that way, Debbie proved to be another kind of role model, a role model for taking care of your friends.'

Harry writes of Phillips in *Making Tracks*: 'The period of 1975–80 was a time in which people insisted on being allowed to do what they weren't supposed to do. Anya symbolized that period. She was a powerful energy source that's now missing from the scene, an example of how intense willpower is charisma.'

CHAPTER THREE
Blondiemania

When David Byrne of the band Talking Heads remembers early Blondie performances at CBGB's, he chooses his words carefully. 'You could tell they had a voracious appetite for pop music – all different genres, and at the beginning they didn't have the chops to pull it off.' A very polite way of saying that when they were first starting out, Blondie had two strikes against them – their enthusiasm was greater than their musical skill, and by the standards of the burgeoning punk scene, they were pure pop.

Byrne contends however that there was a brief period at CBGB's, from 1974–6, when the audiences and the bands were very non judgemental. He says, 'I think it was that sense of openness that the bands and the audience shared to different kinds of music. What they had in common was . . . there were no *virtuosos*, and it was more important just to express yourself with the limited means available to you ... honesty and wit were more important than half-hour guitar solos or pyrotechnics.' But that blissful pre-punk period only lasted a couple of years, says Byrne. 'Then some bands started having more success, so that if two bands were playing together, one would be the standard opening act for the more popular one.'

And at first, Blondie was not one of the more popular bands. Although they were among the first bands to play CBGB's on a regular basis, they were considered by many of the scenes' champions to be poor relations to the really edgy, punk bands of the time. Music journalist Lisa Robinson, one of the most prolific writers at the time, admits, 'When I, my husband, Richard Robinson and Lenny Kaye started *Rock Scene*, we wrote a lot about the Talking Heads, Television, the Ramones and Patti Smith. Blondie was more of a pop band and we kind of ignored them. I mean, Patti was more of an artiste, the Ramones were sicker, David Byrne was weirder and Tom Verlaine was elusive. Debbie was just this gorgeous goddess and we didn't take her seriously at first.' Robinson's statement reflects a third strike against Blondie – they had a phenomenally beautiful female lead singer. As hard as it is to imagine beauty being a liability in any situation, Deborah Harry's remarkable good looks made her suspect at CBGB's.

The fourth strike against Blondie, and the one that almost cast them out of music, was they seemed to be plagued by casual disasters – the kind of stuff that was so funny, you could cry. Music writer Carola Dibbell recalls, 'When I was doing research for my essay on women in punk [included in the *Rolling Stone: Women in Rock* book], one thing people would always say about Blondie was there would always be some royal screw-up, like they were supposed to go on at ten and they'd go on at four, or right before a show, their sound system would explode.' Blondie's co-founders, Harry and Stein also lost all of their original collaborators during their first year together. Their drummer left them to go to medical school, then their most assured musician, bassist Fred Smith, left to join the band everyone thought would break out of punk and make it big – Television. Harry says in *Making Tracks*, 'After Fred quit, we got very paranoid. We felt everybody in the scene was against us, and stayed depressed for a month. We threw our hands up in the air and said, What's the use? It's too ridiculous, this is really hard.'

There were of course, people on the scene who liked

Blondie right from the start, like writer and scene maker [and sometime scene stealer] Glenn O'Brien. 'I loved Blondie,' says O'Brien, 'I mean, I loved other bands too, but Blondie had great songs and that pop potential. Plus, Debbie was just so gorgeous and Clem was a total pop star.'

O'Brien speaks of New Jersey native and *virtuoso* drummer, Clem Burke. Burke first met Harry and Stein in 1974 at an old New York hang-out called Club 82, where New York legends a generation before Blondie, like the New York Dolls and Jayne (then Wayne) County played. Burke heard that they had placed an ad in the New York weekly, the *Village Voice*, looking for a 'freak energy rock drummer', so he found the ad and went to the audition. Burke was just nineteen and the last person to try out for Blondie. He was also the only one they wanted to work with, partly because he was the best drummer they'd heard that day, but partly because Burke had decreed that his greatest musical influence was drummer Keith Moon. The then long-haired Burke rehearsed for a couple of weeks with Harry, Stein and bassist Fred Smith, but their first gig together as a foursome was tragically Smith's last. It was Burke's nagging and vote of confidence that actually convinced Harry and Stein they should keep Blondie going.

As the cliché goes, every ending is also a new beginning. The departure of Blondie's original drummer made room for Burke, then Fred Smith's exit made room for Burke's hometown buddy, a stud of a young buck named Gary Valentine. Valentine started hanging out at Blondie rehearsals, hit it off with Stein, and quickly got absorbed into the ranks as bassist. Valentine had the arrogance and boy beauty of a major rock god. Later, he would reveal that he also had the ego of one. Valentine brought a few songs he'd composed to the band, and added another strong personality to the Blondie line-up as well as a bit of male eye candy.

The final addition to Blondie came in early 1975 when 20-

year-old pre-med student Jimmy Destri joined the band. Destri's sister, Donna, who subsequently sang back-up on several of Blondie's albums, was in a band called The Fast and was a friend of Harry's. She told Harry her brother was a good keyboardist. As it turned out, Destri had played in several bands before Blondie, including another CBGB's pop band Milk 'n' Cookies, but he had gone back to pre-med and working as an intern in a hospital because he didn't think music was going to get him anywhere. Still, he couldn't fight the fact that music, not medicine, made him happy. Although he never became Dr Destri, which may or may not be the world's loss, Destri and his Farfisa organ would be vital in developing Blondie's signature sound. Destri would also help write several of Blondie's hit songs.

The line-up of Harry, Stein, Burke, Valentine and Destri clicked musically and aesthetically. All the boys cut their long hair and unified their mod urban greasers look. Harry and Stein, who were respectively ten and five years older than Burke, Valentine and Destri, were living together in a loft on the Bowery near CBGB's. This soon became the Blondie headquarters and crashing pad. The close proximity to the vibrant New York music scene of CBGB's helped motivate Blondie to get serious – they pulled themselves together and practiced every day for more than a year, doing whatever odd jobs they could find to supplement the meager amount of money they were making playing music. Blondie's average pay was about $60 a gig, which then had to be split among Blondie's five members. For Harry, odd jobs included working as a barmaid and doing piece work soldering belt buckles.

By the Summer of 1976, Blondie had sharpened up their sound and their look, and had developed a local following. Sexy pictures of Harry taken by Stein appeared in *Punk* and *Creem* magazines, sparking interest in the band. Since the New York press and the music press had started writing about the scene at CBGB's, it followed suit that the music industry would start sniffing around, looking for the band that might be able to sell the CBGB sound to a bigger audience.

Producers of the 1976 Ramones self-titled debut album, Marty Thau and Craig Leon, thought Blondie might be the ticket. Suddenly, some of the original strikes against Blondie started to work in their favor. Blondie knew they weren't great musicians, so they practiced hard and developed clever songs. Being the underdogs of the scene also developed their drive. They were a pop band with punk roots, instead of a punk band, which Thau and Leon knew they could sell. Deborah Harry was too beautiful to be punk, but her sex appeal helped make Blondie appealing to people who were prejudiced against punk. And the band had had so much bad luck in its first couple of years together, they'd cleared out the bad karma and made room for lots of good.

Thau and Leon were introduced to Blondie by producer Richard Gottehrer, who had produced a CBGB's compilation album, which didn't include Blondie. Among others, Gottehrer had previously produced the girl-group hit single 'My Boyfriend's Back' for the Crystals, and wanted to work with Blondie to bring out their accessible pop sound. Thau and Leon decided to test the waters by letting Gottehrer produce two Blondie singles, 'X-Offender' and 'In The Sun', which were then released on a small American top forties label, which was co-owned by 50s teen idol Frankie Vali, Private Stock Records.

Even though the singles didn't hit, Gottehrer convinced Private Stock to sign Blondie and release a full album with an attendant publicity campaign showing off Deborah Harry's pin-up good looks. For a band whose aspiration at the time was to be as big as Television, getting signed was incredibly exciting. The fact that Private Stock and Gottehrer believed in Blondie enough to record an album must have felt like an amazing validation, especially after two years of playing second fiddle to almost everyone at CBGB's. High on that feeling, Blondie made the mistake many young artists make. They had nothing to lose and everything to gain, so they signed a legally binding contract, marrying them to Gottehrer and Private Stock Records, without having any legal representation of their own.

Working in the Plaza Sound Studio in Radio City Music Hall during August and September of 1976 really felt like the big time for Blondie, who had barely even performed on a real stage before (the stage at CBGB's was about six foot square), much less been in a real recording studio. As is the case with many first albums, Blondie knew the songs they were recording backwards and forwards, but studio time helped them clean up their music technically. The studio also showcased Harry's velvety voice, which was sometimes drowned out during live shows by the loud, exuberant band.

Gottehrer worked at a very relaxed pace, maybe a little too relaxed for Blondie, as with the impatience of hungry young wolves, they just wanted to get the album out in the world. Harry, Stein, Burke, Destri and Valentine started to take themselves more seriously at the same time, they joked with each other that the album would probably end up in a 99-cent discount bin. With the record 'Blondie' finished and scheduled to come out in January of 1977, the band knew they needed someone who was going to be on their side and who would help them interface with the record label and take care of business. What Blondie needed was a manager.

I WANNA MAKE YOU A STAR

'I'm the anti-Christ,' says Peter Leeds sardonically, when asked to discuss his tumultuous two years, 1977 to 1979, as Blondie's manager. What he means is that he's the villain in the Blondie story, at least as it was told by Harry and Stein in *Making Tracks*. But he suggests that since 1981, when that book was written, there are others who may also be worthy of daggers from Deborah Harry and Chris Stein. From Leeds' perspective, he was just doing his job, taking a band with modest expectations and bringing them to worldwide prominence. Leeds says, 'I didn't care about their expectations. If they were content to play Max's and CBGB's their whole life that's okay, but it wasn't enough for me.' In *Making Tracks*, Harry and Stein say Leeds treated them like children, and Leeds admits several times that he made decisions for their own good without consulting them. In general however, he speaks very highly of Deborah Harry's talent, and admits that although he has also worked with Judy Collins and Roberta Flack, Blondie is the most successful act he's ever represented.

Leeds, a New York native, has been managing talent since he was in High School. He became the manager of Deborah Harry's first band, The Wind in the Willows, in 1967 through his association with publicist, Dominic Scicilia. Leeds recalls that based on his early impressions of Harry, he had no idea what she would become. 'Debbie had brown hair and she always hid. [The Willows] were a seven piece band and she always stood behind somebody on stage.' After the Willows were over, Leeds had no contact with Harry until Christmas 1976. Leeds was managing a musician named Harris Wilder who was signed to Private Stock Records. Blondie had just finished recording their first album for Private Stock, and both Harry and Leeds attended the label's holiday party. Leeds first ran into Richard Gottehrer who told him about a new band he was working with called Blondie. Leeds says, 'I knew about Blondie because they had been in the press a bit.' Next Leeds runs into Harry. 'I talk with Debbie and she introduces me to the rest of the band. I haven't seen her since 1969 and I had no idea Blondie was her band.'

The irony is that even after this bizarre coincidence, Leeds almost didn't become Blondie's manager. Harry had reservations even then because after meeting with Leeds, the band decided to go with another manager, Sid Bernstein. That is until Leeds convinced them to come back to him. He says the key thing was that he really believed they could be big. He says, 'They wanted to have hit records and be stars and I thought they had a shot, principally because they were so out there in all their performances, and Debbie was so great at this point. I don't know what happened to her [after the Willows]. It was just an ugly duckling into a beautiful swan type thing. It was just meant to be.'

Leeds says the first thing he did was have a meeting with Larry Uttal, the head of Private Stock. 'A manager's job is to get the record company to do more and to get the producer to produce good records. I'm not telling you that I could have gone into the studio with the band and made records as good as Richard, that's just not what I do. But I am good at beating up the record company and getting whatever there is to get and more. With Private Stock, there was nothing to get. We were always in conflict.' When Leeds came aboard, the first album and the album jacket were already completed and about to come out. Then the first major blow-up hit. Leeds says, 'You know that poster of Debbie in the see-through blouse? I get a call from Debbie about it with lots of expletives. Private Stock is going to release this poster. I listen to her, but secretly, I think it's a great idea.' Harry says in *Making Tracks* that Blondie told the label they wanted a promo poster which featured the entire band instead, and asked them not to put it out. Private Stock put out the poster anyway.

Leeds says there was nothing he could do about that crisis, but the next run-in with the record company was just around the corner. Leeds secured Blondie a spot on an American TV show called *Don Kirschner's Rock Concert*, which aired on NBC Saturdays at midnight. Leeds badgered Kirschner, who finally agreed to run a video of Blondie, the only problem was that Blondie had no videos to air. Leeds asked Private Stock to finance a last-minute video shoot. Leeds recalls, 'The conversations weren't pleasant. I don't feel like I have any obligation to anyone but my client so if you, the record company, don't like me, I don't care. It's about me serving my client and me supporting myself and my family.' Leeds says he financed the shoot himself. 'We hired a studio somewhere on 57th Street on the westside, Bob Gruen did the camera, Dominic [Scicilia] was the director and Stephen Sprouse made a background.' Blondie was filmed playing four songs including 'X-Offender', 'In The Sun' and 'In The Flesh'. These videos would later play a role in helping break the band in Australia, but first, the band had to make an impression some place a little closer to home, in the American recording industry capitol of Los Angeles.

BLOWING THEM AWAY IN LA

Rodney Bingenheimer is a Los Angeles DJ legend and quite a character. He began his airwaves career at radio station KROQ in 1976, a job that would be the gateway to living out his own rock star fantasies. Today KROQ is a major Los Angeles radio station, but when Bingenheimer first started there, they were so low budget they would sometimes go off the air for three hours at a time due to 'technical difficulties'. Because Bingenheimer had good taste and was an early champion of all kinds of new music, later in life he ended up not only hanging out with various music legends, but he even played on stage and recorded songs with some of them including Blondie. Bingenheimer recalls, 'Once, as a thank you, Blondie did a single with me called "Little GTO", on Bop Records in 1979. It was me singing lead vocals and Debbie backing me up. Because of their record contract, it was credited as Rodney and The Brunettes.'

Blondie had good reason to be thankful to Bingenheimer, whose claim to fame in the Blondie story is twofold. He was the first DJ to play Blondie on the radio. 'I played "X-Offender" on KROQ even before they signed to Private Stock. I don't even know how I got it. I just loved the beginning – with her talking – like the punk Ronettes.' Word got back to Blondie in New York that they had a DJ on their side and Bingenheimer says excitedly that they then sent him an autographed Blondie album. 'So I interviewed them over the phone and I got them booked at a show for KROQ in LA.' It was this show that got Blondie to the West Coast, and it was in LA that the energy of Blondiemania first started to build.

Deborah Harry says in *Making Tracks*, 'Going to LA was a big deal for us at the time. We played the Whiskey for a week and blew everybody away, and then we got another week with the Ramones and that was also a big success. Everyone in LA was ready for us, as nothing was happening there at the time. They had all been hearing about us via Rodney, who'd been pushing us on the radio, so they were curious and the shows were sold out.'

Blondie were treated like royalty in LA – a refreshing change from New York where people had the attitude of, Oh Blondie, yeah, seen them a million times. Two people who discovered Blondie during that trip were students Theresa Kereakes and Pleasant Gehman, who together worked on a punk fanzine called *Lobotomy* (1977–81). Gehman, now a novelist and music journalist in Los Angeles, says, 'It was mostly about music, but our ideas of music stretched from Blondie and the Ramones to free give-away 45s [from fast food restaurants]. I was still in High School and couldn't even type then, so the whole thing was cut and pasted-up on our living room floor.' Kereakes, now a television executive in New York, was a UCLA student who soon became *Lobotomy*'s head photographer. 'I wanted to be [Warhol photographer] Chris Makos. I just wanted to be there and take the pictures and document LA's punk rock scene, which at the time was centered around clubs like the Starwood, the Masque and of course, the Whiskey, which is where Pleasant and I first saw Blondie.' After that first taste of the band, Gehman says, 'We were like dead-heads over Blondie, and followed them everywhere. There wasn't all that much going on out here at the time, but more than that, Blondie was just made for LA with songs like "In The Sun". In New York, they had that whole arty faction that looked down on Blondie. We had that whole fuck art, let's dance type thing out here and Blondie was perfect for us.'

Kereakes and Gehman used *Lobotomy* as their excuse to hang out with musicians they liked, which apparently wasn't difficult. Gehman says, 'If you liked a band back then, it was normal to expect to meet them. Plus, the bands I was interested in were on these tiny branch labels and there were no publicists or handlers or anything. I was seventeen and really cavalier about things then. I thought if I liked someone's music, we'd be really good friends.' Kereakes adds that the LA punk scene was a pretty intimate circle of about a hundred core people, who all knew each other and partied together on a regular basis. She says, 'There were always parties to go to after the shows at Joan Jett or someone's house. My parents had given me a car and I didn't want to crash it, so I was always the designated driver. That's why I remember stuff no one else does.'

Not so with other people from the scene. Lance Loud, the grown-up son from the 60s American real-life TV series, *The Loud Family*, had a band and was a star on the LA scene, along with Runaways member, Joan Jett. When asked to comment on that time, both Loud and Jett laughed and said, 'Sorry, I don't remember a thing.'

What Gehman remembers is interviewing Blondie for

Lobotomy at a house party locked in someone's bathroom. She remembers doing qualudes with Jett and Jimmy Destri, who she says had a mad crush on Jett. She remembers passing out with Destri in a room at the Tropicana Hotel and waking up in the middle of the night to find the room flooded with six inches of water – 'Sneakers and packs of cigarettes were just floating around the bed!' Of Clem Burke, Gehman's strongest memory is of the innovation he demonstrated when it came to styling his hair. 'Once I was taking Jimmy and Clem somewhere and I went to get them and it took us a whole hour to get out of the hotel room because Clem had to fix his hair. He put on three kinds of gel, then hairspray, then, as he'd been eating potato chips, he wiped his hands and the bag on his hair. To finish it off, he'd tease and blow-dry.' She laughs, 'He said he was trying to make himself look like a cockatoo.'

Of Harry and Stein, who partied with young fans less than the young bachelors in the band, Gehman remembers, 'I'd take Debbie to junk stores and we had the exact same taste in clothes.' Kereakes has pictures of Harry wearing a pink and lime striped mini dress, which looks like a Stephen Sprouse design, but was actually a thrift store find from Gehman and herself. Gehman says that Harry became a kind of motherly figure to her. 'One night there was a party at the Tropicana and I'd passed out by the pool. So in the morning, I go knocking on Debbie's door to use the phone or use the bathroom or something. She comes to the door with no make-up and her hair all messed-up, wearing just a yellow and black t-shirt, a little gold necklace of a skull and crossbones and panties. I can't believe how beautiful she is, even at like 9 a.m. with her hair all messed-up. She was like, 'Oh my God, come in. Do you want an egg?'

Kereakes remembers Harry saying things to her young fans like, it's cold outside, wear a sweater, or you should stay in school. She also remembers Harry being extraordinarily accommodating to them. 'There were always times when we knew she'd rather be alone or that she was tired of having all of us around, but she never said anything. She was always kind and she never made you feel self-conscious for being a fan. I think Pleasant and I looked to her as a model of behavior in every way.'

Harry and Blondie soaked up all the love they got in LA like sunshine, and they realized that young people were Blondie's key audience. As the first New York band to play the Whiskey, they revolutionized the scene's aesthetic. As Harry says in *Making Tracks*, 'When we arrived, most kids were wearing bell-bottom pants, but by the end of the first week, the girls were wearing mini skirts, while the boys were suddenly packed into straight-legged tight pants and sporting skinny ties.'

While shaking up LA, Blondie caught the eye of two producers. The first was hit factory legend Phil Spector who saw one of Blondie's shows at the Whiskey and thought they were great. Rodney Bingenheimer remembers, 'I brought Debbie and the band to Phil Spector's house. He was ranting and raving – he wanted to produce Blondie but I didn't think Debbie was into it.' Blondie got a real kick out of meeting Spector, but apparently he was so manic during that visit, they couldn't imagine working with him.

The second producer to become infatuated with Blondie was Mike Chapman, who had worked with British bands like Sweet and female rocker Suzi Quatro. Peter Leeds says Chapman came to see Blondie at the Whiskey every night they played there. Leeds and Chapman started talking and it was clear that Chapman had a real affinity for Blondie's sound. Leeds liked him enough to extend a promise. Leeds says, 'I wrote Mike Chapman a note on a napkin that said if I ever got Blondie out of the producer relationship with [Richard] Gottehrer, he could produce the band. He kept that napkin framed by his desk.'

It was in LA that Leeds formalized his relationship with Blondie. They were uneasy about Leeds – headstrong Gary

Valentine was particularly unhappy – but, high on the energy of their LA trip and unwilling to stop the ball from rolling, they pressed ahead and signed a contract with him that they would live to regret.

The next break for Blondie came out of the blue while they were still in LA and must have felt like part of LA's good vibrations. David Bowie had been working with punk legend Iggy Pop in Berlin and they heard Blondie's album and decided they wanted Blondie to open for Pop's US Tour, on which Bowie would be Pop's piano player. Harry and Stein in particular were over the moon about the prospect of working with two of their favorite artists.

When Blondie returned to New York from LA after just three weeks, something had changed irrevocably for the band. *Punk* magazine's John Holmstrom says Chris Stein explained that the audiences in LA were nothing like CBGB's – they'd yell and scream and clap and it got Blondie to break through and come alive on stage. It was a particularly important development for Deborah Harry who was reportedly a little wooden during performances. Holmstrom thinks that part of why LA was so liberating for Blondie was it gave them more room. He says, 'The stage at CBGB's was very small and as Debbie said to me once, I didn't move because I couldn't move. They weren't the same band after LA. They came back and they played the Palladium and they really took to the big stage. They couldn't play the small stage anymore.'

A SECOND HOME IN THE UK

In March 1977, Blondie left New York to go on tour with Iggy Pop and David Bowie. Stops on that tour included Montreal, Toronto, Boston, New York, Philadelphia, Cleveland, Detroit, Seattle, Portland, Vancouver, San Francisco, and finally ended in mid-April in LA. Blondie's

LA fans wanted more, so the band stayed on an extra week to do shows at the Whiskey. One night they were joined by members of Iggy Pop's band, Joan Jett and Rodney Bingenheimer for an on-stage jam session.

The Iggy Pop tour not only gave Blondie their first taste of life on the road, but it gave them the opportunity to watch Pop and Bowie and how they handled their fans and their fame. What they learned by example was to practice generosity whenever possible, balanced by a true passion for the music and a respect for good equipment. Blondie was so impressed by Bowie, they hoped he might be able to produce their next album, even though they were still under contract to Gottehrer.

The Iggy Pop US tour was followed in May 1977 by Blondie's first English tour, opening for their CBGB's siblings, Television. Peter Leeds can't recall exactly how this deal came about, 'The European Tour came out of nowhere. We went with Television, maybe because Blondie and Television were playing together at CBGB's, because I didn't know Television or their manager, Jane Friedman.' This accidental pairing would prove to be a real turning point for Blondie. Although LA's small punk scene had responded well to Blondie, that was only a big splash in a small pond. A hundred kids in LA didn't have the power to put Blondie on the American music charts when Blondie was totally at odds with the kind of music that was being played on the radio in America. Plus their association with punk scared off music business people who'd never been able to keep a punk band successfully on a tour schedule or sell their records.

The English tour began with a warm-up gig in Bournemouth on May 20, where Squeeze opened for them. Immediately Blondie saw audiences go wild. Just like in LA, the crowds were younger and more interested in feeling good than looking cool. The first official stop on the tour was the Apollo Theatre in Glasgow. It was there that

Blondie realized Television had no intention of sharing any of their limelight. The tour was all about Television, and Blondie had to fit in around their needs and desires. The bands, who knew each other fairly well from CBGB's, were even to travel in separate buses. Blondie was filled with apprehension. As Harry says in *Making Tracks*, 'The headliners are in control of how much power, sound, lights and time the opening band gets. In this situation, bands can either work together, like we did with Iggy and Bowie, or try to outdo each other.' Television, threatened by Blondie's fresh post-LA buzz, were set on doing the latter. But it was a battle they were destined to lose.

After Glasgow, the tour made stops in Newcastle, Sheffield and Manchester. Blondie took a while to warm up, especially since they were feeling a distinct chill from Television, but two things started to happen. They started to get press, some of it good, some of it bad, but the difference from American press was that journalists were considering the band in more sophisticated terms, analyzing and criticizing the music, the lyrics and Blondie's visual presentation. Likewise, the fans were picking up on Blondie's Warholian irony, like the camp sarcasm of 'Rip Her To Shreds' and the pop politics of a sympathetic ode to a sex, or 'X-Offender'. They even got the smartness of Harry's Blondie character. Harry says in *Making Tracks*, 'I was also beginning to find English kids somewhat more literate and sophisticated than Americans. They clock everything and were catching the nuances in the phrasing of the music and words I was singing. They appreciated our act right away, making Britain Blondie's second home.'

There was another reason Blondie worked so well in Britain. At the time, the country seemed to be in the midst of a general malaise. Blondie's music was cathartic for the kids' feelings of hopelessness and boredom, providing a confection of fun and rebellion with a subtext of rage. Rage against rules, rage against conformity, rage against stupidity, rage against feeling pain. Blondie tapped into this energy themselves too. Feeling exhausted and a little stir crazy from the myopia of touring, they actually trashed their hotel rooms. Blondie was beginning to realize that rock 'n'roll was also going to be hard, hard work.

THE CHRYSALIS

By the time the tour reached London, Television felt the British press were turning on them, while Blondie started to get rave reviews. Blondie's manager, Peter Leeds was amazed. 'I didn't realize the importance of Europe until after that trip.' The combination of seeing Blondies' potential abroad and Leeds' frustrations with Private Stock gave him a clear idea of what was next – a move to a label that could support Blondie's affinity with Europe. Leeds decided the right label for the job was Chrysalis, which was run by Terry Ellis. 'I wanted Terry Ellis partly because he had a band called the Babies and he had them everywhere. Also, he had been Jethro Tull's manager and I knew he would relate to management, and because I knew that Europe would be vital and he was an Englishman.' Meanwhile, Private Stock President, Lavvy Uttal, further angered Leeds by asking for copies of the videos Blondie made to send out as a promotional tool, even though the record company wouldn't cover the cost of making them. Since that's why they existed, Leeds gave the videos to Private Stock to distribute anyway.

Leeds' method for getting Terry Ellis' attention was slightly unconventional, even for rock 'n'roll. 'There was a lot of Blondie press when we got back from Europe. So somehow I got Terry Ellis' home address and I started sending him clippings and photographs of the band and of Deborah Harry – just that, no notes, no return address, nothing.'

Leeds intention was to arouse Ellis' curiosity to the point where Ellis would come to them. Eventually, he did. But while the anonymous mail teasers may have helped, the real clincher in the deal was that Blondie suddenly had a surprise hit song in Australia. Leeds explains that somehow the Blondie video had found its way to a music television show in Australia where they decided to feature it. 'So the announcer said, "Here's a new band from America and here's their first single, 'X-Offender'!" but they made a mistake and they played "In The Flesh". They cued up the wrong song on the tape and that became the hit. It was a freak incident – no one had anything to do with it. The gods were just smiling on us.'

Ellis made enquiries through a third party about whether or not Blondie might be able to get out of their record deal with Private Stock, and Leeds let them know he wasn't sure if they could get out of the deal, but that he wanted them to. So Leeds invited Ellis to watch Blondie play in New York. The night Ellis saw Blondie, they had no idea he was there and Leeds says he didn't even introduce Ellis to the band. But Ellis liked what he saw. In particular, he was in awe of Deborah Harry, who he felt could be a major star.

As Leeds drew closer to a deal with Chrysalis, Blondie was about to go into the studio with Richard Gottehrer to record their second album, *Plastic Letters*. But first they had to deal with the problem posed by the wilful Gary Valentine. Peter Leeds, who butted heads with Valentine constantly, decided to fire him from Blondie. Leeds says, 'Blondie had nothing to do with [throwing Gary Valentine out]. They wouldn't have let me throw him out if I had asked them. He was too much of a long-time friend of Clem's.' Leeds says that his main contention with Valentine was that he wanted to be a solo player. 'Gary had no regard for how his wild stage antics affected the other band members.' Leeds says, 'When he jumped around on stage, Jimmy's organ went out of tune. And, the final straw was one night at the Whiskey – you know how the tuning pegs of a bass are real big and stick out at the end? Well, he came within an inch of taking out Deborah's left eye.' Leeds says Valentine was also unhappy because he didn't want to be a bass player, he wanted to play guitar and he was threatened by Deborah Harry becoming more and more of the focus of the band. Leeds says, 'He didn't understand why he wasn't as important as Deborah Harry. So I fired him and then I told the band, the same thing as the Chrysalis deal. I did it then I told them.'

The way Leeds got Blondie out of their Private Stock deal was fairly simple. He recalls, 'I'm in a meeting with Larry Uttal and I say, We're not going to make any money together, the band isn't going to be a success here, I want to buy the band's contract out. So Larry says, It's not for sale, and I say, Everything is for sale it's just a question of price. He says, Okay, I want a million dollars. And I say, Larry, we're not talking about fucking Led Zeppelin for Christ sakes! They sold no records and no concert tickets – what are you holding on to? So he says he needs the weekend to think about it. On Monday he says, Okay, $400,000.'

What wasn't simple was convincing the band that it was the right move at the right time. Even though they weren't happy with Private Stock either, Blondie was starting to suspect that Leeds blurred the line between working for Blondie or even working with Blondie, and feeling like he owned Blondie. Leeds defends himself by saying, 'It was my job to make them successful. Blondie didn't know where they were going, they didn't know what they were doing next week. I have no apologies to make and no regrets. If I hadn't moved them around, they would never have become the success that they did.'

Leeds broke the news to Blondie while they were in the studio working with Gottehrer. After talking with the band, Leeds confronted Gottehrer. '[Gottehrer] says, If you're leaving Private Stock you can buy me out too. We settled on

$100,000 and he sold his rights to the publishing and his rights to the production. Then Terry [Ellis] put up the half million dollars, plus a little extra for the band, we made a deal and Blondie's career began.'

In *Making Tracks*, Harry speaks of a midnight covert contract signing at some big lawyer's office. At the end of the night, Blondie was signed to Chrysalis and owed them a half million dollars for the buy-out from Private Stock. At dawn, as the contract negotiations finally closed, Blondie trashed the office of the lawyer where they had been cooped-up for hours and hours. Maybe they realized the music business was going to be full of moments like this, when they would be forced to be some place they didn't want to be, swimming with sharks. Or maybe it was a combination of a rush of power and a rush of fear over what was to come.

WHISTLESTOP TOUR OF THE WORLD

Blondie made *Plastic Letters* without Gary Valentine, although he left them with a hit song he penned called '(I'm Always Touched By Your) Presence Dear'. Leeds had hired another buddy of Clem Burke's, Frank 'The Freak' Infante, to play bass. After recording was finished, they decided to keep Infante in Blondie and went off to LA to do a few more shows for their devoted fans at the Whiskey. These weren't Blondie's best shows but Chrysalis decided to have them filmed and by chance hired filmmakers John Cassavetes and Sam Shaw to do the job. A little-seen hour-long documentary called *Blondie* was the result.

Infante couldn't really play bass very well, but Blondie decided to keep him on as a rhythm guitarist. They auditioned an English bass player named Nigel Harrison out in LA and were impressed by how quickly he seem to pick up their tunes. They hired him without realizing that he had taped the Blondie show the night before and taught himself all their songs.

As pleased as Blondie was about their new line-up, new record label and their hit single in Australia, they were a little alarmed at how everything was speeding up. As Harry says in *Making Tracks*, 'Soon we were moving too fast to maintain control of what was happening around us and we had to leave it all up to Peter [Leeds]. He'd say, "Oh, I signed a contract and you have to play here." Or, "The record company expects you to go there and do some promo."'

Because of the hit in Australia, Harry was swept away for a two-week publicity tour while the band stayed in New York to rehearse for the first Blondie World Tour. It appears that the decision to send Harry alone was made for practical reasons, as the new additions to the line-up really needed to practice with the band, but it set an uneasy precedent for things to come. Harry got her first taste of what it meant to be interviewed by legions of ignorant, sometimes sexist and often hostile reporters, many of whom assumed she'd be either a dumb blonde or a exhibitionistic slut. For the band, it became clear that the record company and Leeds thought Harry could promote the band on her own, and perhaps even preferred her to.

Spending time alone with Leeds brought some suspicions to light for Harry too. Apparently Leeds thought Harry could be and should be the next all-American sex symbol, smiling and suntanned with big hair – another Farrah Fawcett. Harry felt Leeds had no appreciation of her bohemian edge, which he wanted to cover up and she wanted to keep.

Blondie started their international tour in London, continuing to Australia then on to Thailand where they played New Years' Eve 1977–8. After dates in Japan, Blondie returned to Europe where both 'Denis' and 'Presence Dear' were hits. By this time, Blondie was beyond exhausted, which only added to their anxiety about the way they were being handled by Leeds. Away from New York and their friends, families and peers for such long periods of time, being whipped through new countries and meeting seas of new faces, had made the band feel disconnected and lonely. And to top it all off, all of the Blondie members were broke. The only money they had, they got from Leeds who always made them feel like they were begging for handouts. Any money Blondie made was being funneled back to Chrysalis and being put against their debts and expenses, so no one was sure when they would ever see any substantial money for all of their work.

Harry says in *Making Tracks* that instead of calming them, Leeds made things worse by threatening all of the men in Blondie when they complained, telling them they could all be replaced. It was a devastating blow, especially for Stein who had founded Blondie with Harry. Leeds failed to understand that Harry, Stein, Burke and Destri were Blondie. Blondie was not just a concept of a group of guys in skinny ties and peg-legged pants backing up a beautiful blonde woman, but it was these specific guys backing up this particular beautiful woman – individuals with personalities and talents – that made Blondie work.

When asked about the subject, Leeds is a little defensive. 'All of the band was pissed because of the attention that was focused on [Deborah Harry]. I had long talks with them – Don't you understand, she's the ticket? You know, I don't think they did. None of them appreciated how second rate they were without her. And Clem is an extraordinary drummer, but he's the drummer. She was the ticket.' Leeds also says the band never thanked him for anything he did, all they ever did was complain and make him and themselves miserable. So there are no apologies from Leeds for the way he handled Blondie. He takes credit for making Blondie successful through moving them from Private Stock to Chrysalis and pushing them into endless touring. But he does admit that his actions worked in combination with other key elements: 'A) I couldn't have made them successful without them being extremely talented. B) I couldn't have made them successful without Deborah Harry's face. And C) I couldn't have made them successful without Terry Ellis and Mike Chapman.'

MAKING ARRANGEMENTS

When Blondie returned to New York in February 1978 from the European leg of their World Tour, they faced some devastating news. Even though the six-month tour was a success and they had hit albums and singles in Europe and Asia, they hadn't made any money. They were told that Blondie's only hope for financial success was to break in America, and Chrysalis felt the only way they would make headway in the US was if Deborah Harry personally hit the road as Blondie's goodwill ambassador. When all she wanted to do was sleep for a month, Harry left immediately with Stein in tow for a US promo tour where her mission was to charm radio stations and record stores into promoting Blondie's music. Her only stipulation was that Leeds should not accompany them. To her credit, Harry pulled it off like a pro.

The promo tour continued off and on until May, when Blondie returned once again to the West Coast and then performed their biggest show to date in New York at the Palladium. It was a very gratifying experience for Blondie. All of the band members started receiving a salary of $125 a week, which to them was a fortune. They were thrilled to be back on their home turf, finally getting the respect and validation they wanted from their peers and the people who knew how far they'd come. It was the last golden period for Blondie in terms of being able to casually enjoy their success as one of the CBGB's gang. Soon they would far outdistance their contemporaries and belong to the world.

In June of 1978, Blondie went in the studio with Mike Chapman. After Leeds had made the deal with Chrysalis, he and Terry Ellis had agreed that Chapman, who was well known at the time for his work in Europe and had two number one singles that year on the US charts – Exile's 'Kiss You All Over' and Nick Gilder's 'Hot Child In The City' – was the producer to break Blondie in the US. The band accepted Chapman although, once again, the decision wasn't really in their hands. Leeds says there were some mumblings against Chapman, but, 'They'd all met Mike because he'd been hanging around the Whiskey and they liked him. He's real easy, real fun, bright, energetic, competent and he was very successful at the time.' What Blondie could not have known was that Chapman was a total perfectionist. Leeds recalls, 'The first day we're doing the first track. Whoever counts it off, counts off and they start – Mike Chapman cuts in, "No, No, No – that was very good but not good enough. Let's do it right." It went on like that for several hours. Mike was always such that no one would challenge him, but I think Nigel and Clem were ready to kill him because they had never had someone demand that much discipline from them.'

Harry says in *Making Tracks*, 'We weren't prepared for [Chapman's] level of expertise so we learned an enormous amount about how to record from him. His approach was very different from Gottehrer's. Chapman helped us become more commercial, with tighter arrangements and perfect basic tracks.' Both Chapman and Blondie wanted a number one record in America, so they set out to make the best record they possibly could and they came out with a masterpiece. But the process was hellish and relationships among band members were tense. Part of the problem was that exhaustion had made all of them a little toxic and a little paranoid.

Having to record together may have been a blessing as it kept everyone focused on a common goal. One of the songs they spent the most time refining was a funky James Brown type tune Harry and Stein wrote in 1975 called 'Heart of Glass'. Harry says of the song in *Making Tracks*, 'When we did "Heart of Glass" it wasn't too cool in our social set to play disco, but we did it because we wanted to be uncool. "Heart of Glass" was based around a Roland Rhythm Machine and the backing took over ten hours to get down. We spent three hours just getting the bass drum. It was the hardest song to do on the album and took us the longest in studio hours.'

After the record was finished, tensions remained among the Blondie members, so much so that Leeds says he was forced to come up with a design for cover art that would allow the Blondie band members to be photographed separately. Leeds says, 'I knew I couldn't put them in a photo session together and get a useable photo, so I came up with the *Parallel Lines* album cover, each of them on their own black or white stripe so that we could take the pictures individually. I came up with that idea and it became an award-winning cover. Somewhere in a file, is my original drawing.' Unfortunately, the cover for *Parallel Lines*, which was named after a song Blondie never finished about 'communications, characterizations and the eventual meeting of different influences', remains another sore point for Harry and Stein. The concept was explained to them differently and they never agreed to the idea that all the boys should smile while Harry remained icy. Harry and Stein maintain that they were asked to pick pictures of themselves from the shoot that they liked to be considered for the cover, and Leeds went ahead and used ones they'd rejected.

In July and August, Blondie went on a US tour to Santa Cruz, San Diego, Phoenix, Kansas City, Minneapolis, St Louis, Austin, Dallas, Houston, Detroit, Toronto, Atlanta and Miami with another one of their musical heroes, the Kinks. After that they flew directly to the UK to promote the release of *Parallel Lines*, and sure enough, the second single from the album, 'Hanging On The Telephone' shot to number one in the UK. But much to the record company's dismay, the two singles released in the US went absolutely nowhere. By the time 'Heart of Glass' was released, *Parallel Lines* was deemed a failure in the US. It didn't matter if 'Heart of Glass' charted, it was the third single off the album, which was called dead in the water.

Blondie returned to the US in despair in September 1978. They were still broke despite being successful and famous in the UK and in Europe, and they were even more frazzled and worn out. What mattered most to Harry and Stein was to try and get their lives back in order and back in their control. After nearly a solid year and a half of touring, Harry and Stein finally moved out of a hotel into a real apartment, a small penthouse on 58th Street near Central Park. Next, with the legal advice of their business manager, Bert Padell and their lawyer Marty Silfin, they tried to re-negotiate their contract with Leeds. Leeds says they asked him to relinquish too much authority and that he wanted to leave because the band was making him miserable. The only path for Blondie and Leeds was divorce.

Blondie continued touring in support of *Parallel Lines* and from October 29 to November 16 they played Long Island, Boston, Philadelphia, Buffalo and Cleveland. At the end of the tour they started interviewing other managers. After considering about forty candidates, they decided on Shep Gordon, who had worked with Alice Cooper. Harry says in *Making Tracks* that Gordon won them over by saying less not more. 'Shep said "I'm interested and if you want me to do it, I will." And he didn't want a contract, whereas practically all the others wanted big solid binding five-year contracts with options.'

Harry and Stein felt they'd been burned badly by Leeds, mostly because they felt personally betrayed and disillusioned by his tactics. Being exhausted by his regime of relentless touring and then, constantly being told that they were either broke or that the money was 'in the pipeline' made them feel even more abused. Unfortunately, their exit agreement with Leeds stated that he would earn 20% of the gross off any Blondie or Deborah Harry projects originated at Chrysalis Records – a figure which guaranteed he'd earn more money in perpetuity than the band or the record company. So to add insult to injury, they would feel scalded by Leeds for the rest of their lives.

Of course, Leeds feels burned too. He says, 'I couldn't have accomplished what we did if I had to ask their permission for everything. They don't give me any credit for their success and I don't care.' Contrary to what he says, he actually appears to care very much. 'Everyone at Chrysalis has said to me you are the smartest one – you made the most money and you got out. But I do have regrets. A) I could have made more money if they weren't assholes and I'd have stayed with them, and B) I didn't get to enjoy a lot of things. Like, I never got to stand backstage at a big stadium gig – that all happened after me.'

Just as they were severing their ties with Leeds, Blondie finally got what they'd been working up to – their first hit single in the US, 'Heart of Glass'.

SUCCESS IN THE US

The importance of Blondie breaking in the US was twofold. From a financial perspective, Chrysalis had told the band that unless they were a hit in the US market, they would never really make money. The need to cover their debts to the record company and Leeds, and come out with something for themselves, drove them on this front. It is also possible that the record company exaggerated their situation in an attempt to keep them desperate and therefore motivated. But the second issue was really more one of pride. They had been a hit in every other major market around the world and yet in their home country, they were being largely ignored. For Blondie it just didn't add up. It was one of many things that confounded the band as they were exposed to more of the harsh realities of the music business.

On New Year's Eve 1978–9 Blondie played the Winterland in San Francisco, opening for one of the biggest bands in the US at the time, REO Speedwagon. When they returned to New York, finally, they saw that 'Heart of Glass' was steadily climbing the US charts. What came next were offers for Blondie to appear on nearly every American TV outlet available for musicians, including the *Mike Douglas Show*, *The Merv Griffin Show*, *Late Night with Johnny Carson*, *Dick Clark's American Bandstand* and the *Midnight Special*. All of them finally saw what the rest of the world already knew: Blondie was a great band with great songs young people could really relate to, and Deborah Harry was an incredible, photogenic and telegenic lead singer both men and women would adore.

Getting on TV was always a priority for Blondie. They were a visual band and they knew that it was important to entertain, not just play music. But early on they also figured out that being beamed into the homes of millions of people was a far less physically taxing way to reach them than months and months of grueling tours.

Around this time, Harry also decided to pursue acting. She had always wanted to be a movie star. Harry's dramatic acting debut was in an indie film by Mark Reichert called *Union City* in February 1979. Stein, ever Harry's collaborator, got a chance to write music for the film score, a long-time interest of his. The movie's title track, 'Union City Blue', would appear on Blondie's next album, *Eat to the Beat*. For the rest of the band and for Blondie's record label, Chrysalis, it must have been threatening to see Harry and Stein so easily swept up in other projects, but from the beginning, the duo had always had interests broader than pop music.

Blondie travelled to Europe in March to do TV appearances to promote *Parallel Lines*, which due to bad planning turned out to be as grueling as touring. Because everyone assumed TV was easier than touring, the band was given no recovery time or days off, and they were booked back to back from city to city. Harry says in *Making Tracks*, 'Our schedule moved us even faster from city to city. Sleep was down to five hours a night. Get on a plane at nine a.m. kids! Every night we dined on great exotic European meals, so we ended up having low blood pressure, which makes it hard to wake up in the morning. We were now the biggest pop stars in Europe, zooming around in limousines to the best restaurants, but meanwhile, we were totally zonked out and unable to eat, feeling like we were a hundred years old. Everything seems to balance out. You always pay for what you get. And as you get to know what the price is, you get a better idea of how far you want to go and how much you want to pay.'

After winning so many uphill battles in her career – fighting to get signed, fighting to get away from Private Stock to Chrysalis, fighting to break in Europe and Asia, fighting to make a better record than they'd ever made before with Mike Chapman, fighting to get away from Peter Leeds and finally, fighting to get on the charts and on the radio in the US, Harry was clearly wondering when the combat would end. And if that was never going to happen, was all this struggle worth it?

Blondie was in Italy when they heard that 'Heart of Glass' finally hit number one in the US. With only one month to recoup in New York, Blondie made a video for the song and in May went into the studio to record *Eat to the Beat*. Coincidentally, working in neighboring studios at the Power Station were the Kinks, Bruce Springsteen and Nile Rodgers and Bernard Edwards of Chic (who would later work with Harry and Stein on Harry's solo projects). Mike Chapman and the band knew each other well this second time around, so even though Chapman was going through a prickly divorce, and there were mounting tensions in the band, things were smoother in the studio.

After the recording of *Eat to the Beat* was complete, Blondie set out to do a round of shows in US cities. Harry says in *Making Tracks* that the stage shows were spruced up with help from a choreographer, an old New York cohort named Tony Ingrassia, who had worked with the Stilettos. Blondie also travelled first class the whole way. The only thorn in their side was their opening band, Rockpile, who resented their status and took offence at every perceived slight. By all accounts Harry and the band enjoyed themselves on the *Eat to the Beat* Tour, which was followed by the group's cameo in the Meatlof movie, *Roadie*.

Next, the band returned to New York to create one of the first rock video albums – videos to accompany each song on *Eat to the Beat*. As this project married Harry's love of music and movies, she enjoyed the process immensely. Although there were limited outlets for music videos at the time in the US, as there was as yet no MTV, the videos would eventually help boost Blondie's profile worldwide. Videos had served them well back when the 'In The Flesh' video made the single become a hit in Australia, and again, sending videos out around the world was easier than touring or even making TV appearances.

However, Blondie did do a small tour in Europe where a single off *Eat to the Beat* was already number one – 'Dreaming', perhaps the most perfect Blondie song ever. It was in London on this tour that Blondie felt the full force of Blondiemania. A Blondie record signing at Our Price Records on Kensington High Street attracted thousands of screaming fans, creating a massive traffic jam. Film footage from this event shows Harry sticking her head out the window above the screaming crowd, laughing and waving – she appears incredulous. Blondie even had to employ a bodyguard for Harry, although in *Making Tracks* she maintains that she never felt vulnerable in public. In an odd parallel, it was during this visit to London that Blondie had a chance encounter with Beatle Paul McCartney and his wife Linda, outside their hotel as they were boarding the tour bus.

Blondie played a triumphant New Year's Eve 1979–80 show at the Apollo in Glasgow, which was filmed by the BBC, and then wrapped up their European Tour in London at the Hammersmith Odeon where they were treated as part of the rock 'n'roll elite. These were tremendous shows for Blondie, and in *Making Tracks*, Harry says reflectively, 'In truth, our British fans made us pop stars.'

BEGINNING OF THE END

In January of 1980, Blondie was at the peak of its success and by all accounts, although there were still tensions in the band, they were enjoying it. Therefore, it's hard to piece together all of the factors that led to their very public crash and burn just two years later.

1980 continued on a high note with disco maven Gorgio Moroder asking Blondie to do the theme song for a new Paul Schrader movie, *American Gigolo*. Moroder had first offered the song to Stevie Nicks, but after she declined, he called to offer it to Harry. It was their first job as guns for hire, and the effort would produce Blondie's biggest hit of all time – 'Call Me'. The title of the song was copped from the movie's gigolo antihero, played by Richard Gere. Harry liked the movie a lot, but rejected Moroder's lyric ideas and rewrote the song herself. 'Call Me' was then recorded in two days in New York, incorporating a synthesizer track Moroder had made in LA. 'Call Me' became Blondie's second number one single in the US, and *Billboard*'s number one song of the year.

Harry and Stein were happy with the success of 'Call

Me', but the rest of Blondie regarded the song as too commercial, and tensions inside the band were at an all time high. Blondie took a break and all the band members used the time to branch out on their own and use their success to either help other artists, or finally do some work with other collaborators. Blondie also tried to renegotiate their record deal with Chrysalis at this juncture, as they felt they still weren't seeing all the money they were owed and they wanted a better royalty rate.

When the band came back together to work on *Autoamerican*, all of the members of Blondie had had some time to reflect on their success and discovered they weren't entirely comfortable with it. Even though they had worked hard, perhaps they all felt a little guilty about how big they'd become. This translated into the need to push themselves even more to prove they were deserving of their hype. And while they remain cavalier about it, the venom from their New York peers about Blondie 'selling out' to disco must have taken some toll. Regardless, Harry and Stein in particular did not want to rest on their laurels. If anything, they wanted to use their name to push even newer hybrids of music into the mainstream. Still, they couldn't be naive about record sales either, so the convergence of all these issues, plus the input of the 'seventh Blondie' – producer Mike Chapman, gave birth to the mature and futuristic *Autoamerican*.

Autoamerican has also been cited as the album where Blondie started getting a little 'weird', but from Harry and Stein's perspective, what good was success if it couldn't buy them more artistic freedom? Other band members were less enthusiastic about the ideas in the album, and just wanted to make more good music. Ultimately, *Autoamerican* was successful in incorporating both. To everyone's surprise, the risky songs did the best anyway. The reggae-influenced cover of 'The Tide Is High' went to number one in the US, which was only made less phenomenal when 'Rapture', the first number one rap song in the pop charts, followed it.

But even with the success of these two unusual singles, Harry and Stein didn't feel like they got to exorcise all their creative demons. After all, as long as they were part of Blondie, they had to sound like Blondie (at least enough to make their record company happy), and they had to consider the other members of the band who certainly had a big say in any direction Blondie took. Also with Blondie, Harry and Stein had to put their songs in the hands of Mike Chapman. Chapman saw his job as picking the hits, so often Harry and Stein's more esoteric efforts were passed over. Even the songs chosen by Chapman were often cleaned up to sound more commercial, which didn't always sit well with Stein. It was the idea of being able to go in the directions they couldn't go in with Blondie that inspired Harry's 1981 solo album, *Koo Koo*. The end product was a fusion of rock and R&B, produced by Chic's Nile Rodgers and Bernard Edwards.

To be fair to the band, Deborah Harry completely changed her look for her solo album's cover and for the videos to promote it, which were made in collaboration with sci-fi surrealist, H. R. Giger. But Harry also changed her image because she felt trapped and dominated by the Blondie character she had so lovingly created. Even as opportunities for Harry in film started to materialize, she realized she was stereotyped by her Blondie image. All movie people thought she could play was a brazen, sexy rock babe and Harry wanted to do more.

Although fame and success had come with enormous pressures, it had also given Deborah Harry a peculiar kind of strength and wisdom. If there was something she started out desperate to prove to herself, it appears she had. Which isn't to say she wasn't thrilled to be working on new projects, but she was now free to do stuff more exclusively for her own enjoyment and the value of the work itself. She says at the end of *Making Tracks*, 'The older I get, the better I feel. I had the weight of the world on me when I was younger, and I was very unsure a lot of the time, out of touch, and half of what I should have been. Now that my other half is here too I'm very happy. I'm glad I'm doing what I'm doing. When I see myself doing something and I'm satisfied with it, it's the best feeling. That's what everybody wants.'

Harry, taking the time to pursue other projects however, did take time away from Blondie, a real sore point for the other members of the band (excluding Stein), who simply didn't have all the options Harry had. Burke, Destri, Infante and Harrison also missed touring, which they felt was an essential part of being musicians, and what they enjoyed most about being in a band. Meanwhile, Harry and Stein, who were also at this point respectively 36 and 31, were tired of touring and liked staying put in New York. Touring with Blondie was also a whole different kind of torture for Harry, who had to do the majority of the work both onstage and offstage, dealing with the press on behalf of the band.

Harry's solo album had also confused the public about whether or not Blondie was breaking up. *Making Tracks* co-author and Andy Warhol biographer Victor Bockris remembers, 'I was talking to Andy at the Factory one day and he says, "Why has Debbie broken up Blondie?" And I said, Andy, Debbie is an intelligent person. She doesn't want to be stuck in a cartoon role her whole life. And he said, "Well, what do you think I do everyday?"'

Warhol's question reflects what a lot of people thought at the time. Deborah Harry had a good thing going with Blondie, they were generating a lot of money and she was the most famous and most photographed woman in the world, perhaps even more so than Princess Diana. So why would she walk away from it? Even today, people have a difficult time accepting that for Harry, this level of fame wasn't the be all and end all. It simply didn't satisfy or suit her. Bockris says, 'I was always very much in support of what Debbie and Chris were doing because I understood they were really sort of Beat characters who just wanted to do what they wanted to do, without necessarily doing what made the most money.'

Koo Koo sold very poorly, in part because the record company didn't push it, fearing it would confuse the public. Harry appeared on the cover as a brunette with four needles piercing her face. As gorgeous as the artwork, a painting by Swiss surrealist H. R. Giger, was, it was banned from several record stores and posters promoting the album. Chrysalis was also being ambivalent about Harry doing any solo work in the first place, especially solo work that was so dramatically different from Blondie. Deborah Harry and Blondie, as they had been for the first five albums, was the formula they knew they could sell, and what they knew the audience wanted. And as much as that view may appear distastefully conservative, part of the blame lies with the mainstream pop audience. Because they proved Chrysalis right. Deborah Harry's hardcore fans would stay with her whatever she did, but the mass audience wanted Blondie.

Without Harry, there was no Blondie in the eyes of the record company and in the eyes of their fans. So the pressure of determining Blondie's future was heaped on Harry's shoulders – if she didn't want to continue, the band did not continue. It was an unfair position for both the band and for Harry to be in, and divisions grew, exacerbated by the record company and various manipulative Blondie handlers who all had their own purposes to serve. Finally, at Stein's urging, Harry agreed to do another Blondie album and tour, even though her heart wasn't in it.

Blondie's sixth album, *The Hunter*, was released in 1982. Differences aside, the band was proud of it. However, like *Koo Koo*, it reflected a darker side of Harry and a much darker Blondie. While the other Blondie albums embodied the spirit of youth, rebellion, frustrated desire and fun for fun's sake (albeit with some nasty subtexts), *The Hunter* was clearly about Blondie feeling like an endangered species. Harry says of the theme of the album, and the single from it called 'The Hunter Gets Captured By The Game': 'We identified as both hunter and hunted, but obviously we were more of the hunted at that point. We were really marked for slaughter and decimated by a bunch of different people right around then, as we had really bad business problems.' Harry further says that dissension behind the scenes at Chrysalis was in part responsible for the album's failure. 'There were changes going on at the record company as well. There are usually personnel changes at a record company every five years and those are deadly to an artist because very often the people who sign you aren't there any more and the new honcho who comes in isn't really interested in old artists.'

And as much money as Blondie had made for Chrysalis, by 1982 they were in Chrysalis' eyes 'old artists'. Harry says the record label was never behind *The Hunter*: 'The record company [Chrysalis] just didn't market it. All of our records were different from what they expected. Every time we handed in a record, they'd say, Uh, we don't hear any singles on this, and hand it back. We handed them *Parallel Lines*, which ultimately had six singles worldwide on it, but they handed it back and said they didn't hear any singles on it. *Autoamerican*, which had "Rapture" and "The Tide Is High" on it was the same way. They were always expecting to hear one thing and they got something else, and at that point, when they got something they didn't expect, because of the bad management and the bad business management we had, things started to waffle.'

Harry refers to the ultimately disappointing relationship Blondie had with Shep Gordon and accountant Burt Padell, the circumstances of which remain veiled in secrecy. Peter Leeds, who is somewhat biased, as Padell helped Blondie negotiate his exit agreement, is the only one who would speak on the record. The way he understands it, Padell and Gordon were also in business together and they served each other's interests over Blondie's.

The combination of continuing business problems and a lack of enthusiasm from the record company might have been enough to break Blondie, but what finally shut them down without really giving them the chance to promote *The Hunter* was Chris Stein's illness. The episode of *Glenn O'Brien's TV Party* referred to in Chapter Two shows Stein picking at a blister on his lip. He is painfully thin and noticeably sickly. O'Brien and Stein joke about how Stein used to weigh 175lbs but is now down to 145lbs, and about how Stein's just gotten out of the 'diet hospital', getting in shape for *The Hunter* Tour. Their light-heartedness doesn't hide a feeling of alarm conveyed by Stein's long-time friend O'Brien. He says of Stein's illness in retrospect, 'No one knew what was going on and it was pretty frightening.'

Stein collapsed after a show early in *The Hunter* Tour and everything stopped. Stein was hospitalized and later diagnosed with the life-threatening illness Pemphigus Vulgaris, a genetic disease which caused his skin to erupt in blisters outside his body and inside his mouth and throat. The condition was eventually treated with steroids, but Harry nursed him from his hospital bedside for months. It took Stein a good four years to physically recover and almost a decade to really get back on his feet again, but he was a changed man. As he says himself in his interview in chapter 7, a changed man for the better.

As for Blondie's demise, O'Brien, who has also written about music for more than 20 years, sums it up this way: 'A lot of things that happened to Blondie happened to a lot of artists in the music business. A lot of great artists get screwed over. It's not like anyone is looking out for young musicians when someone comes along and waves a big check in front of them. In a lot of ways, their bad experiences were typical. How many bands last longer than they did anyway? Not many.'

BLONDIE COMES OUT ON TOP

Blondie has to date sold over 40 million records worldwide, and have had a dozen top ten singles in the UK, Holland, Germany, Australia and the US, including, but not limited to, 'In The Flesh', 'Denis', 'Heart of Glass', 'One Way or Another', 'Dreaming', 'Atomic', 'Rapture', 'The Tide Is High' and 'Call Me'. To top it off, Blondie's 1978 album *Parallel Lines*, has been included in a number of music critics' lists of the 100 greatest pop/rock albums of all time. Some record by any standard but then Blondie never a straightforward pop band, as critics then and since have been quick to recognize.

John Holmstrom: 'I think I was the only one outside Blondie who thought they had a chance in hell of getting a record contract. I was really your average music consumer at the time and I didn't like any of the bands they were pushing as the next big thing. The attitudes of people hanging out at CBGB's were so parochial – "Oh, the Marbles are going to be the big band" or "Milk 'n' Cookies are going to be bigger than the [Bay City] Rollers." People were picking bands that had already peaked. They were as good as they were going to get. Not only did Blondie have a sound I thought could really go somewhere, the main thing I saw was energy.'

David Byrne: 'I think Blondie brought a lot of styles to the pop mainstream that weren't there before. Things they were listening too, they incorporated. When they got really successful, I wondered how they were going to handle it, and for a while, they seemed to be handling it very well. They kept doing what they set out to do and they did it well. They didn't just crash and burn after the first hit song.

And Blondie had a whole sense of being a pop band, but playing at being a pop band as kind of a role. Debbie took on the role of being a glamorous rock 'n' roll singer but it was always with a wink to let you know this was just a part that she was playing. But like any actor, they have to love the character to do it well, and she did. But she was always letting you know, musically and physically, that this was all kind of a game. I don't know if once they became really successful, if that was always picked up by the audience. Debbie and the band kept what they were about, but that part of the message may have been lost.'

Lisa Robinson: 'Of the whole CBGB's scene, Blondie had the most commercial success, so it was easy to sneer and say, well of course they had the biggest success, they sold out the most or they weren't the most left of center or they weren't that interesting. But that was really a silly injustice to them. Blondie really reflected the streets of New York. They did a lot of stuff combining and connecting street stuff that was happening in art, music and fashion. I had never heard of Stephen Sprouse before Debbie. Blondie had rap in their music when that scene was just starting to exist. Plus, it's a huge accomplishment to reach that many people and to create songs people want to hum and dance to. They made great records with great songs and they were able to break out into radio at a time when radio was dominated by bands like Styx, REO Speedwagon and Journey – that's a huge accomplishment. I think they knew exactly what they were doing.'

Kurt Loder: 'Blondie was a phenomenal band – not live, they were a little sloppy live. Well, let's say they were a little punky live, but on records they were just so good. They are also great songwriters. Their lyrics were very unusual – 'In The Flesh' is a very unusual song. They were obviously influenced by a lot of styles. They had a great drummer – Clem Burke, and Gary Valentine was a great bass player – it's too bad he lost his mind. Then

Jimmy Destri had a real unique keyboard sound. I loved them, they were so great! I was unhappy when they broke up.'

Rodney Bingenheimer: 'Blondie is the answer to all your problems! Put on Blondie and your Beach Boy albums to get you out of your depression. They had an influence on music in LA and just on music in general. Any band with a woman in it, and any woman in a band who I've had on my show, say they were influenced by Debbie. But of course, Debbie wasn't happy about it. She was like, They are ripping off my style! And I was like, It's a compliment. I still see her influence everywhere, but it's all gone downhill since Blondie. I hate the 90s in every way and I blame it all on Blondie breaking up.'

CHAPTER FOUR
The Deborah Harry Interview
PART 2

BLONDIEMANIA AT ITS PEAK (1975–82)

How did your life change most from the 70s to the 80s?

Well, in the early 80s, Blondie became so successful, I became a little distanced from the downtown culture, which is why I appreciate it so much now. I became a part of the mechanism of the industry in the early 80s and I didn't know how to handle it. I didn't know how to live with that kind of exposure or that kind of money. It sort of took me away from what made me pop creatively. I found that difficult.

As the most successful band to come out of the CBGB's scene, did you feel alienated from your peers?

Well, alienated I'm not so sure, but certainly distanced. It was a peculiar situation to out-distance all your friends and contemporaries in money that way, because then they are sort of relying on you for money or for this or that, and it does get really heavy.

People don't necessarily think about the burdens that success can bring.

It depends on your nature too. Some people are very happy

Above: HIPPY HARRY: Deborah Harry in the Wind in the Willows, Sun Rise Mountain, New Jersey, 1968. COURTESY OF PAUL KLEIN/JANE RICHTER/ART N FRAME

BLONDIE BOMBSHELL: Deborah Harry electrifies the album covers of *Blondie* (1976), *Plastic Letters* (1977), *Parallel Lines* (1979) and her solo effort, *Def, Dumb and Blonde* (1989)

blondie

PLASTIC
LETTERS

'DIGITALLY REMASTERED INCLUDES BONUS TRACKS'

DEBORAH HARRY

DEF DUMB &
BLONDE

DIGITALLY
REMASTERED

DON'T YOU WANT ME?: Deborah Harry
as cover girl for *High Times* (*above, right*)
(PHOTOGRAPH BY FRANCESCO SCAVULLO © TRANS-HIGH CORPORATION)
COURTESY OF JOHN HOLMSTROM, **as a comic creation for** *Punk* **magazine** (*above, left*)
(ILLUSTRATION BY BOBBY LONDON © PUNK PUBLICATIONS), **and various Blondie collectables**
(***below***) COURTESY OF HOWDY DO COLLECTABLES, NEW YORK AND DEBORAH HARRY DOLL COURTESY
OF BOB SELLSTEDT (PHOTOGRAPH BY JENS MORTENSEN)

bove: POP STAR POP ART: Andy
arhol's portrait of Deborah Harry,
nthetic polymer paint and silkscreen
k on canvas, 1980.

ght: MAIL ME: Rare Debbie Harry
amp from Mali.

Above: BEAUTY AND THE MEAT: Deborah Harry calms the wild Meat (loaf) in Alan Rudolph's 1980 film, *Roadie.*

© RONALD GRANT ARCHIVE

Left: HARRY WIGS OUT: Deborah Harry with Sonny Bono in John Water's 1987 film *Hairspray.*

© MOVIESTORE COLLECTION

Above Left: LOVERS LIP-LOCK: Deborah Harry and Chris Stein display their mutual admiration in the New York City subway, 1977. © ROBERTA BAYLEY

Above Right: SURVIVAL CHIC: Deborah Harry pre-dates 90s safety gear fashion on stage in Berkeley, California, 1977. © THERESA KEREAKES

Below: URBAN BEACH BABE: Deborah Harry unwinds at Coney Island, New York in 1977. © ROBERTA BAYLEY

Left: RAMONEO: Joey Ramone and Deborah Harry pose for *Punk magazine,* New York, 1977. © ROBERTA BAYLEY

Below: THE VIEW FROM HERE: Blondie on stage at CBGBs, New York, 1977.
© ROBERTA BAYLEY

to make a lot of money. I was certainly happy to make a lot of money, but people handle it in different ways. There's a responsibility that comes with it, but I wasn't motivated that way. I guess I wanted to be rich and famous, but I mostly wanted to be famous [laughs].

And what did you enjoy most about success and being famous? When do you most often think to yourself, Hey, I'm having a good time?

Performance, getting to perform – that's it for me. And of course, some moments when acting, when I really got out there in that total magic cellular spot when everything else vanishes and you're totally captivated and in that moment. Those are great times. I guess that's the Alpha Zone? Something like that.

When you look back on your career, what are you most proud of in terms of your contributions to pop music?

I don't know . . . I guess we, not me personally, but Blondie and Mike Chapman, were responsible for creating a lot of areas of new music, a lot of crossover areas.

Were your adopted parents happy for you or worried about you when you became so famous?

Probably all of the above.

Your mother, who was interviewed for the Blondie cover story of Rolling Stone in 1979, was clearly so proud of you.

Yeah.

That piece was venomous though.

I guess, [Jamie James] wrote two pieces for *Rolling Stone* and they were both so rotten, he was fired. Unfortunately, one was about me. He was awful, he was such an asshole – a strutting little pompous git. I had said we couldn't do the interview at a certain time, and he showed up anyway and started doing the interview. So I walked into the room and he was like, Well, I just thought I'd come and hang out! I thought, Oh, this is really wrong, and from that point on it was all downhill. He was invasive of our rehearsal time and our space, and after I said he couldn't hang out, that's when he got out the hatchet. But I've been chopped up quite a bit since then and it doesn't phase me anymore. It's just part of the ritual.

It's interesting how many different kinds of music you've done over the years – jazz, Cole Porter, rap, rock, pop . . .

Well, to me as a singer, a song is a song. I know there are different phrasings and different attitudes, but as a singer, I approach it from the emotion of the piece and when I do that, I actually come out as a better singer than if I try to be a tech-nician.

I saw you once on The Muppet Show *singing the 'Rainbow Connection'. What is the weirdest celebrity cameo that you've done?*

I never got near winning a Grammy Award, but one year they asked me to present an award and I appeared with George Burns. And we did this joke, and that was a moment for me. We did a little routine that George wrote, and I don't remember exactly what it was, but I'm sure I fucked it up.

Is there anything that you haven't been asked to do that you wish they'd ask you to do, like sing the national anthem at a big football game or something? You know, Whitney Houston was once offered a million dollars to sing at a mass Moonie wedding. She didn't show up though.

[pause] I'm stunned into silence . . .

Since you've already played Vegas, what would be odd for you to be asked to do at this point – host The Rose Bowl Parade?

I can't imagine them asking me to host the Rose Bowl

unless they had an ulterior motive to use me as target practice for a pie-throwing contest. Those shows are so circus-like. I did a show in Europe [in 1997] called *The Night of The Proms*, where I sang Blondie songs with an 80-piece orchestra and a 50-piece choir and a little rock band incorporated into the ensemble, and I felt like I should have had a whip and a chair on stage with me. I don't know if that would have gone with my songs, but for that event, I really felt like it would have been right. It was wild.

PICTURE THIS

What are your favorite pictures of yourself?

I don't know if I have one particular favorite, but I sort of like the ones that Mapplethorpe did. It's interesting to see how each photographer sees you and how you respond to them. The other thing I like is the moodiness of Chris's pictures. They are so intimate and so personal and tender. They have an intimate quality to them.

What about pictures of you when you're screaming, mouth open – very proactive?

Yeah, most of the ones I really like are the ones that are live shots that capture something when you're not prepared and you're not posing. It's really a moment and good photography. I've got one on my fridge like that. A fan took it from the audience. I'm bellowing into the microphone and my face is totally distorted and my teeth are bared and my hair is all sweaty and stringy but it's great. I just love it. I think it's a really cool picture – it's the real deal. You can't pose that, there's just no way. It's like when you catch a dancer in mid-flight.

But I never liked myself in pictures until I started wearing make-up, you know? I hated the way that I looked. People are weird aren't they? I'm weird. I loathed the sound of my voice for years too. I think it was only after Chris started taking pictures of me that I learned to relax with it and understand what the process was. I never seemed to work with [any photographer] who made me feel comfortable – it was always sort of nerve racking.

It must have seemed very strange to you then when people started announcing that you were one of the most beautiful people in the world?

Very bizarre, yes.

What ever happened with the original cover art for Plastic Letters, *which was rejected by your record label, Private Stock?*

I don't know if I have the pictures we took or if the record company has them. It was shot in that huge parking lot on Santa Monica Boulevard [in LA]. When it was in construction, it was right across the street from the Tropicana Hotel. They were building this huge parking lot and there was just this unworldly kind of structure there with these huge pillars and ramps and things. I made this dress from a pillowcase and red gaffer tape. It really looked great. Then somebody came around with an old convertible and we just started hanging around this car. It looked fabulous! It sort of reminded me of what the Plasmatics did later, but they [the label] hated it. It was too extreme.

Did your good friend Anya Phillips make the pink dress on the cover of Plastic Letters?

Anya made the pattern for that dress and I actually made it from her design. But I used a little different technique than she used – I actually sewed it. She use to just punch holes in the fabric and tie little knots and do it all with strings, which was all very spidery and wonderful. But I was a little worried about that, as the one who had to jump around in it. I wanted it a little more substantial. Not that it was noticeable, but she was like [mildly disapproving tone], Oh, well, I would have never done this. I would have just done that.

She did the dress in 'The Hardest Part' video too right? By the way, is that you in that video?

Yeah, why?

In some interview I read or some fan club newsletter, you refer to the fact that another girl played your part in that video.

Oh, I was probably just being cute. Disgusting isn't it? I also have a pair of pants and a halter top of Anya's that I used for that song I did for Scarface – it's white and really fantastic. What was that song called? I might have done that with Giorgio [Moroder]? Gosh, it's just too much stuff, you know? You get moving really fast for eight years and things just pile up and when you get back, you just don't want to look at it.

Over the years, have you kept your own collection of all the Blondie press and Blondie memorabilia?

Well, we had our archive stored in Chris's basement and then, a couple of years ago, he had a flood – like four or five feet of water and all these tapes and pictures were ruined. We saved as much as we could. Everything jarred memories, but it was just a big nightmare that everything was in peril. I mean, some of the tapes we sent to be rebaked and we had to hang these posters out to dry. You just start pulling it out and it's all a big montage of what you've done, who you've met and where you've been. You start going like, Oh, San Francisco – that was really good. If we did it with everyone in the band, then you'd have the total story with everyone talking about the same night. That would be really interesting and really funny [sighs]. We did a lot of stupid rock 'n' roll stuff.

So, I wanted to talk about designer Stephen Sprouse. He declined to be interviewed for the book, but the two of you had such a major collaboration.

Well, Stephen was great when we first met in the 70s. He's kinda shy but he really knows what he wants, he's just really hesitant to spit it out. In old pictures, before Stephen, you can see I was sort of dressing in like cowboy boots with an old 40s dress – I was really all over the place, wearing whatever caught my eye.

But some of your old looks were really great, like ripped t-shirts and underwear with boots.

Yeah, some of it worked. But Stephen got me started with those really high over the knee boots. And Stephen was great because he took me and said, 'Here, wear these boots and this mini skirt and these big Italian shades'. It was simple.

You had your own fashion flair. Why did you put so much trust in his opinion?

[laughs] Because he could draw really well. He'd won some big design award when he was fourteen or fifteen, so as soon as he graduated from High School, he went to work for Halston. He worked on a lot of Halston's designs – a lot of Halston was Stephen.

He lived with you in the loft on the Bowery didn't he?

Yeah, he was living on the third or fourth floor. It was a crazy place – I don't know how he lived up there – there was no heat.

You did so many things that we now think of as good fashion – the found and customized clothes, the ripped t-shirt and knickers sort of punk look, the red, white and black power 80s look, and then the op art, asymmetrical, monochromatic look. But was there anything that stands out for you now as bad fashion – like, Wow, what was I thinking?

[pauses] Well, I'm sure there were times that something I wore should have had a better sense of line or whatever, but you'd have to show me pictures and then I could analyze it and rip it apart.

Rip yourself to shreds?

[laughs] Yeah, but you know, I just don't think about it that much. Stephen was great because he would send me out with drawings and show me how to mix and match everything and all the alternatives, so it was so concise and so perfect, that I wouldn't have to think too much. The only thing was I got really sick of wearing black, but then he got into all those pop colors.

Yes, there are pictures of you from 1981 in an anti-black outfit that was neon green and you wore a neon green wig too.

Well, that was my *Koo Koo* stage and I had to do something different from Blondie, so I used to coordinate everything – the outfits and the wigs were all the same color. Candy Price Pratts [former fashion editor at American *Vogue*] gave me all these synthetic wigs when they first came out, so I had all these crazy colored wigs. Candy lived in the building both Stephen and I moved into on 58th Street. I've been very fortunate and it's all been very serendipitous that I've ended up living with all these people who are so talented and so generous. Stephen just loved rock 'n' roll and rock 'n' roll really feeds him. When he's working he always has music blasting. I regret that we've had a falling out, and I don't know if it's my fault, but it's really unfortunate.

Were sneakers the punk shoe?

They were for the Ramones.

What about dark glasses? How did that start as one of your signature looks?

Well, shades have always been really cool. I started wearing glasses and I guess it was sort of this pop look. Then, when we were living downtown on the Bowery there were these junk stores that were actually very, very good. There were actually fences that operated from these junk stores, so the junk was meaningless, it was just piled in there. Us kids would walk around and see all this crazy shit and that became our gear. So one time they had this load of Japanese golf glasses that were big, chunky old things from the 40s and 50s, and those became like the signature glasses because they looked fantastic. I have a wide face and most glasses don't fit me, so I found these glasses for wide faces and was like, Here they are – glasses for me!

You still wear those today, so how many pairs did you buy?

I don't know, but I should have bought more.

Were they only black with black frames?

There were hornrimmed ones too and I got them both.

Later, did glasses become a shield to hide behind when the spotlight of fame got too intense?

Well, they are really convenient when you've just got off an airplane or just got up in the morning and you haven't put your make-up on and you look fucked up. They always look cool and they are always very rock 'n' roll.

What about the dark roots? You are credited with being the first to purposefully wear dark roots with your platinum hair.

Mostly I was into sectioning and having sections of color. The roots well, I really didn't mind having two-tone hair so I would let it go for a while, but what I was really trying to achieve was stripes, like animal stripes, but I just never had

88

the patience to put the bleach on that carefully. For myself, I wanted animal [growls] on my head.

Thus, the lion wig for The Hunter *later. For that album cover, you were supposed to have morphed lion faces too, right?*

Yeah, we just couldn't find someone who could really image it without making us look like cute little Walt Disney characters. We wanted it to be really good-looking, wild and tribal.

THE STORY BEHIND THE SONGS

Is 'Platinum Blonde' the first song you ever wrote?

Yes, it is. [she recites the full lyrics]

I want to be a platinum blonde
Just like all the sexy stars
Marilyn and Jean, Jayne, Mae and Marlene
They proved it, they really had fun
In a luminescent dayglow shade
I'll walk into a bar and I'll have it made
Cause if that's all it takes – a double processed blonde
I want to be a platinum blonde
I want to be a platinum blonde
I even tried wearing a wig for a while
It was the right color but not the right style
I'm going to get some peroxide at the beauty supply

[she's laughing] That's pretty much it. It just repeats. There's another song I wrote called 'Puerto Rico' around that same time, it's really sick and very camp. I like that one. 'In The Flesh' was a part of that early stage. There was another song that we used to do in the Stilettos that Elda wrote that was a scream called 'Wednesday Panties' that was just so sweet. It went . . .

Monday, pink Monday
Tuesday bluuuuuue
Thursday, Friday, Saturday, Sunday
Wednesday, what happened to you?
I left my Wednesday panties in Passaic
Passaic, New Jersey [laughs]

[more laughs] *Yeah! What about 'You Look Good In Blue'? Who looks good in blue? Is it you?*

No, I don't think so. That's one of Jimmy [Destri]'s. All his songs are pretty much about women and relationships.

Well, you do look good in blue too. How about 'I Didn't Have The Nerve To Say No'?

Well, that's a problem I relate to. I think I even wrote that one? [Hums a few notes] I can't remember how they all go. But it's all self-contained in the title. A lot of people can't say no and it gets them into really bad spots. There's this friend of mine who can't say no and she constantly lets people down. You ask her for something and get involved in this whole process of getting something done and – it doesn't happen. But she can't do it, she can't just say, No!

I thought that song might have been inspired by your experiences in Japan where they don't even have a word for 'No' – a whole culture that can't say no. You say in your book, Making Tracks: The Rise of Blondie, *that you'd say no to your handlers in Japan and they'd totally ignore it and just state the same request three different ways. But I guess that's really more of a technique for not letting someone else say no.*

Oh, yeah. I've been through all that bullshit too [laughs].

Okay, what about everybody's early favorite – 'Rip Her To Shreds'?

That one is kind of autobiographical. It's about the girls at CB's [CBGB's] – myself as well, gossiping and taking the bitchy queen kind of approach. It was meant in good fun. Like, 'She's so dull, rip her to shreds' – [it's kind of like an inner voice] talking about yourself at the same time. Scary! This is a funny story, when I first went to Australia, they couldn't wait for me to rip my clothes off, because they heard I did that when I sang that song. These people were so horny!

They thought you were some kind of sex-crazed slut?

That was fine though, you know, I had my moments.

'One Way or Another'?

That one is about this stalker boyfriend I had. I broke up with him and he became a stalker and he was really good at it. He worked at a job where he was inhaling chemical fumes all day, and then he would drink at night, so he'd get really insane and then he'd start after me.

You mean call you every hour on the hour or physically come after you?

Both, I mean, everything. He was so wild, I had to move out of New Jersey! So it might have been the first stalker song ever written, although I don't think they even called it stalking in those days. I think we just called them pests.

What about 'Will Anything Happen'?

I think that was Jimmy's song too, so it must have been about some woman.

It wasn't a collective cry from the band about your career? It's on Parallel Lines, *your US breakthrough album?*

No, sorry.

'Just Go Away'?

[starts singing] 'Don't go away mad, Don't go away sad,

Just go away . . .' I think that says it all. You know – Just leave me alone. Exit. Departez-vous. Splitzky. Get off my cloud [laughs].

Was that sentiment directed at anyone in particular?

Oh no, just at people who are annoying in general, or just at the general annoyance factor in life.

'Die Young Stay Pretty'?

I think it's pretty obvious that was directed at all of the famous people we all loved who were so close to the edge, they went over the edge. My personal philosophy has always been to somehow endure. I certainly have pushed the limit as far as taking chances with my physical self, but at the same time, I've always envisioned some kind of longevity and a career that would last longer than five years.

'Atomic'?

Jimmy wrote that one too. He was trying to do something like 'Heart of Glass', and then somehow or another we gave it the spaghetti western treatment. Before that it was just lying there like a dead lox [cured fish]. The lyrics, well, a lot of time I would write while the band were just playing the song and trying to figure it out. I would just be kind of scatting along with them, and I would start going, 'Oooooooh, your hair is beautiful'.

Were you looking at Clem Burke when you came up with that line?

[Jokes] But of course! No, not really.

A fan of Blondie's in LA from 1977, writer Pleasant Gehman, has this great story about all the stuff Clem put in his hair, like the grease from potato chip bags.

Yeah, he had many formulas for his fucking hair. When I

first met him, he was putting beer in his hair and sticking his head in a gas oven, which I thought was kind of fun.

They don't teach that one in beauty school. How about 'Pretty Baby'?

That one was about little Brookie [child model turned actress, Brooke Shields], and maybe a little bit about myself at the time. We went to see that movie, *Pretty Baby*, and Brooke was so outstanding and touching in it. Then we did a photo shoot together with Michael Mackenzie, and she turned out to be such a real person and so sweet. So we wanted to write a song about her.

It's amazing that someone who did some pretty controversial stuff at a young age, managed to hold on to herself and keep herself separate from all that.

I think her mother, Terri, was pretty straight with her and answered all of her questions pretty completely, and her father was a smart, stand-up kind of guy.

'Living In The Real World'?

That's Jimmy again, but he's not living in the real world, and let him stay there. Ouch!

'For Your Eyes Only'?

That was the James Bond thing. We were supposed to do a song for the James Bond movie *For Your Eyes Only*, but we didn't like their song, so we did our own song and they didn't want it. But that's okay, the Sheena Easton song was fine.

Hers was a ballad, a love song, yours was a rock 'n' roll, adventure song. What about 'The Beast'?

Oh, that's a good one. That's just a rap song about the devil, 'the beast', going out for a night like he was just a regular guy.

Which of your songs is the most celebratory? Then, which is the sexiest and which the most twisted?

'Union City' is the most celebratory. It could have almost any words to it, it just sounds so anthemic. Sexy probably would be 'Rapture'. As for dark and twisted, I'd have to give you a list because there's a lot of stuff going on in the music like that. I guess 'The Beast' was a pretty cool one, but that came much later.

And of course, 'Rip Her To Shreds'.

Well, that was more camp, but yeah, everyone got that one. Everybody loves that [makes a witchy laugh sound].

'Rapture' was the first number one rap song. How was that received at the time – did anyone accuse you of cultural appropriation?

Yeah. There were some rumblings about it at the time, and what I learned then [about the press] is that since everyone has to say something about it, everything will be said – good, bad and in between. That was my big discovery.

How did that song come about?

These graffiti artists – like Freddie, Futura and Lee, who had just ventured into CBGB's. Suddenly, there was this other area of crossover, and we were initiated into the rap world. So Chris [Stein] just said, I'm going to write a rap song. At that time, it was all the Sugarhill Gang and they were just ripping off Chic and using those tracks behind their raps. There was no real original music for rap, so Chris just created this crossover format and that was that.

Why do cars come up so much in your music?

I like cars and I'm from the suburbs, so cars are a part of my consciousness. I used to get in the car to have a private moment of peace and quiet and meditate and drive real slowly down a nice, quiet, peaceful road, listening to the radio. I found it very much a part of growing up and having a car is a sense of freedom for me. It's only inner city kids who don't get into cars, for everyone else – if you want to go anywhere and see anything, you've got to have a car. There was no mass transit for me to come into the city – there were buses, but they were all commuting buses. If I wanted to have a night out or something, like get into another reality, I needed the car.

I understand you still like driving yourself around the city.

Well, I don't like getting caught in traffic in midtown or anything, but to go out at night, it's very convenient. You can fill the car up with people and it's like having a living room on wheels. Especially my car – the Blondiemobile – it's as big as some people's bedroom.

CHAPTER FIVE
The Making of an Icon

WHO IS BLONDIE?

Contrary to popular belief, Blondie isn't Deborah Harry's stage name. Officially, BLONDIE IS A GROUP, as t-shirts their management once had made declared, a pop art band held together by founding members, Deborah Harry and Chris Stein.

But if you thought Deborah Harry was Blondie, actually, you've got good reason to be confused. Blondie was a name coined by horny construction workers and macho motorists who'd routinely call out to the platinum Harry – 'Hey blondie!' Although Blondie eventually became the band's name, Harry first conceived of 'Blondie' as the name of her developing stage persona. Harry had been informally molding her cartoon-like alter ego from the time she joined the Stilettos in 1972. 'Blondie' was simply the way she wanted to present herself on stage, and the Blondie character embodied elements of the woman Harry wanted to be with elements of the woman she was.

As Harry told Victor Bockris in her 1981 autobiography *Making Tracks*: 'I wanted to create this character who was primarily having fun, even though she was being maligned by her friends and her heart was being stepped on by members of the opposite, or same, sex.' Harry further wanted to mimic the outrageousness of male rock stars like David Bowie and Mick Jagger, which had never been done at the time. Just because she wanted to be one of the boys however, didn't mean she wanted to look like one. At the same time, she wanted to transcend the tragedy of the great platinum blondes, like Jean Harlow and Marilyn Monroe. 'The initial idea was to be desirable, feminine, and vulnerable, but a resilient, tenacious wit at the same time, rather than a poor female sapped of her strength by heartthrob and unrequited love.'

It was also very important to Harry that 'Blondie' be funny, buoyant, energetic – a cheerleader of rock 'n' roll, who at the same time refused to be 'just a girl'. Harry wanted 'Blondie' to sing in all the voices of the men in the band, and in all of the voices of her audience – male, female, young, old, gay and straight: 'When Blondie did finally hop out on stage as a character she would try to be bisexual or asexual and a lot of times, she would see and do things from the point of view of a third person.' To this day, Harry will still refer to the 'Blondie character' as her identity in the band. For this reason, technically Deborah Harry both is and isn't Blondie.

Admittedly, even without the name Blondie, there was no way anyone was going to miss Deborah Harry. Besides her good looks, she often experimented on stage with costumes and props ranging from a goldfish in a bowl named 'Mr Jaws', to nine-foot high murals of Japanese monsters which she'd rip to shreds, to a wedding dress and crucifix (take note Madonna!). She was and still is a visual genius and performance artist as well as a musician.

The tension between Blondie's identity as a band and the attention and interest showered on its fabulously glamorous front woman, Deborah Harry, would be one of the major factors in the band's demise. By 1976, when they recorded their self-titled debut, Blondie had become an innovative band with an infectious, classic pop sound. Blondie's music stands on its own as a major achievement. But the world probably wouldn't have taken notice of

Blondie if not for the style, personal charisma, voice and beauty of Deborah Harry. And herein lies the eternal paradox of Blondie: yes, Blondie made Deborah Harry, but conversely, Deborah Harry also made Blondie.

Although Deborah Harry's phenomenal run with the band Blondie from 1976 to 1982 is what made her world famous, Blondie did not make Deborah Harry an icon. Surprising but true, Blondie's profile and string of hit songs can't account for the level of celebrity Harry still has in 1999, a level of prestige and notoriety which is out of proportion to her actual commercial success. As Harry has said herself, she's far more famous than she is successful.

Many people as well known as Harry, and certainly many who made more money than she did, never become icons. In fact, most celebrities, especially those who've come to prominence in the 90s, enjoy a few years of success, then simply fade away with a couple of hit songs or a seminal movie or television role as their legacy. It's not that these people aren't talented or that audiences don't appreciate their work. It's just that they failed, for whatever reasons, to tap into people's psyches and stimulate their fantasies and desires to a level where they could become a symbol of their time.

For Deborah Harry, the timing of her meteoric rise dove-tailed perfectly with the end of the 70s and a culture 'ready for the 80s'. Looking for something new to separate their generation from the one before it, young people around the world said goodbye to disco and said hello to its electronically enhanced cousin, New Wave. New Wave also offered an equally glamorous fashion alternative to disco, and unequivocally, the first queen of the urban New Wave sound and look was Deborah Harry.

But even that defining moment and the New Wave she rode in on, don't account for Harry's lasting influence. It's only now, 20 years since she first made her mark on the pop culture landscape, that we can begin to fully appreciate the layers of Harry's persona. Peeling away at them, one finds a hundred points of access to Deborah Harry. She embodies a recognizable element from all decades she's lived in – she's a 50s bad girl, a 60s free thinker, a 70s punk, an 80s pop star and a 90s post-modern artist.

What other artist can make music that simultaneously sounds like new wave, punk, rock, rap, girl group, garage band, disco, Euro disco and dance trax? And, at the same time, reflects the sensibilities of a movie star, a sex symbol, a beatnik, a feminist, a nerd, a fashion icon, an entrepreneur, and an agitator? It would appear that Harry was in fact post-modern, before most people knew what that meant.

The more you know about Deborah Harry, the more you realize there is to know about her. Men and women, young and old, gay and straight have all found something about Harry that makes them keep coming back for more. It's these elements of her persona and her life story, separate from but connected to Blondie, that are the building blocks of Deborah Harry's iconography.

SEDUCTRESS

First and foremost, what was obvious to the world, was that Deborah Harry was a babe. She was surreally beautiful, but that wasn't what made her devastatingly sexy. After all, there are many beautiful women in the world who are not sexy, who appear like pieces of art under glass, fragile, delicate and pristine. You like looking at them but you don't want to muss them. Not so Deborah Harry. She was already plenty mussed and ready to make the first move.

What made Harry sexy, at least superficially was the way she looked, but what hooked people was her knowingness and her disarmingly frank sexuality, which hypnotized people like a drug. Harry was no tease, in fact, she was probably more woman than most men would know what to do with. That made her dangerous and intoxicating and utterly desirable. English writer Paul Burston adds, 'She was also tough – a prototype to Madonna. Girls enjoyed her as well. She wasn't just a blonde simpering sex object. She put herself across as sexy and in control.'

Of course sexuality is a tangled web and what flips a switch for one person may turn the electricity off for someone else. Burston sounds like he's talking about chocolate cake when he describes what became an obsession for him: 'First it was her lips. She has the most amazing shaped mouth. She could look so sexy with the way her top lip sort of perked up. And then when she sang, she'd make these grimaces and her mouth would just get so big – like a letterbox. I thought she was just so sexy. Everybody wanted her. You either wanted to fuck her or be her.'

Her lips, her hair, her fashion choices, her music, her life story, what she would say in interviews, etc, it all added up to make Deborah Harry unbelievably appealing. But the fact that she fuelled the sexual fantasies of men and boys cannot be under-estimated as a factor in making her an icon and contributing to Blondie's success. Ashley Heath, Fashion Editor and Creative Director of *The Face* magazine and a self-described 'massive Blondie fan', has the perfect story to illustrate this point. 'When Deborah Harry first toured Britain, Blondie played Glasgow's Barrowlands, a really early Blondie stronghold. Subsequent to that, Glasgow had a really strong pop scene with bands like Postcard Records, Orange Juice and Altered Images, who were all influenced by Blondie. So the music was ultimately very important, but when she played the first gig in Glasgow, she was wearing a t-shirt with a rip down one side and the whole crowd, which was quite a hardcore music crowd and mostly lads, all moved to one side of the stage because they literally wanted to see Debbie Harry's tits. Really, they wanted to see her tits more than they wanted to hear the songs at that point.'

But Harry wasn't just on the receiving end of crass and lurid sexual longing. In the late 70s, Harry penned an essay for *High Times* magazine, called 'I Wish I'd Invented Sex' which celebrated one of her favorite pastimes, and in some interviews, she'd list her exercise routine as 'swimming and fucking'. She also spoke openly about her frustrated sexual life as a teenager and what it felt like to suffer under the stigma of 'good girls don't'. In a 1996 *High Times* interview with *Making Tracks* author, Victor Bockris, Harry says of that time, 'I was really oversexed. Really charged and hot to trot. Later on, when I got my driver's license, I used to drive up to this sleazy town near Paterson [New Jersey] and would walk up and down this street called "Cunt Mile". I would get picked up by and make out with different guys in back seats of cars to get my rocks off because I was so horny and couldn't make out with anybody from my town.'

For a female celebrity to speak like this is still revolutionary. Harry wasn't just sexy on stage to sell records, she broke the silence about female desire, sexuality and horniness in a way unmatched even by Madonna, who in her own book *Sex* (1992), mostly talked about her fantasies framed by erotic 'art' photos. Meanwhile, Harry spoke about her own sexuality with such frankness she'd make a biker blush.

SURVIVOR

Victor Bockris, is trying to explain why Deborah Harry will, like a line out of the 1980 pop song 'Fame' declares, live forever: 'I think that when Debbie Harry arrived, people felt like she was going to be there forever and she is. It's not a rational thing, so you can't really pin down why. She's just part of the American Dream.'

Indeed, Harry's life story echoes a number of classic

fairytale themes, which in no small part endeared her to her public. As an adopted child, Harry fantasized that her real mother was Marilyn Monroe, an icon she idolized as a child. Although Harry's adopted parents were loving, she never fitted into New Jersey 50s suburbia. Whether that had much to do with not knowing her biological parents, is unclear. Harry, shy and insecure, took comfort in creating her own myth – she was special and she had to prove it. In Harry's case, whatever her battles with self-esteem, by virtue of her celebrity, she emerged triumphant from her uncertain beginnings. Or so the story goes. Harry has laughed at the pop psychology that has emerged in profiles of herself throughout the years, but the mystery of Deborah Harry's parentage, and the fact that the people who produced such an extraordinary child have no idea what their 'mistake' gave the world, adds a bittersweet twist to her tale.

Over the years, some stories about Deborah Harry have tried to make the case that she started out an ugly duckling and turned into a swan. Demonstrably, it's untrue. While Harry has tomboy tendencies and her weight has fluctuated all her life, by all accounts (except her own), Harry was always beautiful – as a baby, as a girl, even as a teenager. The only part of the ugly duckling/swan tale that might apply to Harry is that in her early 20s, Harry simply lacked the confidence and the flair for exhibitionism (as well as the platinum hair and skimpy fashions) she would later flaunt in Blondie. A late bloomer, Harry really came into her own in her late 20s and early 30s. Before Blondie Harry had lived hand to mouth and had been a waitress, a beautician, a Playboy Bunny and a junkie and survived it all. The fact that Harry was 35 in 1980, during the height of her success with Blondie, is certainly divine inspiration to struggling artists over 30 all over the world. Plus, off-stage and off-camera, even Deborah Harry didn't look like Deborah Harry. Although naturally beautiful, Harry certainly never walked around looking like she did in Blondie 24 hours a day. But that didn't stop a whole generation of women from thinking that she did, and wishing that they could be as beautiful and glamorous.

While beauty and the beast characterizations of Deborah Harry and Chris Stein's relationship are insulting to them both, as Harry's long-time boyfriend, Stein was certainly the envy of men everywhere in the world. But it was the relationship itself that most people envied. That Stein and Harry had in each other both romantic and creative partners, and reached such spectacular levels of success together, made them both seem like the luckiest people alive.

But then Stein got sick. And, although there are plenty of people who made too much of the fact that Harry nursed Stein during his two-year battle with his skin disease, to Harry herself it was a simply an act of love and commitment. Harry is uncomfortable with being praised for something that in her mind was just the right, normal, decent thing to do.

It was the press who really went crazy with the story, however, after a reporter caught sight of Harry in 1982 while at a New York hospital covering the birth of Mick Jagger and Jerry Hall's new baby. Reports of Harry's bedside vigils, which included her feeding him baby food through a straw and sleeping on a cot in Stein's hospital room, accompanied by pictures of Harry in a black headscarf and glasses, looking like a widow in mourning, ran in papers all over the world. It was declared that she had nobly 'given up her career for Stein'.

Although Harry didn't make a conscious choice to end her career, Stein's disease was all consuming from 1982 until 1985. It was just a two-and-a-half-year break, but when Harry was ready to return to work, a number of other female pop stars had emerged and it seemed like there wasn't room enough in the marketplace for all of them.

Filmmaker John Waters sums it up this way: 'When she blinked and took a break during the height of her career, when Chris got sick, 50 people stole her act and ran off with it. That's what happened. Then about 100 people stole her look.'

MANNEQUIN

Even without any prompting, John Waters zeroes in on Deborah Harry's iconic look. 'She had that very famous hairdo which is what I'm always attracted to people for. She made roots – she really was the first woman to have blonde hair with dark roots. She was a beautiful woman who almost purposely broke all the beauty rules and still looked like a new kind of gorgeous.' Of course Harry's new kind of gorgeous had some familiar elements, but as Waters says so eloquently, 'Maybe she felt influenced by Marilyn [Monroe] but I never felt that when I looked at her. To me she was something new. She was the lovechild of nobody but her own great imagination.'

Ashley Heath also emphasises that not only was Debbie Harry an original, she was an original of her own creation. '[Debbie Harry] is a visual genius, and I don't think it denigrates her or the music to say that fashion is very, very important to Blondie. The packaging and presentation of the music was crucial, and I don't think people ever gave Debbie Harry the credit she deserves for it.'

The problem, says Heath, lies in the fact that people too often confused Debbie Harry the woman with Debbie Harry or 'Blondie' the stage performer. He says, 'I don't really think it's stated enough that "Blondie" the character was this total stage creation. People really identified Debbie with this sexy ex-waitress, ex-hooker, junkie image she had on stage and in videos. The truth is, as much as Bowie before her, she dressed for the part. So why do we give credit to Madonna for coming up with all these looks over a fifteen-year period, when Madonna, in my opinion as someone very interested in fashion and style, got nowhere near creating the iconic looks Debbie Harry did in a five-year period?'

Deborah Harry's instinct for fashion was first confirmed when Harry was just a teenager. *Making Tracks* co-author Victor Bockris says, 'She told me that when she was in High School, she designed a fuzzy vest for herself and a month later, Sonny & Cher came out with the same thing and it became all the rage. So she knew she had some instinct for what was going to happen and what was going to be right now.' Indeed, Harry experimented, sometimes with disastrous results, with hair colors and extreme fashions, which she says resulted in her suburban friends refusing to be seen in public with her. Isn't this a story all fashion-forward people can relate to – being made fun of one year, and then being copied the next?

In the late 60s, Harry went through a natural, hippy stage where, as she was seen in her first band, The Wind in the Willows. Promotion shots from this time show Harry favoring the brown hair, no make-up and baggy clothes look. It was coming out of that period in the early 70s where Harry began her thrift-shop chic, which was aided and abetted during the mid-70s by her ideal partner in crime, designer Stephen Sprouse. Together, Harry and Sprouse streamlined Harry's look and made her infamous zebra dress from a pillowcase they found in the trash. Next Sprouse directed her early ripped t-shirt and thigh-high boots look, and as she ascended, he designed Harry's signature dresses, including her infamous asymmetrical strap dress from the 'Heart of Glass' video.

Victor Bockris says, 'Stephen Sprouse lived with Debbie on the Bowery and he designed her clothes and was really the first person who understood how Debbie should look.' In *Making Tracks*, Harry says: 'I asked Steve what his ideas on dressing people are and he said, "I just call it modern, almost a uniform, be it a dress or a suit. I think that's the future. We have less and less time to choose, so five outfits of the same thing, is a good idea. It's hard to find clothes that aren't overdesigned. I don't like to see designers get carried away with whatever they are doing. Like putting you in minis was modern looking to me. The sixties appealed to me for all that bright color and op art. I like bright colors in monochromatic use that became a backdrop for the person wearing them." '

Harry's yellow dress in the 'Picture This' video and solid blue unitard and matching sheer blouse in the 'Dreaming' video are examples of Sprouse's monochromatic color ensembles. Sprouse declined to be interviewed for this book, choosing only to issue the comment: 'Deborah Harry is one of the great legends of the punk rock movement', but without doubt, he and Harry made fashion history together. In fact, pictures of Harry's look from the late 70s look contemporary today because Sprouse's designs have a minimalism and simplicity to them which make them as modern as anything that has been designed since. Also, Harry's look from that time is literally contemporary, as her look has been reincarnated on the catwalks and in high fashion magazines by designers, stylists and photographers over the past three years.

As Ashley Heath says, 'That look Debbie Harry had in 1978 or 1979 has been copped-off by so much 90s fashion. Like that safety gear, knee-pad look she wore is just so Helmut Lang. I think he would be the first to admit that Blondie had a great look, and his work has been very, very in the spirit of Debbie Harry.' Heath also places Harry as the originator of what he calls 'knicker fashion'. 'You look at the work of the sort of trendy fashion photographers, the kind of people who shoot for *The Face*, and cop-off from art photography, and you see so much knicker fashion over the last five years and Debbie Harry did so much of that look –

knickers and a t-shirt. There are fashion stylists now who literally make hundreds of thousands of pounds using these style decisions – Let's just put the model in knickers and a t-shirt – and Debbie Harry did that look twenty years ago.'

Downtown New York designer, Maja Hanson, is too young to even remember Deborah Harry from 1978, but uses Harry iconography to inspire the risqué women's wear designs she now creates for the likes of Madonna, Courtney Love, Tina Turner, Marilyn Manson and actress Rose McGowan. 'I love her. Rock 'n' roll is always an influence but Debbie Harry is a great tough girl, one of the originals. I think more than anything, her attitude is so cool – just the expression in her eyes, the way she carries herself. I think it says, I'm not going to take any shit.'

While that attitude is always present in Hanson's take no prisoners, femme fatale designs, her collection from Spring 1997 in particular was a homage to Debbie Harry. Although Hanson had become a Blondie fan, she researched this show by going through the Blondie clipping file at the public library and looked at a lot of stuff she was wearing in her Sprouse period. She says, 'I pulled some colors from stuff I saw, like bright red, and I made this one very Debbie Harry dress – it's like red jersey with a layer of fishnet over it. I also used asymmetrical, jagged hems, but more refined versions of what she wore. Then just the hair, the make-up and the expression that the girls used – all of it was very her.' Hanson also saw Harry's influence everywhere that season. 'I think a lot of things that she wore that were really strong-shouldered, almost break-dancer stuff influenced a lot of designers when everyone started getting inspired by 80s fashion.'

That same season, designer John Bartlett was showing an uptown version of 80s inspired fashion. His collection was all sex, slink and swagger, a red, black and white power romp in luxury fabrics, softened by a dash of 50s high camp via dialogue from old movies like *The Bad Seed*. Bartlett, also an admirer of Harry's, sums up the elements of her Blondie style which influenced him: 'Her style was such that it was never flamboyant like a Cyndi Lauper, it was much more modern, very clean lines, very sexy. She was like a fashion designer's dream and she transcended time and transcended trends. The way that she dressed or the way that she looked – you couldn't say she was a punk or she was new wave, she was always ahead of the curve without looking out of place. Her image really challenged the way people looked at beauty and femininity. Some of her pictures now still look very contemporary. I was looking at a retrospective of Madonna videos on TV recently, and so many of them look dated, whereas Debbie Harry's look isn't dated at all.'

But Harry's influence on Bartlett isn't limited to his designs on the runway. Bartlett discovered Blondie as a teenager living in Cincinatti and he says Deborah Harry raised his expectations for his own future. 'I think as a Freshman in High School I asked my parents for Blondie records for Christmas. At that time, Blondie and Debbie Harry represented everything that was not Ohio, everything that was progressive and New York. I was just starting to explore my own look and have my own experiences and she was such a formative influence! I was so disconnected from all the things I wanted to be and she was like my lifeline to the world I was imagining I could live in some day. She embodied the fashion ideal, the music ideal, the lifestyle – she was surrounded by sexy guys, and she seemed to have everything you could want.'

When he finally did move to New York in 1985 to begin his fashion career, as an omen of the good things to come, Bartlett actually ran into Harry. He recalls, 'I met [photographer] Chris Makos and he invited me to this party he was having. It was in the penthouse of the Morgan Hotel and the first person I remember seeing at this party was Deborah Harry sitting on this couch, and I was like, "Oh, this is it – I've arrived! I can die now." It was like the pinnacle of finally coming to New York.'

Todd Oldham is another New York designer who owes a debt of inspiration to Deborah Harry. As a teenager living in Denver, Oldham discovered Blondie but initially, it was the fashion, not the music that captured him. He says, 'I saw the *Plastic Letters* album cover and I was speechless. I had never seen someone look like Debbie Harry. She was gorgeous and I bought it even though I had no idea what it was. I brought it home and I looked at the credits to see who had done the dress and it was Anya Phillips.'

Anya Phillips, as described in more detail in Chapter Two, was a close friend of Harry's and a purveyor of the bad girl lifestyle, which included rock 'n' roll, the creation of the Mudd Club and designing clothes as unique as she was. As Harry describes in Chapter Four, Phillips' designs were often not sewn, but held together by an intricate lacing of strings. Far from being a haphazard technique however, Phillips designed to avoid sewing. She had a very strong sense of concept with everything she did, and she probably thought sewing was the easy way out in terms of making clothes. Phillips also designed Harry's sexy black outfit in 'The Hardest Part' video, which was really more of a bikini with flaps, than a dress. Phillips, who also worked as a dominatrix, pioneered the dominatrix aesthetic in street and club fashion. By all accounts, Phillips was a ferocious woman and she designed ferociously sexy clothes.

Oldham says he was certainly intrigued: 'Somewhere there was a picture of Debbie and Anya – maybe in the liner notes, and Anya Phillips really inspired me to push it [with making clothes] because the edges were just cut on that dress. So *Plastic Letters* was a full experience for me because the music was so fresh, Debbie looked like no one I'd ever seen – I was instantly stunned and enamoured, she had all these hot dudes behind her, and then of course, there was that pink dress.'

Like Bartlett, Oldham moved to New York and ended up coming face to face with Deborah Harry. Actually, all these years later, Oldham is now Harry's neighbor, which has only increased his regard for her. 'I see Debbie Harry every other morning just walking her dog, we live in the same building. With no make-up and having just rolled out of bed, she looks amazing. Even her morning outfit, which is probably whatever is by the bed, is cool – it's the way she wears it. She always had that little extra without doing anything. You look back at different artists and you think how great that they represented that particular time, but Debbie Harry was so transcendent and effortless. I've never seen a bad picture of her, and there has never been a bad Blondie moment.'

MUSE

Deborah Harry did not die young in order to stay pretty, as the Blondie song she wrote decreed. First of all, she stayed pretty being alive, but then again, who needs to leave a good-looking corpse when your beauty has been captured in thousands of photographs?

If there's a photographer who appreciates the elements of what makes someone an icon, it's David LaChapelle. His portraits of celebrities, like the one he took of Deborah Harry used on this book's cover, incorporate elements of their legend, shot with a sense of humor and an absolute respect for beauty. In Harry's case, LaChapelle had a personal relationship with Harry as a fan. He says, 'She meant a lot to me when I was a kid. She was the alternative to everything going on in the late 70s. She was the coolest thing and the most beautiful person – looking at her videos, I couldn't imagine anyone more beautiful.'

LaChapelle, who at the time was a bus boy at Studio 54,

saw Harry occasionally, but he didn't get the chance to do one of his signature portraits of her until 1993. 'It was a really big deal when I got to photograph her. *Details* [magazine] asked me to do it. I was really, really excited because I loved her.' LaChapelle says he wanted to take Harry back to her quintessential Blondie look for the photo session, which he describes as 'a cool eclectic New Yorker – punk rock with a little bit of hip hop and disco thrown in and super, super glamorous'.

The enthusiasm the prospect of shooting Deborah Harry inspired in La Chapelle is shared by many other great photographers. Over the past twenty-five years, Harry has been shot by an assortment of influential photographers including, but not limited to, Robert Mapplethorpe, Francesco Scavullo, Annie Lebowitz, Arthur Elgort, the Earl of Litchfield, Greg Gorman, Lynn Goldsmith, Bob Gruen, Chris Makos and Jill Furmanovsky. There are literally enough photos of Harry – who before Madonna was the most photographed woman in the world in the 80s, reportedly even more so than Lady Diana – to fill an empty swimming pool. But perhaps none of them captured her so well as LaChapelle, whose photo also tells her story.

LaChapelle explains, 'The taxi cab was obviously very New York, like she is, but she's reckless and crazy, like real rock 'n' roll, so it was like this wrecked cab. The telephone booth with the phone off the hook is a reference to "Call Me". Then there's the New York skyline in the background, where it all happened for her, although we shot in New Jersey and she's from New Jersey too.'

What comes through in the photo is also how LaChapelle sees Harry: 'I think that she's the definition of cool – they should put her picture in the dictionary beside the word. Debbie Harry just encompassed it. You can see bits and pieces of her in all the female performers who came up in the 80s and you can see they were all inspired by her. She had this modern quality, the things she sang about and the way she looked. She looked detached and like she didn't give a fuck – she was the opposite of eager to please. But then, her life was about the opposite of being detached and aloof. She was feeling it, and when Chris Stein got sick, she had her priorities in the right place.'

LaChapelle, who had never met Harry before the shoot, was impressed by her respect for his vision. He says, 'I remember her willingness to be shot the way I wanted her to be shot and to look the way I wanted her to look. Her hair was different, and I wanted to get this iconic picture of Blondie, this cartoon character that she wasn't living 24 hours a day, but which was a part of her. And she was willing to go right back into it and let me photograph that side of her.'

It is exactly this spirit of collaboration that has inspired so many photographers who have worked with Harry, along with, of course, her incredible face and the kind of respect people have for her. But unlike many celebrities, LaChapelle discovered that when you shoot Harry, she does not arrive with any excess baggage. He says, 'She didn't come with publicists or anything, she came alone and represented herself. I got the feeling that she tries to have a good time with whatever she does. I think she's been through some really hard times in her life, and she realizes it's a photo shoot, it's not a difficult thing and she doesn't have to make it difficult.'

For a woman as celebrated for her beauty as Harry has been, LaChapelle was also impressed by her lack of vanity. He says, 'She's also not one of these people who fell apart when they got older. She was a great beauty – in 1979 they called her the Face of the 80s and the most beautiful woman in the world, whatever. She's disarmingly normal considering what she's been through and unneurotic, unlike other women I've photographed who were heralded as great beauties when they were younger. She was the ultimate cool subject.'

Another photographer who appreciates how cool Harry is, is New York scene photographer Patrick McMullan. McMullan took over the Page Five column in Andy Warhol's *Interview* in 1987. In the years since, McMullan has had a virtual monopoly on party photography in national and regional American magazines including *Vanity Fair*, *Harper's Bazaar*, *New York* and *Ocean Drive*.

McMullan, also a downtown New York fixture, remembers when he first started seeing Blondie in the late 70s: 'There were always pictures of her in ads in the music section of the [*Village*] *Voice* for Blondie, and Debbie stood out as the Marilyn Monroe of rock 'n' roll. Then, after *Parallel Lines*, I started to notice that they played Blondie at every chic party – it was always that album because of the great energy in the music.'

It was starting in about 1985, after Blondie's break-up and Chris Stein's illness, that McMullan started taking pictures of Harry. 'She started to come back out again for openings and events, just hanging out not performing. She was definitely the biggest New York celebrity at that time, and she kind of crossed over a lot of barriers. Just as Sean Puffy Combs in 1998 is everyone's favorite rap world personality and he can go everywhere and is welcome anywhere, Debbie was both downtown and uptown and everyone's favorite blonde. She was always fun and easy, very real but still very glamorous. Debbie was always a favorite of photographers.'

McMullan's photographs help illuminate Harry's activities during a time when outside of New York, she was keeping a relatively low profile. This was an awkward time for Harry. She had basically been out of the public eye for three years and was settling into her post-Blondie persona, simply being Deborah Harry. Observing and interacting with Harry at public events, McMullan got to know her well. 'She likes to be a little contrary about things, but it's all in fun. She's smart, much smarter and wittier than you might think.' He laughs, 'She is a little on the crude side, not in a bad way, but in a cool, punk way.' McMullan adds, 'And she also has a real avant-garde side to her that she wants to develop, which is probably stronger than her commercial side.'

FREAK

As much as Deborah Harry fits into mainstream ideals of beauty and style, she was noteworthy for her willingness to throw 'pretty' out the window in favor of something a little extreme, obscene, cheap, silly or even downright ugly. Paul Burston says, 'She was always parodying herself, even when she was officially slim and officially sexy. She played around with her image a lot too, the thing Madonna obviously made a massive career out of, but sometimes she'd look really freakish. She'd have her hair just butchered-off or she'd wear something really unflattering. It wasn't restrained or playing it safe, she was transgressive.'

Perhaps the first time Harry's mainstream public really understood how far from Blondie she was willing to go was when H. R. Giger fashioned the cover art for Harry's 1981 solo album, *Koo Koo*. The album cover, which showed Harry's head and face pierced by four skewers, was banned in the UK from high streets and London Transport for being 'offensive' and 'likely to disturb children and old people' according to a July 1981 piece in the British *Daily Mirror*.

H. R. Giger, who now has his own museum in Gruyère, Switzerland, recalls how the collaboration between he and Harry originated. 'I had just won the Oscar for *Alien*, and I was in New York City having a show [of *Alien* artworks] and Debbie Harry and Chris Stein approached me and we were talking and talking and I thought I might do a portrait of her. So about a year later, they said that they would like to have something for her album, *Koo Koo*.'

Harry was quite a fan of *Alien*, as she considered Sigourney Weaver's role in the film akin to something she'd love to do herself, and she and Stein were also science fiction enthusiasts. They also had a fetish for pagan symbols, especially skulls, which were a recurring theme in jewelry Harry wore around that time. Harry knew that she wanted to make a radical change in her image for her solo album to distinguish Deborah Harry from Blondie, and Giger seemed like the perfect solution.

Harry gave Giger free reign and he went right to work after he received a head shot of Harry from British photographer Brian Aris. Giger recalls, 'I remember she wanted to change the name from Blondie to Deborah Harry, so the first thing was to change her hair color. I asked her to make a portrait of herself to give to me. At the time, a friend of mine was a doctor who made acupuncture where they went into your ears with little needles. I was very impressed by this, so I took very big needles and I used them for her portrait – I stuck them through her picture. Then I airbrushed it so that it looked like the needles went through her head to suggest stimulation, to turn on the four elements – Earth, Air, Fire, Water.'

Harry, of course, got the concept right away and was really excited about unveiling this new image of herself, not because it was shocking as much as it was such a departure from Blondie. It was also the first time Harry had complete control choosing an album's cover art. Giger says, 'She was very pleased but, I think some people thought it was like voodoo, when you stick needles into a doll and make magic, but that's not what I meant by it.'

Next Harry travelled to Switzerland to make two music videos with Giger for her *Koo Koo* singles 'Now I Know You Know' and 'Backfired'. Harry and Stein enjoyed the time they spent with Giger and his wife Mia, and they were duly impressed by Giger's home and studio, which on the outside looked like the other houses in the area, but once inside were absolute monuments to his personal vision, from the customized black alien chairs in his dining room to his garden, overrun with organic plant chaos. The garden also featured perhaps the only sci-fi fountain in the world, which looked like it was molded from flesh. Harry says that the fountain made Giger's presence known in the neighborhood: 'When the fountain erupts, the whole block trembles.' If Harry was enthralled by Giger's garden, Giger was amused by seeing her enjoy it. He says, 'She was sitting in my garden typing an article for Andy Warhol's *Interview* magazine – clack, clack, clack on the keys. It was one of my best moments.'

Of the videos themselves, Giger says, 'Working with Debbie was very good, she was very professional. I had worked with the human form before and made costumes for the theater, but I thought Debbie looked really beautiful, really strong.'

Unfortunately, many of Harry's fans didn't appreciate this new direction. In the *Daily Mirror* piece Harry defended the cover by saying, 'It's ridiculous to ban something like this when you consider the sort of posters around which exploit women and advertise violent films.' Giger was no stranger to controversy and the reaction to this latest work was typical of the panic his work had always inspired, but for golden girl Harry, *Koo Koo* marked the beginning of Harry being at odds with the populist appeal of Blondie. This dark, sadomasochistic image of Harry would be strengthened a year later with the release of David Cronenberg's film *Videodrome*.

Harry was simply exploring her more esoteric interests and challenging herself as an artist, but as Victor Bockris says, 'Those nails through her cheeks upset people. All of a sudden she went from being sexy and fun and Hollywood to being dark and gothic and frightening.' Harry had no idea of the backlash that would follow her entering into collaborations with two artists she simply admired – Giger and Cronenberg, but *Koo Koo* and *Videodrome* really set a precedent for Harry, that she would pursue aesthetics that intrigued her, lend herself to images that were cutting edge, regardless of how they compromised her commercial viability.

In the years during Harry's solo career, from 1985 to 1998, when she released four albums – *Rockbird* (1986), *Once More Into The Bleach* (1989), *Def, Dumb & Blonde* (1989) and *Debravation* (1993), she never regained the notoriety she had with Blondie. As Bockris says, 'Her hardcore fans like everything she does and they've followed her through the years, but Blondie had an enormous audience, Deborah Harry never had a big audience.' As tragic as this may have seemed to everyone for whom the kind of celebrity Deborah Harry had with Blondie is seen as the be all and end all, Harry used her opportunity as fallen pop star to once again connect with her roots in the downtown art, music and club scenes.

One of her lifelines to what was happening two generations after CBGB's was a young designer named Michael Schmidt. Schmidt, also an adopted child, was a huge fan of Harry's as a teenager growing up in Kansas City, and officially met Harry in New York in 1985. 'I had a friend – Eric Jackson, who was assistant to Guzman [a photographer who had worked with Harry since the 70s]. When they were photographing Debbie for the cover of *Rockbird*, they needed someone to come in the day before the shoot and sit in on the lighting test. Eric asked me if I would do it, so I went there and wore a blonde wig, the actual Stephen Sprouse dress Debbie wears on the cover and tons of make-up. I was in drag as Debbie!' Schmidt laughs, 'I used to have the test Polaroid's, but damn if I know where they are now.'

Schmidt came back the next day and hung out with Harry during the shoot, but technically, he had met her seven years previously. 'The first concert I ever went to was Blondie [the *Parallel Lines* Tour, 1978]. It was when I was 16 years old. I remember everything – it was amazing! Of course, we were in the nosebleed seats, but it didn't matter – when she came out on stage, I let out this squeal. Half the back section turned around. I was having this transcendental experience. After the show, I was walking back to the car, I saw this group of people and it just occurred to me that they were waiting for Blondie to come out. I stood out there for about 40 minutes until they came out to get into their limo. Chris and Debbie came out, they signed a few autographs, she was walking past me and she turned to look at me and said 'Hello', and I leaned over and kissed her on the cheek. They got in the car and went away and I cried and cried for so long – you can't imagine. Needless to say, that was the highlight of my entire life at that point.'

At the time Schmidt met Harry in New York, he was making jewelry for a company called Erikson Beaman, where his talents eventually made him head designer. He started making chainmail clothes on the side, as he had always been interested in working with metal and adapting it for unusual use. He says, 'So it just kind of snowballed. I started selling stuff to this little store in SoHo, and one day, Cher was walking by and saw a dress of mine and wanted me to make all of this stuff for her. Then Cher started giving my stuff as gifts, to people like Bon Jovi and all these bands she was working with at the time.' In 1988 Schmidt moved to LA to help Bon Jovi launch a line of rock 'n' roll clothing. As that project was terminally delayed, he started making one of a kind, custom items for celebrities including Madonna and Tina Turner. He says, 'Those were fun years for me, but I never liked LA and I couldn't wait to get back to NY. So, as soon as my contract expired, I moved back to New York in 1991.'

As Harry had given Schmidt her number at the *Rockbird* shoot, over the years they kept in touch and became friends. Harry found in Schmidt a kind of youthful energy, confidence and an edge that she admired, and when he returned to New York, they began hanging out on a regular basis. Although their relationship was platonic, Schmidt was often Harry's 'date' in public, accompanying her to events like the 1991 New York première of Madonna's film *Truth or Dare*. An *MTV News* clip from the after party for *Truth or Dare* shows Harry and Schmidt being interviewed by *MTV News* anchor, Kurt Loder. While Harry is laidback when Loder asks her about Madonna, saying, 'Oh, she's great but I've only met her a couple of times', Schmidt is quick to insert that Madonna had come to see a recent solo show of Harry's. He explains, '[Madonna] is not a kind, giving person, or at least she wasn't at that time, so I wanted people to know that Madonna was a fan of Debbie's.'

Schmidt's loyalty to Harry and his creative genius ended up fostering a personal and professional collaboration between them. He says, 'The first dress I made for her was the razor blade dress in 1993.' When asked what about Harry inspired the dress, Schmidt says, 'Oh, you know how inspiration is, it just pops up out of nowhere. Razor blades were still metal, and I wanted to branch out from chainmail. I also wanted to do something really aggressive looking because Debbie can pull off things that are really hard. So I told her, I've got this idea you are not going to believe – we have to do a dress out of razor blades. Of course, she went for the idea immediately.' Schmidt's labor of love for his muse and mentor required him to dull each of the 3,000 razor blades by hand with sandpaper and then sew them on the black undergarment. He says proudly, 'Whenever she wears that dress, people just freak.'

Harry still wears the razor blade dress today and in fact was photographed in it at the 1998 *Q* Music Awards in London. The dress symbolizes who Harry really is – an artist who takes risks. Schmidt's other designs for Harry include a bandage/bondage dress, a chainmail top made of little links that are skull and crossbones, and a chrome corset – pieces which inspired some of his best work. 'Her interests are very dark. She and Chris [Stein] are both intrigued by the most twisted stuff and it's great. If I could make her a dress out of human bones, believe me, I would and she would love it! I get to explore a whole other part of my psyche working with her – places in my mind I don't ordinarily get to go because no one else would respond it. Cher did a little bit, but not as completely as Debbie.'

Schmidt maintains that in the 90s, Harry's stage persona is just a dressed-up extension of who she really is. He says, 'Her image is uncalculated, it's just her personal style.' He thinks that the reason people still have a hard time giving her credit for all her accomplishments is a societal bias against beauty. Schmidt says, 'The problem for a lot of attractive people, like Marilyn Monroe, is that people won't take them seriously. Beauty can be very threatening. Debbie is so smart she borders on genius level, Chris too. They are like aliens, people from another world.'

DIVA

Much to his own surprise, as a one-time rabid fan who in his high school shop class once made an engraved plaque that said, 'Debbie Harry, I'm going to getcha, getcha, getcha!', Michael Schmidt ended up living with Deborah Harry for two years, from 1994 to 1996. He explains, 'I was looking for a place to live and Debbie had this enormous apartment. She travelled a lot, so she was looking for someone who'd be there and look after the pets, so I moved in.' It was during that time, waking up every morning with Harry's Warhol portraits staring him down, that Schmidt began the rock nightclub SqueezeBox. As detailed in chapter 9, SqueezeBox became a vibrant, vital hang-out for Harry to get reconnected and re-inspired.

It was also through hanging out at downtown clubs like SqueezeBox and Jackie 60, and performing at the outdoor music festival Wigstock (also detailed in chapter 9) that Harry reinvigorated one of her most loyal fan bases – her gay following. Harry, like most intelligent women in entertainment, has always had an eye for talented gay men who have influenced and have helped her realize her personal style. Conversely, gay men have gravitated towards Deborah Harry, and have stayed loyal fans, even more so as she's gotten older.

Paul Burston offers this theory: 'It's like they say in *Follies*, you're a vamp, you get older and then you're camp – it's the progression of a diva. Gay men still get her, we always will. Like whenever Debbie Harry was on *Top Of The Pops*, all the straight boys would be like, "Oh, I'd like to give her one!", and you felt like you and Debbie had a private joke between yourselves that these straight guys didn't get. It was like a little conspiracy – she was using her sexuality to get them to buy the records, but we're the real fans, and we're the ones who really understand what she's doing.'

Harry also widened her gay audience when she reinvented herself and Blondie with remixed dance tracks of such popular hits as 'Heart of Glass' and 'Dreaming'. These remixes were particularly successful in gay discos around the world. Burston confirms, 'The Blondie remixes were produced by Diddy, a gay producer who first did "Atomic" himself, which was just a massive song in the UK.'

Village Voice gossip columnist Michael Musto, who is often called upon to arbitor gay issues, says he thinks Harry's movies really helped her turn a corner with the gay audience: 'I think she was more of a gay icon once she was involved in John Waters' films *Polyester* and *Hairspray*. But even prior to that, there was a kind of catty, drag queen quality to some of Blondie's music, like "Rip Her To Shreds" and "Die Young Stay Pretty". As a gay music aficionado myself, we seem to like two types – the fraught with neurosis, on the verge of emotional collapse Liza Minelli type, and then we like the opposite, the "I Will Survive" Gloria

Gaynor type. Debbie fits in with that fierce ruling diva thing. She sang the flip-side version of what gay icons like Judy Garland did. Judy sang, "Oh my God, the man got away and I'm going to kill myself!", and Debbie sang, "If the man leaves, so what?"'

Downtown performer Joey Arias is remembering what it was like to share the catwalk with Harry in 1994 for a Thierry Mugler fashion show in Vienna. 'She came out and they did her up all Victorian-like and she looked incredible. But,' Arias laughs, 'I remember Thierry freaking-out for a second because she was getting bigger press for the show than he was.' Arias, who has known Harry since the CBGB days, believes Harry is as much a fashion icon or a rock icon as she is a gay icon. He says, 'Harry is no more gay icon than she is straight icon. She's a multi-icon – she's like a diamond, she has many facets, it depends on whose holding her. Everyone sees something different in her and she just allows herself to be handled.'

SUPER SPOKESMODEL

During her years with Blondie, Deborah Harry became such a fashion darling that in 1980 she was even asked to lend her name to a line of designer jeans. At the time, designer jeans were all the rage, with Brooke Shields touting, 'Nothing comes between me and my Calvins' for Calvin Klein, and such now forgotten labels as Sergio Valenti and Jordache pushing their jeans with equally sex-saturated ad campaigns. The line Harry lent her name to was called Murjani, and Deborah Harry junior size Murjani jeans retailed for a mere $36 a pair.

Harry says in *Making Tracks* that she was getting a number of offers at the time, and decided to go with Murjani because they promised her and Chris Stein creative control of the TV commercials promoting the pants.

Unfortunately, after they completed one spot, the president of Murjani, Warren Hirsch, left the company, taking creative control with him. The one commercial that they did develop was quite provocative however, and featured Harry walking down rainy streets while her voice-over whispered, 'If you know where you're going, you know what to wear.' At the end of the 60-second advert, Harry arrives at a club, gets up on stage and then caustically screams out the same line.

In the years that followed Murjani, Harry would also do two other TV endorsements – one for Revlon make-up's 'Unforgettable Women' campaign, which seemed to make sense, and one for Sara Lee, which showed Harry pulling fresh-baked Sara Lee goods out of an oven, which seemed to make no sense at all. How does a glamorous rock star end up pushing the fine art of baking? But this twist on Harry's persona shouldn't really raise any eyebrows. While Deborah Harry never tried to be anything except more of herself, that included being an actress.

CHAPTER SIX
The Character Actress

Throughout her rise to superstardom, the press labeled Deborah Harry the 'punk Garbo' and the 'rock 'n' roll Marilyn'. Those were the terms they used to allude to Harry's hybrid of 50s blonde bombshell and 80s self-styled pop diva, but unwittingly, they also intimated at her future as an actress.

Perhaps it was inevitable. Deborah Harry's musical talents aside, she was simply riveting to watch. Her wide face was a pale and luminous palette for her deep-set bedroom eyes, cupid's bow mouth and severely arched brows. Harry was stunning, and to this day reigns, unequivocally, as one of the most beautiful women ever in rock 'n' roll. Add to that a distinctive, velvety smooth voice and a unique way of phrasing her words, alternately sweet and razor sharp. Likewise, her persona projected femininity and vulnerability, while being tough and street smart. Catlike, Harry could glide and slink, then suddenly, turn and scratch. It was a combination that fed the fantasy lives of both women and men, who wanted to be her or just plain wanted her. She had so much character, it was easy to conclude that the medium that might showcase Deborah Harry best of all was film.

As Blondie ascended in the late 70s, Harry received a

number of unsolicited scripts. Blondie's numerous videos and TV appearances had clearly stimulated filmmakers' imaginations. As the 80s rolled around, Harry was keen to make the jump from vinyl to celluloid. Having already over-ridden her natural shyness and got in touch with her extro-vert side within, she was eager to perform more than the cartoonish vamp she'd created for Blondie. In fact, she was tiring of that role, as was evident in the image change she'd made for the videos from her first solo album, *Koo Koo* (1981). Both 'Backfired' and 'Now I Know You Know', projected a darker, kinkier Harry in a collaboration with the Academy Award-winning *Alien* production designer, H. R. Giger. But Harry would discover that even though the movie industry beckoned, the field's relentless typecasting and her relative lack of acting experience were setting her up for another uphill battle.

As a result, Harry's roles in film thus far, with a few notable exceptions, have shown us only a glimmer of what she might be capable of as an actress. But, conversely, they have added dimensions to her persona outside of Blondie, which have only increased her allure. While many of the movies Harry has appeared in weren't even B movies – they were more like B minus movies – there actually is some method to her madness. If you take each project apart, behind the scenes you'll find a director or someone else in the cast who Harry really wanted to work with, or an orig-inal script or role that was much more than the finished film made of it.

As any Deborah Harry enthusiast can tell you, in general, her movie roles fall into three loose and sometimes over-lapping genres. Firstly, there are those where Harry essen-tially appears in a cameo role or as herself; secondly, there are the cult classic/schlock horror movies where Harry camps it up for laughs and thirdly, and perhaps most sig-nificantly, her dramatic roles in which she really is acting and, in most cases, rather finely.

125

THE CAMEOS

The majority of Harry's film roles are no more than glorified cameos. It seems that her Blondie image was too powerful to shake. Plus, she played that character so well, it's not difficult to understand why directors and audiences wanted to see it again and again. While she is electrifying on screen in many of these roles, they don't really challenge Harry or challenge the audience to do anything but tap into that place that loved Blondie and always will. For example, one of Harry's first film appearances is in Amos Poe's *The Foreigner* (1977). She appears as ethereal mystery woman, Dee Trik. Shot on no budget in 16mm and in black and white, the vague plot line of *The Foreigner* is just about impossible to follow. But the story is secondary to the beautiful, blown-out, grainy images of New York's lower East Side and some of punk's more colorful characters, like Anya Phillips as Doll and Patty Astor as Harlow. In one segment Harry, holding a cigarette, asks the Foreigner for a light. She's gorgeous, even though her hair is a gigantic blonde frizz and she's sporting an unflattering look she favored at the time – the androgynous mod with a shoulder-padded jacket and skinny black tie. She even sings – first a French ballad and then a ditty in German, thus making Harry's one scene in *The Foreigner* seem like stolen footage from a vintage music video.

Her performance in *The Foreigner* is echoed by her performance nine years later in another movie by a New York indie director named Amos – Amos Kollack. Although Harry was already an established icon when *Forever Lulu* (1986) was shot, she once again plays the role of the muse of few words and big, breezy hair. *Lulu* opens with Harry being photographed – a big tease as this is a knowing reference to her being a rock star in real life, and has little relevance to her character in the movie. Harry only appears in the background of the movie as the film's star, Hanna

Schygulla – bleached blonde here to be a Harry *dopple-gänger* – struggles to unravel some half-witted intrigue. Near the end of the film, Harry does have a line or two, but her real purpose in *Lulu* seems to be to dress up the movie and give it some New York street cred. As if to say, if Deborah Harry's there, it must the real insiders' New York.

Harry also signifies New York cool in Martin Scorsese's short film *Life Lessons*, part one of the trilogy *New York Stories* (1989). Harry appears again in just one scene. She's standing in the crowd at a trendy downtown art space called Blind Alley after a typically 80s, self-important performance monologue by the always impressive Steve Buscemi. Her mere presence and the fact that she mutters the lead character's name is enough simply to validate the event as 'cutting edge'.

Harry bestows her rock 'n' roll credibility on Joan Freeman's *Satisfaction* (1988), a movie that becomes a comedy by default. Featuring future Academy Award winning actors, Liam Neeson and Julia Roberts, the movie tells the story of a wannabe group of working class girlfriends who form a band. You can see why Harry would lend herself to a film about young women trying to take themselves and their music seriously – *Satisfaction*'s heart is in the right place. Harry, Neeson and Roberts all played second fiddle to the star of the movie, Justine Bateman. Justine who? Well, years later, she's not a household name, but at the time she was a regular on the American TV series *Family Ties*. And just like Bateman, *Satisfaction* is a little too suburban in its sensibilities to pull off its 'underdogs come out on top' story. Bateman and Roberts are hardly convincing as musicians, and Liam Neeson, over-acting as an ageing songwriter invigorated by Bateman's musical talent, is downright embarrassing. But Harry, who appears in one scene as Neeson's jealous ex-lover, manages to shine. Platinum blonde and dead glamorous, she's convincingly world weary and bitter. However minuscule the role,

Harry's performance is definitely a precursor to those she would deliver in later movies, such as James Mangold's *Heavy* (1996).

In Alan Rudolph's Meatloaf vehicle, *Roadie* (1980), Blondie performed a fantastic cover version of 'Ring of Fire'. *Roadie* was filmed at the height of Blondie's success and it is a glorious moment to have captured on film. They are so great to watch that one wishes there was a lot more of Blondie in the movie. Especially more of Harry, who is enchanting in one scene where she's sitting around wisecracking and having a beer with Meatloaf.

THE CULT CLASSICS

Two of Deborah Harry's most important film roles fall into the cult classic queen category – her major motion picture debut in David Cronenberg's *Videodrome* (1982), and John Waters' *Hairspray* (1987). Both of these movies are looked at in more detail later in this chapter. The cult classic roles are important elements of Harry's persona, as they fed her image as someone who was in on the joke of popular culture, not just a product of it. If Harry's image in Blondie at times verged on the beautiful ice queen, these roles exposed her sense of humor, her ability to be dowdy, her penchant for camp extremes and her own nerdy interest in sci-fi and the occult. Best of all, one can tell in these films that Harry is enjoying herself.

The love child of *Videodrome* and *Hairspray* was, for Harry, called *Tales From The Darkside: The Movie* (1991). Harry played a middle-aged, middle-class suburban housewitch, who has captured one of the neighborhood kids in her kitchen dungeon and plans to throw him into the oven for her dinner party entrée. In an attempt to avoid his own gutting and stuffing, the little boy keeps stalling her by retelling little horror stories (or 'Tales From The

Darkside'). After *Hairspray*, filmmakers caught on to the idea that not only was Harry available for supporting roles, she was very good at playing the villain. Harry's role is deeply ironic, a casting move as odd and as shrewd as the fact that Harry once appeared in a Sara Lee commercial. *Tales* was a moderate hit and also featured an impressive list of actors including Julianne Moore, Christian Slater and Steve Buscemi. As Harry appeared first in the film, she got top billing over all of them.

Soon after *Tales*, Harry appeared in the schlock horror film *Body Bags* (1993). This is not a high point in Harry's acting career, as she attacks the role of a pushy nurse working for a wacko hair growth specialist as if it were a carnival ride. But the role is interesting for two reasons – it was Harry's opportunity to work with director John Carpenter, who was experiencing a bit of a slump of his own after creating such classics as *Halloween* (1979) and *Escape from New York* (1981). Carpenter actually appears in the film, narrating between the three segments in dead-drag. Such schlock legends as Roger Corman, Wes Craven and Sam Raimi also have cameos along with actors like David Naughton (*American Werewolf in London*), Mark Hamill (*Star Wars*) and the ballad mistress who stole the theme song for *For Your Eyes Only* from Blondie, Sheena Easton. The other in-joke of the film is that Harry's nurse turns out to be a brain-eating alien. Altogether fitting as Harry wrote about a head-eating Martian in Blondie's 1980 hit song 'Rapture'.

THE HEAVYWEIGHTS

Ironically, one of Harry's meatiest roles came her way in 1978, right after Blondie finally scored their first US number one hit 'Heart of Glass' – *Union City* (1979), a small indie film by Mark Reichert. Full of anxiety over adjusting her performance quality from the stage to the screen, Harry still managed to deliver a notable performance. The role of a depressed New Jersey housewife from the 50s, whose controlling husband was on the brink of madness, was a role to which Harry could relate. It was, in some respects, the woman she might have been if a restless spirit and rock 'n' roll hadn't provided broader horizons. The role required Harry to be a brunette, and losing the blonde of Blondie set an important precedent. For it was *Union City* that inspired Harry's roles in the three most important films of her acting career to date – *Videodrome*, *Hairspray* and *Heavy*.

VIDEODROME

Deborah Harry was quoted in *US* magazine in 1980 as saying that the ultimate movie role for her would be 'the sort of character Sigourney Weaver played in *Alien*. She was strong yet feminine.' A year later she would get cast in her own science fiction epic, and although *Videodrome* was a movie devoid of aliens, it would certainly alienate a good number of her mainstream fans. Now that almost two decades have passed since the movie was released, it has emerged as an untouchable cult classic. A luscious jumble of ideas about the seductive power and the corrupting nature of television and video, it's clear that neither cult film maker, David Cronenberg, or Deborah Harry, the actress, were settling for an easy or a safe direction.

A movie about a cable TV programmer and his descent into madness after being exposed to a mind-altering and possibly mind-controlling TV broadcast, promised a winning combination of orgasmic gore, fetish sex and social critique. *Videodrome*'s star, James Woods, was still hot from his stellar performance in *The Onion Field* (1979), and David Cronenberg had just enjoyed success with his popular exploding head opus, *Scanners* (1980). *Videodrome* was also billed as Deborah Harry's major motion picture debut.

Harry played a character named Nicki Brand, a sexy shrink based on a TV personality Cronenberg had met while doing promotion for his previous films. Cronenberg explains, 'This talkshow host had her own kind of star quality and charisma, and she was very blatantly sexual, which is why we started looking at non-actors for the role because we needed someone who exuded those qualities and who had that kind of persona.'

Harry more than fit the bill, but Cronenberg did, however, have to defend her from critics who thought she might bring too much personality to the role. He recalls, 'There's a thing you run into now where people talk about an actor bringing a lot of "baggage" to a role. It drives me crazy. For M Butterfly, Warren Beatty wanted to play [the Jeremy Irons] role, and that was an interesting idea, but people would say, Beatty is known for his philandering – how could you possible cast him in a role where he is supposed to be so naive, he can't even tell a woman from a man? That's an extreme example, but it's as though people fear an actor's persona will interfere with the character they play. So, I was really not wanting to deal with Debbie's rock star background other than that Blondie fans might be interested in coming to see her act because they hadn't seen her do that before.'

Harry wanted the role of Nicki Brand partly because she was an admirer of Cronenberg's work. She signed up to do *Videodrome* based on this connection with Cronenberg, and a very rough draft of the script. Cronenberg says, 'I don't think she was approaching it the way a normal actor would – dealing with the movie as a whole. Over the years, I've had actors turn down roles in my films, even though I know they really want to work with me. An actor lives through a role, and it was a good role, but it wasn't a completely developed one when Debbie signed on.'

What Cronenberg means is that he was literally writing the script as they were shooting the film. 'That's how we did things back then – I fondly refer to those days as the Tax Shelter Era. You know, in October and November, all these dentists and doctors would realize they'd made too much money and they were going to have to pay a lot of taxes unless they could find a tax shelter, so they'd want to invest in movies. You couldn't finance one movie all year, and then suddenly, you could finance three. Producers would call and say, We've got the money and we shoot in three weeks!' Cronenberg admits these weren't the best of circumstances for Harry to be working under, especially for her first lead role. 'I was trying to find the movie as we were making it, shooting out of sequence and such – I'm amazed it turned out as coherent as it did! But Debbie floated with it all very well.'

If that wasn't stressful enough, the movie actually required quite a different kind of performance from Harry than her previous acting endeavors or her stage act with Blondie. 'At first, I had to tell her everything. I mean, she did a lot of things with her eyebrows – don't forget Blondie was kind of camp and exaggerated. So at one point she said, kind of exasperated, "So everything I ever learned about performing won't work?" And I said, "Worse, it not only won't work, it's destroying the film."' But Cronenberg was confident she could do whatever the role required and Harry was up for the challenge. 'I looked at her in *Union City*, so I knew she could do it. Plus, she's extremely bright and very tough in a good way and she really wanted to do it.'

Contrary to what the press may have said at the time, Cronenberg remembers that *Videodrome*'s graphic sex scenes weren't a problem at all: 'Oh those were relatively easy. The physical stuff was more familiar for her as a stage performer – not that she has ever done anything like what she did in the movie on stage, but the subtle dialogue things were more challenging for her.' Cronenberg also recalls that Harry and her co-star, James Woods, got along very well: 'There was a lot of bantering and joking around. She was certainly not intimidated by anyone and she wasn't intimidated by the nudity at all.' Cronenberg recalls one funny exchange between her and Jimmy Woods: 'There's this scene where the Jimmy Woods character develops this kind of slit in his stomach and has things disappear in there. So after a long day, he was getting cranky having to wear all this special effects stuff, so he says to Debbie, You know, I ceased being an actor. Now I'm just a bearer of the slit. And she said, Yeah, now you know how it feels. I thought this was very funny since he was always pestering her.' Cronenberg emphasizes that while Harry was a newcomer to acting, she still packed quite a punch. 'It wasn't like she was some naive little thing coming on the set. It was a level playing field and she certainly had respect.'

Harry proved herself to be a formidable presence as well as an unusual pop star. But Cronenberg also appreciated that about her. 'I knew of her association with William Burroughs, which was interesting later when I made *Naked Lunch* and got to meet Burroughs, but I knew her approach to what she was doing was more than just being a recording artist. It was obvious that she was interested in rock music as a social statement and a social force as well as just trying to hang on, which we all do. But it was a much broader understanding, and may I say, intellectual approach of what rock music could be and how it could intertwine with other art forms and other artists like Burroughs. And of course, Burroughs had a long history of being involved with rock figures and performers of all kind. Debbie came with a very broad understanding of what she could bring to the movie – it was a good fit.'

It may been a good fit but that didn't make it a hit. *Videodrome* was financially and critically lackluster, but none of it, as the reviews of the film attest to, was Harry's fault. She had no problem filling out the persona of Nicki Brand and handled herself with panache. Unfortunately though, in the finished film, it's unclear whether or not Nicki Brand is a real person or a fantasy created to undermine Woods'. Relegated to video temptress, Harry's screen time fades towards the end of the film as sinister chaos reigns. David Cronenberg who had previously created cult favorites such as *Rabid* (1976) and *Scanners* (1980) recovered well from the controversy and animosity that *Videodrome* inspired. He has since gone on to create other such creepy and visionary films as *The Fly* (1986), *Dead Ringers* (1988) and *Crash* (1996). Much like Harry herself, *Videodrome* is getting better with age and has recently appeared in several critics picks of the Top 20 cult movies of all time.

HAIRSPRAY

Baltimore's pride and joy, filmmaker John Waters, recalls, 'During her early years with Blondie, I knew of [Debbie] and I was a fan, but I did not know her. I think I went to CBGB's maybe four times in my life, so it wasn't like I hung around that scene, but I always loved her.' He laughs, 'She had that great hairdo, which is what I'm always attracted to people for.'

As impossible as it seems that at any time in their lives Deborah Harry and John Waters did not know each other, their paths crossed for the first time in 1980. According to Waters, that year, a mutual friend hooked them up to work on the music for Waters' 1981 film, *Polyester*. 'Tab Hunter sang the title song "Polyester", Chris [Stein] wrote the music and Debbie wrote the lyrics. I remember the day Tab Hunter recorded it – Debbie was right there and it was like old wave meets new wave.' He laughs, 'So after that, I kinda wrote the part [of Velma Von Tussle] in *Hairspray* with her in mind.'

Hairspray (1987) is to date both Harry and Waters' most popular and most accessible film to date. Waters says in mock horror, 'Children liked that movie. I accidentally made a children's film!' A send-up of Baltimore in the 60s, with a positive message about integration, *Hairspray* added a new dimension to Harry's acting career by proving that she could be very, very funny. Although Harry had demonstrated her penchant for camp in the Stilettos and Blondie, after years of playing herself in film cameos, her role in *Hairspray* really underlined the fact that Harry was in on the joke. The film marked new territory for Harry in other ways too. Velma Von Tussle was a matron – a middle-aged stage mother who would do anything to push her mediocre daughter into the limelight. It was a bit of casting against type for a sex symbol like Harry, whose previous roles all played on her rock babe persona.

While more mainstream directors stereotyped Harry after her kinky role in *Videodrome*, Waters saw her potential: 'That's the film that sold me on Debbie Harry as an actress.' But even for Waters, securing Harry's services was a bit of a trial. He recalls: 'She had a killer agent at the time – Stanley Arkin, and he was just the scariest, most aggressive agent you could have.' He laughs, 'I met with him and he made all kinds of demands, and I said, "But, we don't have that kind of money!" He turned out to be a lot of bark, not bite. Then Debbie called me and said she wanted to do it anyway.'

Again, Harry was determined to make her own career choices, despite what her handlers might have thought was in her best interests. Waters: 'She really wanted to do *Hairspray*, regardless of the fact that it may not have been the perfect next step or the exact order she should have done things to benefit her music career, because anytime you confuse people by doing more than one thing, it sometimes works against you.'

But Harry was not the only pop star who turned up in the film slightly out of context. The Cars lead singer Ric Ocasek appeared in cameo as a beatnik, and Sonny Bono played Harry's husband, Mr Von Tussel, a bit of a coup for Waters, since Bono was already retired from the business with a thriving political career as the Mayor of Palm Springs, California. Waters recalls: 'I remember, I said to Debbie, I really want to get Sonny Bono, and she said, "Just tell him I'll blow him", which made me laugh so hard! It just took me by surprise. She was kidding, of course, and it never became an issue because he said yes right away.'

Deborah Harry had always had a strong connection with gay audiences, but after *Hairspray*, it was clear that Harry was a bonafide gay icon. Waters explains: 'She looked great and was talented and gay men always like that. I think gay men have always liked her maybe because it was easy to get dressed like her, even though no one could ever really look like her. You could do the Debbie Harry look – the hairdo, you could imitate the clothes. Hundreds of people stole her look anyway – every rock star did. But, I still,' he says with much affection, 'don't think of her as a gay icon, she's just an icon.'

HEAVY

If *Hairspray* proved Deborah Harry's ability to play for laughs, *Heavy* (1995) proved, beyond any reasonable doubt, her ability to simply act. The first step in the transformation from icon to actor for Harry was her willingness to play a character who not only wasn't blonde, but who wasn't beautiful. Director James Mangold explains, 'Debbie in real life looks way better than [the character she played]. So one of the bravest things was that Debbie, being a figure of glamour and a devastatingly beautiful woman, let that all go. She let me be unkind to her with the camera and she wasn't frightened of putting a pretty edgy, unglamorous persona on screen. I was really impressed by that.'

Harry impressed a lot of people with her role as the

faded roadside waitress Dolores in *Heavy*. American tag team critics Siskel & Ebert based their review of the film around Harry's performance – and this was a film which also starred Shelley Winters, Liv Tyler and Pruitt Taylor Vince. Harry also found a fan in one very tough reviewer, as Mangold explains: 'I loved the fact that Janet Maslin in the *New York Times* liked Debbie. Janet Maslin does not rave, but she gave Debbie a little backhanded compliment. She put Debbie with Shelley [Winters] and said something to the effect that the two people we've seen a lot of big performances from have turned in very restrained ones.'

The general response to Harry's performance in *Heavy* was very positive, but many reviews contained a note of surprise, which underlines how limited people's opinions of Harry as an actress really were. Part of it was Harry's giant rock star persona, part of it, the kind of roles she'd played before. Mangold himself was the first to doubt Harry's ability to play the role. He admits, 'I have to be completely honest. I was a giant Debbie Harry fan musically, but moviewise, I was skeptical.' The idea to audition Harry for the role came from Liv Tyler's mother and CBGB's scenester, Bebe Buell. As *Videodrome* and *Hairspray* were such different genres of film from *Heavy*, Mangold didn't think that Harry would have enough to bring to the part. But actually meeting Harry changed Mangold's mind: 'I found her to be an incredibly soulful person and so down to earth and not in the way people say that about rock stars, but very within herself, very objective about the world and very feeling.'

As he does with every actor he works with, Mangold read with Harry and based his decision to cast her on the strength of her performance. But he was aware how others were going to view her: 'If Debbie was going to be in the movie, I knew people were going to be looking at her with an extra set of ammo, thinking, Oh, it's just stunt casting. So my feeling was she had to do something so human, so reserved, so tender that she shut them up for good. And she did. Her upstate roots show. In fact, part of her connection to the project is that she once actually worked as short order waitress in an upstate New York diner. I think she's brilliant in *Heavy*.'

On the set of *Heavy*, Harry continued to impress Mangold: 'Perhaps this is illustrative of what she's like as a person as opposed to the persona of Blondie, but Debbie was very much like my Peptol Bismol on the set – very even tempered, incredibly smooth, incredibly attentive! Some of the actors were star struck, but Debbie was very relaxed and she united everyone. Shelley loved Debbie – I remember she was talking about how she'd love to direct a remake of *Blue Angel* with Debbie – she was a big Debbie Harry fan. Liv looked to her like an older sister. They share a birthday and Liv had known her for years. So Debbie became a binding agent for the cast – you know there was Evan Dando from Lemonheads from the rock 'n' roll world as well.' Perhaps the biggest test of all was that the movie crew loved Harry. 'Crews measure someone by how high-maintenance or low-maintenance they are, and Debbie was low,' recalls Mangold. 'Also, she made everyone laugh a few times – once when she was sweeping up glass from the floor she started to joke about being on her knees and giving blow-jobs – she loves telling sex jokes.'

The magic behind the scenes at *Heavy* translated onto screen too. The film turned out to be a ticket to the big time for Mangold, who was relatively unknown before *Heavy* catapulted him into the limelight. 'I didn't know what people were going to say about this movie at all. While we were shooting it I really had doubts. Meanwhile Liv Tyler, who was sixteen at the time, used to jump around singing, We're going to Caaannes! She turned out to be right.'

Mangold's next film, *Copland* (1997), would attract actors like Ray Liotta, Harvey Keitel and Sylvester Stallone. It was widely publicized that Harry also had a role in *Copland*, reviving *Heavy*'s Dolores – proof positive of Mangold's regard for her, but mysteriously, she all but disappeared from the film. What happened? 'It's a tragic tale. I've talked to Debbie about it a couple of times but I imagine it was a disappointment,' Mangold says wistfully. 'The role was only four or five lines, but for me and Debbie it was the thrill of bringing Dolores back and putting her in the next movie. What unfortunately happened was the first cut of the movie was about two and a half hours long, and it just so happened that it was most of Debbie's scenes that got taken out in the edit. The cruellest part was that her last clip got removed from the final cut. It had nothing to do with Debbie, but we had to tighten one section by 20 seconds and it was the last place in the movie where she was speaking.' Mangold says Harry put in a great performance as a saucy barmaid who flirted with all the cops before they went home to their wives. Perhaps one day he'll restore her if he's able to release a Director's Cut of the film.

Mangold says that Harry's presence on the *Copland* set was also very poignant for him: 'There was a bittersweet quality to having Debbie on the set because it made me realize how dramatically the scale had changed between *Heavy* and *Copland*. Suddenly, Debbie is in a room with me and Ray Liotta, Harvey Kietel and Sly Stallone and the crew was like seven times larger.' As was the budget Mangold got to work with. He says, 'There were moments I'd lock eyes with her, and I felt like Wow! It was only a year previous that we'd been on the set of this other movie wondering if it was ever going to be seen by anyone.'

Liv Tyler has also gone on to great success in Hollywood, but so far Harry has yet to capitalize on her film career. Mangold takes a practical view of why Harry's rave reviews haven't yet helped her secure more substantial film roles: 'The movie business is very particular. There were five brilliant actors in *Heavy* – Debbie, Joe Grifasi, Pruitt

Taylor Vince, Shelley Winters and Liv Tyler. It seems to be more to do with what Hollywood is doing right now that Liv Tyler has had the most work – she's in the right age group, she's an ingenue.' Mangold sighs, 'Also, let's be honest – *Heavy* wasn't *Armageddon*. You can't convince a studio to hire an actress based on a movie like that – it was too small. But the roles in major studio films for actresses out of their 20s are far and few between, and there are a lot of actresses vying for those roles. But,' he adds passionately, 'I'll be shocked if Debbie doesn't do some more phenomenal film roles. In fact, I'll be shocked if she doesn't do one for me.'

SIX WAYS TO SUNDAY

To date, Adam Bernstein's *Six Ways To Sunday* is Harry's single follow-up to her notable performance in the film *Heavy*. According to director, Bernstein, who met Harry in 1988 when he co-directed the music video for her song 'Liar, Liar', which appeared on the *Married To The Mob* soundtrack, it wasn't until he saw *Heavy* that he was convinced she was right for his film. 'Up to that point, I thought of Debbie as more of a comic actress,' says the New York based Bernstein. 'But she gave such a great, gritty performance in Mangold's movie. She completely transformed herself.'

In *Six Ways*, Harry plays a tragically possessive mother named Kate Odum, who is damaged beyond repair after her husband runs off, leaving her to provide for her only child. The object of her menacing co-dependent affections is her 20-something-year-old son Harry Odum, played by impressive newcomer and Prada model, Norman Reedus. Reedus is clearly the star of this heavy-handed black comedy, but Harry makes a strong showing as the pathological matriarch.

Bernstein remembers meeting with Harry to discuss the

possibility of her taking the role: 'I sent Debbie the script for *Six Ways* through her agent. She remembered me and agreed to meet and discuss the part of Kate. Debbie told me she loved the role. I tried to soft sell some of the more violent moments in the film.' Much to Bernstein's surprise, Harry came back at him and said she'd like to do the part, but only if the violence was full-out, shocking and extreme. 'You have to appreciate that,' says Bernstein.

Six Ways was shot in five weeks in New York during the winter of 1997, although Harry was only required for two. 'The movie's puny budget forced us into a strange schedule,' says Bernstein. 'Every actor, it seemed, had to shoot their death scene on his or her first day of work. Debbie's character hangs herself at the end of the film and she insisted on doing this herself (rather than cheat with a double). She had to hang in a harness which pinched painfully in the groin.' Bernstein further describes Harry's approach to acting as akin to a jazz soloist: 'She doesn't approach her part with icy precision. She waves and riffs around moments, experimenting with each take. In the end she gives you something amazingly raw and real and vulnerable.'

Although Harry doesn't display as much depth and feeling in *Six Ways* as she did in *Heavy*, the film does mark a progression for her. *Six Ways* doesn't fit comfortably in any one genre of Deborah Harry movie. Rather it combines elements of the glorified cameo (Kate Odum is an over the hill lounge singer) and the cult/camp classic with elements that are uncomfortably dark and yet which clearly prove that Harry's come a long way as an actress. *Six Ways To Sunday* is also notable as Harry's least glamorous role ever – she appears shapeless and haggard in a series of puffy bathrobes and slips with her hair bunched up at the back of her head in a forgotten chignon. But just as she proved with *Heavy*, we can see her more clearly as an actress when we aren't seeing her as Blondie.

141

CASSAVETES FILMS BLONDIE LIVE

When Blondie left Private Stock Records, their new label, Chrysalis Records, commissioned a short promotional film about the band from now deceased film legend John Cassavetes. Cassavetes shot the band performing live at LA's Whiskey A Go-Go in 1977. Although not widely released, this is a prestigious little piece of Blondie history and another example of how Deborah Harry crossed the path of another formidable artist and visionary.

GLENN O'BRIEN'S LOST TREASURE

Glenn O'Brien, writer and host of the infamous cable access show *Glenn O'Brien's TV Party* (see chapter 2), holds another obscure piece of Deborah Harry's film career – *Glenn O'Brien's New York Beat Movie*. Back in the early 80s, O'Brien made a film which Harry appeared in but which has never been released. O'Brien explains: '[The designer] Fiorucci got really excited about what was happening downtown in New York and thought that we should make a film about it. So he secured a large amount of money from the Rizzoli family in Italy to make this movie starring Jean Michel Basquiat as a struggling young artist.' O'Brien says the film, named after his 'Beat' column in *Interview* magazine, featured a *mélange* of downtown denizens – everybody who was anybody, including musicians like Kid Creole and bands like The Contortions, DNA and Blondie. Harry has a special role in the film as a bag lady who entices Basquiat to kiss her in the final scene. 'She tells him that if he kisses her, he can have anything he wants, so he kisses her and he begins to walk away and then – poof! Debbie turns into this princess and Basquiat finds a suitcase full of money.' O'Brien says the film was never released because the funders in Italy were arrested for being a part of P2 – a plot to overthrow the Italian government. The film sat in a vault in Italy for years, but in 1998, O'Brien was able to secure the film again and hopes to release it in the next couple of years. 'The production values are good, but it does need some work,' he says.

WHO IS HARRY SMITH?

This 1998 documentary by Dutch filmmaker J. C. Hilversum aims to celebrate the only two significant women with real power and presence in the New York punk scene – Deborah Harry and Patti Smith. With a European's sense of glee, the filmmaker uses Harry biographer and Smith biographer, Victor Bockris, to loosely narrate the accomplishments and the contrasts between Smith and Harry and some of the more historic sites of New York punk history. The best thing about the film is that it includes original interview footage with both Harry and Smith, although they never appear on screen together. Smith has a better part in this film as she's a stronger spokesperson for herself and clearly gave the filmmaker more access to her life.

Harry suffers by comparison as she has never been one to pontificate about her own virtues and analyze herself. But if she loses out verbally she makes up for it visually by the sheer power of her screen presence. Clips of her appearances in films like *Six Ways To Sunday* and *Heavy*, clips of her performing in the 1997 *Night of the Proms* tour, and of her performing with the Jazz Passengers, portray Harry's life and her career as vibrant, experimental and very much alive. The film contains some obscure performance footage from Dutch TV shows. The highlight of the entire film is a moment when Harry is presented on a Dutch TV in a large gold box. When the front side of the box falls open, a very animated Harry is sitting inside with her beloved dog, Chi Chi. An absurd and hilarious moment.

Following Harry's high-profile role in the much-maligned film *Videodrome*, she made her Broadway debut in the spring of 1983 in an ill-fated stage production which opened and closed after one night. The play was titled *Teaneck Tanzi: The Venus Flytrap* and co-starred the late, great comedian Andy Kaufman. Harry says candidly, 'When I look back, during that time, I did all these things that were really interesting but not successful – not good business. But it was great working with Andy, he was very charming and sweet.'

Kaufman, like Harry, was a known professional wrestling enthusiast – they both appreciated the theatricality of the sport. Harry says, 'I can remember even as a child watching wrestling on my little black and white TV. It was always theatrical. It's the battle between good and evil – there are good guys and bad guys, and good guys can become bad guys – they switch around. It's like the soaps.' Harry was such a big wrestling fan, she even appeared on the cover of *Wrestling Magazine* with the now deceased WWF wrestler, Andre the Giant. A love of wrestling drew both Harry and Kaufman to the project, which told the story of a young married woman's life through a series of dramatic wrestling matches. Kaufman played The Ref, and Harry shared the lead role of Teaneck Tanzi with actress Caitlin Clarke.

After a successful run in London under the title *Trafford Tanzi*, the Claire Luckham script was Americanized and brought to Broadway. Obviously backers of the project were optimistic, as big money was spent renovating the interior of the Nederlander Theater, now home to the long-running hit musical, *RENT*. *Village Voice* columnist, Michael Musto, is one of the few people who actually saw the show: 'As I recall, all the leads were wrestlers, and wrestling was used as a metaphor for relationships. It was wacky and over the top, and too offbeat and British for Broadway. The audiences and the critics just didn't know what to make of it. I didn't even know what to make of it, I just went because my friend Zora Rasmussen was in it.'

Zora Rasmussen, who played Tanzi's mom, agrees that the play wasn't right for Broadway: 'They should have put it somewhere Off or Off-Off Broadway first, but instead, they spent way too much money building this huge wrestling ring. We were in previews forever, trying to make it work.' Unfortunately, *Teaneck Tanzi* never did.

Regardless of the production going South, Rasmussen has nothing but good things to say about Harry: 'We didn't know what to expect [before we began rehearsals], but she's very real, very vulnerable, and very nice. But I played her mother, what else am I going to say [laughs]? No really, she was such a doll.' But Rasmussen also remembers that it was a tenuous time for Harry: 'I think her career was in a bit of a downslide, and [Chris Stein] was really sick at the time. Plus, [Teaneck Tanzi] was a very demanding role, demanding enough that two actresses had to play it.' The role actually required Harry to perform such vigorous wrestling moves as full Nelsons, leglocks, head butts, backbreakers and bridges. It was reported in a New York paper that Harry was actually injured in early rehearsals when she was knocked on the head while wrestling with Kaufman.

Harry recovered just fine from her bumps and bruises, but the play's failure, following the less than rapturous reception to *Videodrome*, did have some impact on her career. Michael Musto: 'I'm sorry [*Teaneck Tanzi*] was Debbie's only experience on Broadway. The play came out right after *Videodrome* and they were both so esoteric. The two of those projects together made her less appealing to the mainstream. But the thing about Debbie is she didn't aspire to the mainstream.'

Ironically, as was the case with *Videodrome*, even though the play was canceled, Harry's performance was not the problem. Perhaps her taste in material is, but her choices reflect the very sensibility that has made her an everlasting icon of cool.

Harry was quoted in the *New York Post* on April 28, 1993, after the play was canceled, as saying: 'The critics probably thought the play was too lowbrow for Broadway, but I really had a good time doing it. I'm in great physical shape ... and seriously thinking of doing something more with wrestling.'

CHAPTER SEVEN
Interview with Chris Stein

HEART AND SOUL: DEBORAH HARRY
AND CHRIS STEIN

Deborah Harry will be the first to tell you that there is no Deborah Harry story without her soulmate and partner in love, life and music, Chris Stein. But while Harry and Stein briefly performed as Angel and the Snake, a name that was probably a joke, Stein was no Svengali. Stein did not design or create Deborah Harry or tell her what to do. In fact, at the time they met in 1973, Harry was already a worldly wise woman of 28 and Stein a mere baby-faced 23-year-old art school student. If anything, Harry had more to give to Stein, but both have characterized their partnership as entirely mutual, and a source of strength before, during and after their success with Blondie.

CBGB's door person, photographer and one-time Blondie office manager, Roberta Bayley, recalls: 'I think it would have been impossible for them if they weren't together and didn't have each other. Debbie and Chris had a really good, supportive relationship. They were very, very close and had a passion for each other for many years.' Although their romantic relationship dissolved in the mid-80s, they continue to defy convention as close friends and collaborators today.

The relationship that would form the foundation of Blondie actually began as an act of intervention. Deborah

147

Harry was being stalked by a possessive former boyfriend (who would later inspire the song 'One Way or Another'), and Chris Stein offered his friendship and the comfort of his presence. His intentions may not have been entirely chivalrous – after seeing the Stilettos perform at a long-forgotten bar called the Boburn Tavern, he was captivated by Harry. Harry was drawn to Stein as well, a gravitational pull that seemed to both to simply be fate. As romantic as that sounds, Stein first proved himself to be a friend at a time when a lot of men weren't able to see beyond Harry's beauty. Stein joined the Stilettos based in part on his interest in Harry, but sparks flew only after there was a hard-won trust between them. As Harry says in *Making Tracks*, 'I liked living with [Stein] because he wasn't overly possessive. He didn't have an extreme macho attitude and we had fun together. We laughed at the same things, yet we had differences of opinion and respect for each other.'

Over the years it has perhaps been a little too easy for the public to speculate that Stein was the brains of the operation and Harry was just the beauty, but in fact, the magic of their relationship was that Harry and Stein found in each other intellectual equals. Stein does have an extraordinary mind with a vast capacity for information and analysis, and a kind of impatience with the world that one generally associates with someone who is close to genius. Stein, the only child of two frustrated artists active in the trade union movement of the 30s, had a liberal, lefty Brooklyn upbringing and a rebellious adolescence. Stein was so much at odds with the world that it eventually led him to have a nervous breakdown at age 20, after which he was briefly institutionalized. But even that unfortunate dark spot in Stein's life supports the profile of him as a gifted, if somewhat tortured, artist. Stein always had a good head for conceptualizing new hybrids of ideas and influences, which were perfectly showcased in Blondie's groundbreaking music and move into music video.

Maybe the public finds it easier to see Stein as a genius –

both because he is a man and because he actually looks like what people think smart people are supposed to look like, a little geeky and slightly brooding – than to accept that Harry could be just as intelligent. First of all, it seems unfair that she could have that luminous face and be brainy too, but she is. Harry is just as interested in ideas as Stein, which she expresses in Blondie's original song lyrics, 80 per cent of which she wrote on her own. Harry's lyrics are just as poetic and clever as those of her contemporary Patti Smith, although Smith favors dark subjects and Harry makes light of hers. Harry's intelligence finds a very physical expression, visually borrowing from celluloid icons of the past, yet offering the public something entirely modern. Harry also has a real genius for instinctively knowing how to provoke and please an audience. She always intuitively knew what her audiences wanted from her – a persona bigger than life, a bad girl who was on their side.

Together, two exceptional and somewhat eccentric people like Harry and Stein were able to find a comfortable mix of contentious creativity and collaborative unity. As Harry says in *Making Tracks*, 'Chris and I balance each other out. His logic never fails to put things in perspective for me . . . He's also a much more laidback person. In turn, I'm able to deal with the kinds of things he worries about. So we help each other. He's sane where I'm crazy and I'm sane where he's crazy.'

Harry would ultimately become a much more prominent public figure than Stein, for which she deserves full credit. But Stein shares in Harry's success. *Making Tracks* co-author Victor Bockris sums it up this way: 'Chris is in no way a Svengali figure. Debbie is a much stronger personality, but they are collaborators. Collaboration is really the emotional engine of so much creativity. In Debbie's case, it's Chris. The whole heart and soul of the thing and the ability to go forward and move on had a lot to do with Chris's drive.'

Interviewing Stein was essential to any real understanding

of Harry. He invited me into his infamous Bohemian apartment, stuffed with his various collections (of art and of blades), and talked openly about what he describes as the 'central relationship of my whole life'.

THE RELATIONSHIP

Let's start at the beginning – the inevitable – the night you first saw Debbie singing with the Stilettos at the Boburn Tavern in 1974. Your relationship begins that night because soon after that, you join the Stilettos and the rest is history. So, at the time, were you still in your glitter-glam rock phase with the long hair, make-up and platform boots?

Yeah, but I didn't wear platforms very much, because they were uncomfortable – at least the ones that looked good were uncomfortable. But I did wear black kohl around my eyes like everybody else at the time.

Was Debbie blonde at the time?

No, she had short brown hair – like a boy's haircut. A few months later she dyed it blonde, like Twiggy, and had it kind of plastered down to her head. At the time, she was still working at this beauty parlour in New Jersey.

What kind of place was the Boburn Tavern?

It wasn't anything, it's just that Elda [Gentile, Stilettos founder] and Holly Woodlawn had the loft upstairs, so they asked the owner if they could perform in the pool room in the back. It was an anonymous little bar but in those days people were always inventing places to play.

How would people get the word out so that they'd have an audience?

Well, sometimes there wouldn't be much of one, but friends would come. Elda would invite people while she was out socializing and that's actually how I heard about it. At the time I was dating this girl named Elvira, who used to be the girlfriend of Billy Murcia [AKA Billy Doll], the drummer from the Dolls. We went out for about nine months – she had a little daughter I really liked. Anyway, Elda had invited her to the show, so I went too.

Did meeting Debbie end that relationship?

Yeah, but it wasn't serious. I just really liked her kid.

Had you had a serious, soulmate type of relationship before Debbie?

No, and certainly Debbie has been the central relationship of my whole life. I can't imagine having anything like that again.

A lot is made of the fact that you and Debbie were friends first.

Yeah, I think it was about three months before we were actually intimate.

How was it that you were able to be friends with women at a time when most men just weren't interested in women's minds and women's feelings? As an only child – did you have a strong relationship with your artist mother?

Yeah, my mother is pretty much of a character, but you know, maybe it was some kind of deviousness on my part.

But of all the ploys to get women, being friends with them is a pretty decent way to go.

Yeah, but all the so-called obnoxious qualities of men, I find obnoxious also – all the bullshit camaraderie and all that crap. I don't know if that's my upbringing or just intellectualizing it, but I find the locker room mentality pretty disgusting. So I've always preferred the company of women.

On an intellectual level?

Yes, I always thought it was a big fallacy – I mean, there are differences between men and women, but one is not inferior to the other. There's certainly a ying and yang thing going on and one is the complement of the other, but sexism, racism – it's all bullshit.

Seymour Stein [former President of Sire Records and Vice-President of Warner Bros Records] referred to Debbie as the 'Tammy Wynette of rock' for standing by her man when you got sick in 1982.

Every time we would do a new record, Seymour Stein would always fucking give Debbie these really schlocky suggestions like you should do 'My Boyfriend's Back'. Really cornball stuff. I'm always surprised by him.

Debbie took two years off to take care of you when you were sick with Pemphigus. Does it bother you that it often gets characterized as Debbie 'gave up her career' for you?

Well, it's true what they say – Americans really like to see their heroes get knocked down. Part of the interest in us now is that people think we died and came back. I was watching the VH1 [*Behind The Music* documentary] about Bruce Springsteen and they were desperately trying to make out how the guy suffered and he hadn't really suffered through anything. So the best they could come up with for Bruce's dark period was that he was 'desperately trying to understand himself' or some other really stupid shit. But with us it was really tangible – he got sick and the band broke up and they were all fucked up. People like that, they like to have their heroes get knocked down and beat up.

But does it ever make you mad that her taking care of you gets blamed for 'ruining her career' when clearly, there were other forces at work here too – the band had already deteriorated and Debbie was tired of doing Blondie before you got sick?

No, it's what it is. Earlier on, we actually had a few conversations with [our new] record company and they were like, you should play this up and get more sympathy out of it, which was really obnoxious. But it is kind of absurd, this whole thing with Debbie. Like I've said before, we had a really strong relationship when I got sick and I think it's normal that someone would take care of their partner in that situation.

People admire Debbie for doing it because it was such a normal, caring, human thing to do but it wasn't necessarily what the 'most photographed woman of the early 80s' and a huge superstar was expected to do. It really showed people where her priorities were.

It's not superhuman, but she really did all that shit – she slept on a cot at my bedside in the hospital, etc. But I certainly would have done the same for her.

The other thing people have tried to suggest over the years is that you had some kind of Svengali relationship with Debbie.

I know and that's nuts. It was very much a trade-off. Debbie was the ambassador. She always knew what people wanted and she's physically appealing and she was able to connect us to people. I had certain musical tastes and I had a better instinct for what was going to happen artistically, but I was always too fucking blunt. So we filled each other out with what the other one was lacking. But I certainly wasn't in control. Debbie always told me what to do and frequently still does [laughs]. Yeah, I pushed her in certain directions, but she also pushed. Plus, the Svengali thing suggests that the whole thing was preconceived and it wasn't – we were just making it up as we went along.

The kind of relationship you had as friends, lovers and creative partners is such an ideal for a lot of people, an ideal they never achieve.

I always thought us working together helped the relationship because so many people get competitive in relationships. Once one is off doing something else, it's like the other has to sacrifice something to support the other. I always thought that being successful with the band helped our relationship rather than the reverse.

Is it odd then being back in Blondie but not being in a relationship with Debbie?

No, it's the same thing really. We're so close, we just don't live together. I talk to Debbie every day, at least once or twice. It depends, but she can come and take anything she wants out of here. We trade off stuff all the time, trade paintings. Like she has the Giger painting that's the insert in the *Koo Koo* album – that's a pretty cool one, and I have the one that's the album cover.

[At this point my conversation with Stein segues into his art collection and his blade collection. He is clearly more comfortable and forth-coming talking about art than about Deborah Harry, but it isn't that he's melancholy about her or even that he's bored by having to answer the same old questions he's been asked a million times; one just gets the sense that his deeper feelings and observations about her are private. I also get the feeling that me asking Stein questions about Harry is akin to being asked questions about a family member – someone you know so intimately, it's kind of hard to understand what all the fuss is about. A copy of the newly reissued Blondie autobiography, Making Tracks, which happens to by lying out on the futon, offers the perfect excuse to segue into talking about the band's early years.]

THE EARLY YEARS

The funny thing about the new 1998 edition of Making Tracks is that it has this smiley picture of Debbie on it. Did they ask you to find an 'up' picture of her?

No, it's just that [the publishers] wanted to change the cover. I would have left it alone but because it was the second edition they wanted a different cover. This was the only picture from that time that I could find that I liked. It is taken somewhere backstage in Philadelphia at one of our first out of town gigs.

I understand that when Making Tracks *was originally published in 1982 no one would review it?*

Yeah, no one did pay much attention to it back then, but now that they've re-released it it's getting a great response.

Did you consider updating it or adding to it?

No, we didn't do anything – there's just the new thing up front – Victor's interview. It's really funny. But the book is kind of a whitewash – there's really no negativity in it at all. The tone of it is very fan oriented. We left out a lot of stuff, certainly stuff about us getting stoned. People are more into the anti-hero thing now. And in interviews now, I'll talk about anything. No one even cares about drug use anymore. In fact I heard Marilyn Manson plays up his drug use and talks about more than he fucking even does. He thinks it sounds good and it looks good for his image. I think that's funny. It's really come full circle.

There are pictures of Debbie with Chrissie Hynde, Viv from the Slits, Poly Styrene, Siouxsie Sioux and Pauline Black of Selecter – where did they all get together?

In England. A magazine set up a photo shoot and they all showed up and did an interview together. They invited Kate Bush too but she didn't show up. Everyone else showed up, but I think she was just being aloof.

There are these pictures of you and Devo. Did you ever do any music with Devo?

No, I always just knew those guys, they were always

pretty great. When they were doing the 'Satisfaction' video, we just happened to be in Akron or wherever it was, so we dropped by that shoot. They were a total original thing that got passed over. It's too bad. Mark Mothersbaugh is doing well – he's doing music for [the American cartoon] *Rugrats*, but I don't know what happened to the other guys.

You also took pictures for Punk *magazine. John Holmstrom told me that early on you had a real keen sense of how to market Blondie. Where did that come from?*

I don't know about that. There was no pin-up sensibility in rock 'n' roll and it just seemed obvious. So we did the Punkmate thing and then there was the picture of Debbie in the zebra outfit we sent to *Creem* magazine. Most people saw that before they heard the music.

You talk about footage John Cassavetes and Sam Shaw shot of Blondie – what happened to that?

Cassavetes came and shot us at the Whiskey and made a little short film about us. There was some of it in the VH1 [*Blondie: Behind The Music*] – that scene of Debbie in the white outfit pulling it off. Sam Shaw was the cameraman. He's the guy who shot that famous photo of Marilyn with her dress blowing up.

How did you first get involved in the films of Amos Poe?

He was just around working on the scene. Ivan Kral [guitarist from The Patti Smith Group] was his cameraman. He made a movie called *Night Lunch*, which is really cool, with footage from CBGB's. He's still around and in good shape, he's not all screwed up. He shot some really great early stuff of us in the loft on Bowery. You know that VH1 thing – with the Blondie t-shirts against the wall? That's all his footage.

Was Amos Poe also the cameraman on the cable access show you co-hosted with Glenn O'Brien – TV Party?

He was *a* cameraman – there was no official cameraman on *TV Party*. Jean Michel [Basquiat] did it sometimes, Edo did it a lot. We did about 90 shows and [David] Letterman mentioned it when he first started his show. We always thought he stole some of his sarcastic schtick from us.

What happened with the film Glenn O'Brien made in the late 70s that stars Blondie and Jean Michel Basquiat?

Well, did he tell you he lost all the audio on it?

Really!

Yeah, he wants all of us to lip read and dub over our vocal parts.

But some of the people in it are dead. Like Basquiat.

Yeah, he wants to get the guy who played Basquiat in the *Basquiat* movie to do it. That was a really shitty movie but he had some of [Jean Michel's] mannerisms down. But he didn't have any of his up moments and he didn't have any of his meanness. He was a fucking mean monster who loved to fight and loved to hassle. And the movie didn't have any of his upness. He could also be really charming.

What do you miss about the early years?

Probably just going out and knowing everyone. That doesn't happen anymore, although Mother [New York club] has done a pretty good job of weeding out the bridge and tunnel crowd. I can go in there now and I'll always know a couple of people. But the lack of attention is probably what I miss most. And I miss the atmosphere, there's not a lot of shit left now that has the feeling of New York from the 30s, 40s and 50s – it's all getting scraped away. Back in the 70s you could still get a good feeling for what the city had been like. Now all the links have been cut. Everything is going to get speeded up and plasticized. All the workers will live out in the swamps in New Jersey. They'll build a train line – a sub-subway and the day shift will pass the night shift on the way home to the wastelands of New Jersey.

Was there a point, after Blondie became really successful, when you did something that was just so prototype rock star decadent?

Nah. Not really. Although we did have our own Blondie jet at one point during the last American tour.

So do you think it will be harder for Blondie to have an impact on the younger MTV generation?

No, I think it'll be easier. We just have to keep doing what we've been doing and we'll come out looking unique. I'm happy to lecture young people about what I think they should be doing, I mean all these kids seem to want to be told what to listen to and what to wear! I always had an elder statesman thing. Burroughs was a figure like that for me. Most of my foundations and ideologies come from the 60s. I was just reading this book about Lenny Bruce that Victor [Bockris] lent Debbie and it's pretty good. Sometimes I wish I was ten years older and I had been able to see Lenny Bruce. I was also around for like the tail end of the jazz thing, but I was too young to appreciate it.

It's funny that you say you wish you were older because you missed things that came before your time because so many people wish they'd been around during the CBGB's era. At least, being born and bred in Brooklyn, you were here in New York as a teenager.

Yeah, I was seventeen in 1967 and I got in on the folk thing. I went to San Francisco for the Summer of Love, I went to Woodstock, and when I was seventeen my band opened for The Velvets [the Velvet Underground].

How did that happen?

The Velvets had this gig at this gymnasium uptown and my

friend, Joey Freeman, used to work for Andy Warhol as a gopher. He was this real cute kid with waist length blonde hair and it was his job to go wake Andy up at his house and stuff – he's in a couple of the books. So one day he said to my band in Brooklyn – it didn't have a name it was just a blues band – 'Do you want to play with the Velvets?' People forget it's ironic that that fucking weird leather, metal album came out in 1967 because it was such a contrast to everything that was out around it. Anyway, we took a subway in and they let us use their amps and it was really mellow. Nobody was there – it was this place in the west 90s or 80s. Andy saw us and Joey said later, 'Oh, Andy liked you'. But Andy said he liked everything at that point.

When did you really meet Andy Warhol?

Oh, not until years later after Blondie. Bill (William Burroughs) we knew from the Bowery – where we once lived was a few blocks up from the Bunker. Everyone just gravitated towards each other. Do you know who Vali Myers is? She's mentioned in Tennessee Williams' *The Fugitive*. She's a dancer from Australia and an artist [he shows me a book of her incredible sci-fi, human-animal hybrid, psychedelic paintings]. She's pushing 70 but she looks 40. She's back in Australia now where they are finally embracing her. I guess if anyone was a mentor to me it would be both her and Bill – that's it. Vali inspired me to do these (he indicates a row of plain paper journals, and opens the current one to show me. It's filled with writing, photos and other scraps of paper). She had bits of fur from her animals in her journals as well.

So these are constant reminders of your past?

Yes. I have Anya's [Phillips] ashes downstairs. James [Chance] was always afraid he'd leave them somewhere. He keeps saying he wants them, but he never comes to get them, maybe because they'd make him sad. Anya was a really strong girl who did really powerful things. I'm honored to have them here. She was unique. Eric [Emerson] too. He would've gone on. If he'd stuck with it another five years, he'd have broken through. He was a character. They just went too early.

[At this point, Stein's sometime roommate, artist and musician and general downtown personality, Walter Steding comes in bundled in mittens and scarves. He kindly offers to make us tea. We take a break and Stein invites me downstairs to show me his recording studio. Like his living space, nothing is precious – everything is casually lying around but it's not chaos, it's just relaxed. Stein says proudly, 'This is where most of the recording was done. This is the same equipment I've had for fifteen years.' I noticed about six guitars and I have to stop to look at the gold records. 'Is that the one Iggy shot a hole in?' he says. We go back upstairs to talk more about Harry.]

THE LEGACY

What will Deborah Harry be remembered for?

I think she said it best recently and it's a real simple thing. She wanted to bring the movie starlet sensibility into rock. It hadn't really been done before because all the other women in rock, like Janis, were all coming at it from a male perspective. Janis was almost androgynous – like a guy hippy. So Debbie brought the whole Hollywood/Marilyn sensibility to it. I mean someone would have done it, but it was Debbie.

What doesn't Debbie give herself enough credit for?

I think she doesn't even see how much influence she's had. In a way, she doesn't even consider herself successful or famous. She doesn't see it at all. She has a totally weird psychology anyway, the way she deals with things.

Do you think that not acknowledging being successful or famous helped her survive it? I mean, what can you do with the knowledge that you mean so much to so many people?

You don't think about it much until it's right in front of you, when you're doing a show or something. Plus, I think there's a whole psychic element to having a lot of people think about you. I'm not sure how it affects you. But it's like that whole thing of if you think really hard about someone, maybe they'll call you. So imagine if 100,000 people are thinking about you – it must have some effect. Like if 100,000 guys are having erotic thoughts about Debbie.

That must have been a little weird for you when you and Debbie were together. Were you ever insecure about other guys hitting on Debbie?

Not really, except maybe really early on because we were both good about that. It's funny, but now, I'm getting kind of used to being alone. My last girlfriend drove me so crazy, at this point I'm enjoying being alone, which is kind of a twist because usually I'm always in a relationship.

What are you happy and proud to claim as your influence on Debbie's career?

The whole thing – I mean, I helped her get through all of it. I helped her have a positive outlook about things. To this day, I tend to be more positive about things – maybe that's naive, but she worries a lot. There were a lot of times when we seemed to be at the end and it was really frustrating. I don't know if she would have kept going if it weren't for me. I don't know how I've stayed inspired to do all this. If I were a kid now I wouldn't want to go into rock 'n' roll. Because it's so mundane. When I started out, it was so mysterious. It's just such a part of everything.

Was the Blondie reunion also your idea?

Yeah, apparently, I'm getting blamed for it. I just looked at it realistically. This guy Harry Sandler, who worked with John Mellencamp, he just sort of laid it out and we got a picture of what it would really be and really mean. Plus there was so much interest building up during the 90s.

I understand you had a pretty intense press week recently – CNN, the cover of People *magazine – the Blondie reunion looks like a hit. How does it feel?*

I'm having a good time with it because I was in such a lull. I only did about half as much stuff as Debbie did since Blondie stopped. It took me a long time to recover and get my energy level back up. Then I spent the last few years going to the shrink to figure out why I got stoned for all those years and did all that stuff. I needed to deal with that baggage. We all kinda went crazy after we broke up. Clem didn't, although he's the craziest of us all, but me, Jimmy and Debbie – we all went nuts and had breakdowns. Jimmy had like a two-year lost weekend. Debbie sort of got it out of her system early on, but it took me a much longer time.

So is that why it's only now that all of you can work together again?

Yeah, I think so. We've all needed to get in touch with our own psychology after having had all that disillusionment heaped on our heads when we were so naive about all this stuff. I guess it's just like anyone, when you go out in the world something comes along and totally fucks you over. Everyone who is active in their lives probably has a period of great disillusionment with people and the business structures they come up against. It's nice to get a second chance.

CHAPTER EIGHT
The Wannabes

As an adjective, 'wannabe' is a cruel word. Especially in the context of music, 'She's a wannabe' is a put-down and a slur. It suggests that one artist is the real deal, authentic and original, and all others who work in the same genre are just, well, wannabes – charlatans, counterfeits and copy-cats. Starting with the emergence of Madonna in 1983, 'wannabes' also became a popular media term for young female fans that expressed their devotion to a celebrity by mimicking her appearance. This look-alike, wannabe phenomenon has become a well-documented ritual for young women increasingly looking to popular culture for role models.

Deborah Harry has a particularly interesting relationship to the term wannabe. As the originator of the female pop pin-up archetype, she's the artist who paved the way for Madonna. After Madonna, whose accomplishments changed the world's view of women in pop, there are hundreds of artists who are Madonna wannabes. One could deduce that they are therefore Deborah Harry wannabes, one or two generations removed.

But Deborah Harry was also called a wannabe in her time. As the first beautiful woman to flaunt and own her sexuality and bring a movie star quality to the CBGB's music scene, she was disparagingly referred to as a wannabe punk and even a wannabe singer. And it was Patti

Smith who openly expressed her malice and disapproval towards Harry, considering her to be a rock 'n' roll wannabe.

Evelyn McDonnell, co-editor of the anthology *Rock She Wrote: Women Write About Rock, Pop and Rap*, offers this theory: 'A lot of women in rock – like Patti Smith – are trying to get away from [being judged] by traditional beauty standards. That's very cool, but at the same time Patti is, in an old school kind of way, just incredibly competitive with other women. She was the scrappy tomboy who wanted to be with the guys and wanted to be one of the guys. And when those guys leave you for the blonde showing her tits across the table, you end up hating that blonde. She saw Debbie as one of the blondes.'

Professional jealousy must have also played a role in Smith's unpleasantness – she was obviously deeply threatened by the idea of another woman encroaching on her territory as queen of New York. Especially a woman who was taking such a dramatically different approach from androgynous women in rock like herself. Feminist writer and cultural critic, Mim Udovitch says, 'Debbie Harry reclaimed being femme in an overtly sexual way whereas before it had always been linked to victimization – like Marilyn Monroe. Debbie Harry fucked it up on purpose. There was always something about her look that was deconstructing itself – the roots growing in, the rip in the hose or the slashed t-shirt – that shows that it's artifice. She's not apologetic about being pop either, so there's a sincerity to it, yet she uses the pop idiom to express something that's pretty avant garde.'

Making Tracks co-author, and Patti Smith biographer, Victor Bockris, defends Harry's artistic integrity: 'In the 70s, Patti Smith was supposed to be the real deal and the real punk singer, whereas Debbie was considered to be a cartoon character. But if you look at them now, Debbie is a much more real person than Patti because Patti's not who she appears to be onstage, she a completely different person, a fake. On the other hand, Debbie is who she appears to be – in the best sense, she is Blondie, she is the person singing those songs.'

Bockris also defends Harry's artistic merits: 'Debbie is a very good lyric writer, something no one ever pays attention to. She wrote most of Blondie's lyrics. You hear Patti Smith is a great writer all the time and she is. But Debbie's lyrics are just as good as Patti's, or in some cases, better. Patti's power came from the darkness, Debbie's was in the light. It's easier to get into negativity, wear black, look mean and make it work for you. It's actually harder to take the light path and make it work, and Debbie did. She played the edge, but she played in the light – that's the essence of her strength.'

Bockris maintains that while Harry has great respect for Smith's talents, Smith remains dismissive of Harry: 'I think if you asked Patti about Debbie in 1999, she'd still say negative things about her. You have to remember also that just when Patti Smith left music in 1980, Blondie was the biggest group in the world. In some ways, it was a courageous thing for Patti to do – she left her group, she went to Detroit and got married, but then she had to see Debbie, who she despised, become the most famous woman in the world.'

Smith's inability to cross over into the mainstream does give her more of an underground credibility. For better or worse, she's a very New York character, while Harry played on a much bigger world stage. But as years have gone by, people now see that Smith and Harry, as contemporaries, may have more in common than they have at odds. First of all, both women had tried the groupie route in rock 'n' roll, hanging out with and seducing men from bands they admired as a point of access, but both wanted more. Both women moved on to fronting all-male bands, and as Udovitch points out, both women were then limited to playing roles: 'Debbie Harry was in drag as a woman like Patti Smith was in drag as a man.'

Music writer, Lisa Robinson, also points out that both women, although they achieved different levels of commercial success, were turned off by it. 'Basically, I think on some level Debbie thought success was kind of gross, and Patti did too. Patti couldn't take it, she couldn't do what everyone expected her to. Debbie couldn't or didn't want to either. In both cases, sometimes, you just have to get off the treadmill because you don't even know why you're doing it anymore.'

Knowing what a diminishing term wannabe is, and how much artists have always been inspired by those who came before them, Harry would probably never use it to refer to the hundreds of artists and thousands of fans who proudly claim her as a seminal influence. Still they exist – women and men – whose indebtedness to Harry reveals itself in a whole number of obvious and clandestine ways.

Jancee Dunn, Senior Editor at *Rolling Stone* magazine says, 'I've interviewed a million female artists over the past eight years and her name comes up the most as an influence.' Dunn, who is also an on-camera VJ at MTV's alternative station, M2, admits to being a bit of a Deborah Harry pre-teen wannabe herself. 'I first saw her on *Don Kirshner's Rock Concert* [American TV show] during a slumber party I had when I was twelve and I couldn't fucking believe my eyes! I couldn't get my suburban New Jersey mind around how hip she was. No one I knew even came close to how cool she was, not even Heather Banning, who was this girl in the grade above me who was the coolest girl in school, who smoked in the bathroom and was in a band.'

Eventually, Dunn, like thousands of young girls around the world, took steps to imitate Harry as best they could: 'When I found out she was also from New Jersey, I just about died! I bought *Parallel Lines* and I listened to it incessantly. Then she did that [Murjani] jeans commercial. Well, the next day I went to the Livingston Mall and got a pair of those jeans.' As an adult, Dunn looks back on her Harry infatuation and says, 'One of the things I admired about Debbie was she wasn't afraid of the glamour. She embraced it and worked it and there was nothing wrong with that. She looked like a movie star yet she had that kind of effortlessness that is traditionally male. Maybe she was a neurotic mess underneath, but she was so cool and in control and I desperately wanted to emulate that.' The freshness of Harry means that she is still an interesting subject today. 'Everything I read about her isn't enough. I never burnt out on her, unlike say Courtney Love, who at a certain point you just have to go, Okay, Uncle!'

Mim Udovitch, articulates what is that separates Harry from both Love and Madonna, the female pop stars who most benefited from her legacy. She says, 'Debbie's not as scary because there is something sweet about her image. She doesn't just have that appetite, that unapologetic hunger for attention and the spotlight. She's not going to consume you like Madonna and Courtney Love are.' For better or worse, Harry's was a take it or leave it attitude about love, her looks, money and fame. She sang 'Just Go Away' with Blondie, a far cry from Madonna's 'You Must Love Me'.

But in terms of her influence, Udovitch emphasizes that she was the first to combine Marilyn Monroe and Iggy Pop. Harry once penned an essay for *High Times* magazine, in which she said she wished she'd 'invented sex'. Udovitch believes that in a way, she did. 'Whatever Debbie Harry's actual life, there was something decadent about her persona that suggested wild, late nights. Like she never had trouble getting laid a day in her life and she wasn't turning away from the feast, whether in reality she did or not.' In interviews Harry would list 'fucking' as one of her favorite forms of exercise, an attitude which was nothing short of revolutionary for a woman with so much mainstream exposure. Udovitch says, 'When I was a teenager, it was unthinkable to flaunt your sexuality and own your desires like she did in Blondie, so on a mass culture level, she did invent fucking and she should be proud of it.'

Lucy O'Brien, author of *She Bop: The Definitive History of Women in Rock, Pop and Soul*, says, 'When I was writing the history of women in rock, she really did stand out. She's said, "Oh, I wish it had been me," about Madonna, but I think Debbie, who created this cartoon of a blonde pin-up pop star and then satirized it, was just a bit too early to be playing with such loaded imagery. Madonna was able to keep experimenting and pushing doors open until people finally got it and there was no question of her strength and her control. With Debbie, it was all a bit murky and I think most people read her quite straight as a sexy, bubblegum pop star. A lot of what she was doing was lost at the time, although in retrospect, you can see that the image she was presenting was quite rebellious.'

Deborah Harry also presented herself as a very human icon. She gave the appearance that she was calling her own shots but she never hid that she was fallible and vulnerable. O'Brien says, 'Women like Debbie Harry's openness and frankness, like her talking about her weight fluctuating. Her experiences as a woman reflect the experiences of many women. She's very human and honest.'

As Gail O'Hara, music editor of *Time Out New York* says, 'Her influence was just immense, but a lot of the women who followed on Debbie Harry's heels were really embarrassing, like Dale Bosio from Missing Persons and Teri Nunn from Berlin.' But even more than women who looked like Harry and who copied the Blondie formula of fronting all-male bands, Harry's musical and style influences have been remarked upon in conjunction with artists as diverse as Annie Lennox, Tina Turner and Pat Benatar. Contemporary women in pop such as Liz Phair, P J Harvey, Justine Frischmann of Elastica and Saffron of Republica have cited Harry's inspiration in interviews as well.

According to Evelyn McDonnell, Deborah Harry also has a strong presence among many young, very edgy female musicians: 'L7 made an album called *Triple Platinum*, for which they dyed their hair blonde. Kathleen Hanna from Bikini Kill acts like she was influenced by Deborah – she uses an ironic awareness of her sexuality like Deborah. And Skin from Skunk Anansie also has that awareness of both the rock world and the fashion world.'

THE WOMEN

Joan Jett

Kenny Laguna, Joan Jett's manager, has a story about Joan hanging out in London with Blondie, which he thinks says a lot about Deborah Harry's character. 'It was 1979 in London. Blondie was the hottest band in the world, and Joan was down and out. The Runaways had broken up and the industry was really treating Joan like garbage. So Debbie puts Joan on the guest list to see Blondie's show at Hammersmith Odeon – it was a sold out show and a really big deal. We get to the door and this guy starts giving us a hard time and he clearly knows who Joan is and he's getting a kick out of turning her away. The Blondie bus comes by and they see us standing outside, so they come and take us under their wing. We watched the show from the side of the stage and they treated Joan like a God.

'For the rest of the weekend, they keep Joan, who was like a wounded bird at this point, by their side. Blondie is the toast of London and they present Joan Jett as one of their dear friends. All during this time, 20/20 was filming everything, and Debbie and Chris took great care to push Joan into all the shots, telling them, "This is Joan Jett, she's going to be a big, big star." But meanwhile, Debbie was complaining to Joan about 20/20 saying stuff like, "I can't go to the bathroom without a camera up my ass." So when this big moment comes for 20/20 to interview Joan, she's all stirred up from Debbie telling her what assholes these camera guys are, so when they turn the camera on her she gives them the finger and goes, "Fuck you ABC!" And so *20/20* edited out every bit of Joan Jett.'

Jett laughs and says that even before that incident, she was always on Deborah Harry's side. She was just a teenager when she was fronting the all-female LA rock band, The Runaways, and first saw Blondie in LA in 1977. 'I just loved seeing another woman in rock 'n' roll up there with a strong attitude. She had an edginess, which I could relate to. There was anger, there was tenderness, happiness, all the same things that are in a lot of rock 'n' roll music, but I also saw [she had a] frustration at not being taken seriously.'

Jett knows well what it was like to be a woman in rock at that point, when radio stations would reject any music with a strong female presence by saying, 'We're already playing a woman.' Jett recalls that, right away, she felt comfortable with Harry and the rest of Blondie. 'At the time they came to LA, they knew us, I mean we had already played CBGB's and we might have even met there. They were just really friendly and didn't have a negative vibe towards me or the Runaways, which wasn't the norm'.

Jett was seventeen at the time, and as Harry describes her, 'just a baby', but her house across the street from the LA rock club where Blondie frequently played, the Whiskey, was party central. Apparently, they all had a lot of good times that Jett can barely remember. She does have one funny story to tell however, about the time Chris Stein wanted to take some unconventional pictures of her. 'Actually, Debbie Harry was the first person to get me in a dress and all made up. First of all, dresses were not my thing and I think Debbie even got me in nail polish and everything.' Harry confirms, 'Yeah, we did. I had this black asymmetrical Morticia dress I had made – I sewed it all by hand – it had this little train and we put Joan in it and Chris took pictures of it. She looked great – she's a beautiful girl.'

As a contemporary of Harry's, Jett says she never felt

competitive and she was happy to have a female friend who was also in a band. 'I didn't analyze it, I just knew I got off on the music and I felt like I could relate to her and she made me feel good. As a person, she's very down to earth and it's easy to have conversations with her. Debbie is very approachable, she's never been an untouchable rock star.'

Jett never formally collaborated with Harry, although she played guitar on stage with Blondie one night in 1977 at The Whiskey for a spectacular cover of Iggy Pop's 'I Wanna be Your Dog', and in 1996, Jett and Harry shared a bill at the New York rock club, SqueezeBox. Jimmy Destri, Clem Burke and Nigel Harrison played on Jett's solo debut, *Bad Reputation*, and The Runaways were also briefly managed by Blondie's first manager, Peter Leeds, of which Jett says, 'No comment.'

As for wannabes, Jett says, 'I don't see much that reminds me of Debbie or even where we came from now. To me, Debbie is very unique. Like there's a combination of hardness and softness in her and the way she brought it out on stage. It's her voice, the way she sings, it's a combination of all of that which attracts me to the band and her as a lead singer. Plus, I never got the feeling she was being told what to do by anyone.'

Shirley Manson

'Doesn't every smart woman like Debbie Harry?' says the Scottish lead singer of Garbage, Shirley Manson. 'She has exceptional character and exceptional intelligence yet she was one of the first beautiful pop icons that we'd ever had. There are so many now who have followed in her footsteps, that, in my opinion, don't hold a candle to her. Debbie did it with such style and grace and humor, and she never took herself too seriously. That's what makes her stand out amongst all the pretenders to her throne.'

Manson was actually a convert to the cult of Debbie Harry. She says that she knew very little about Harry before her first band, Goodbye Mr Mackenzie, supported Harry on a British tour in the late 80s. 'I then educated myself,' she laughs, 'I was too young when she was on the charts to have seen her myself, and my peer group were elitist snobs and turned me on to Velvet Underground, Patti Smith, The Stooges, etc, and Blondie was omitted because they had a pop sensibility. I don't think she has received the praise and respect she deserves because the elite crowd looked down on Blondie because they were so pop, and scorn was heaped upon them because they were the most commercial band to emerge from that scene.' With the success of Garbage, Manson knows only too well what that feels like.

But Manson was very impressed by what she saw up close in Harry when touring with her. She says, 'I couldn't believe how ferocious she was on stage – just a ball of energy. She's not so self-conscious about looking pretty, she's more into the whole concept of expressing herself and not just being cool. And of course, she has tremendous depth, which is sadly lacking in most performers. Also, considering the caliber of her stardom, she's so easy and warm. Yet, I'm sure she can be a tiger when she needs to.'

Harry reached out to Manson as well, partly for the sake of tour camaraderie and also because she recognized Manson as a kindred spirit – talented but perhaps a little insecure. Manson was bowled over by Harry's generosity: 'When you're a famous person it's pretty easy to treat others with contempt and make demands and really exorcise your demons. What I find so incredible about her is, here I was in this tiny little band from Scotland that no one gave a shit about and she found time in her day to show interest and extend support.' After that tour, Harry kept an eye out for Manson, and came to see her play with her new band, Angelfish, in New York in the early 90s. Manson recalls, 'Just before I joined Garbage, I was immensely insecure and lacking in confidence, and Debbie came to my shows. I'll never forget – we did a show at Irving Plaza and Debbie came and stood right down front in the mosh pit with the boys and all the kids.' She laughs, 'How can you not fall in love with someone like that?' Manson says around that time, Harry also gave her a pair of angelfish earrings.

Manson and Harry saw each other in London in the fall of 1998 while both Blondie and Garbage were filming *Top of the Pops*. Manson says excitedly, 'She looked absolutely fucking incredible and beautiful, as always, and she said she was amused because she'd been watching my career and she was very proud of me.' Harry speaks of Manson with the respect of one peer to another, and also with the concern of an elder sister, 'Well, Shirley's great. She always was good, better than she knew. She's a terrific singer and I'm very pleased about her success. It doesn't surprise me at all.'

Looking at Manson's frankly outspoken views, unapologetic sexuality and intelligence and trend-setting style, one can conclude that Manson has taken some of the best elements from Deborah Harry's example and made them her own. As one of the few contemporary female rock stars who seems to have talent, beauty and intelligence in equal parts, Manson may, in the course of her career, even add some improvements to the model. Like Harry, success came a little later for Manson, who is currently in her early 30s, and perhaps this maturity will also enable her to map out a long, interesting, risk-taking career in and around pop music.

Manson clearly sees Harry as an important role model: 'I think almost every single female musician owes a lot to Deborah Harry. She's flaunting convention and she's doing it for every woman out there. I find her immensely inspiring. I think she's very brave and at times, that must be very difficult, but I admire her balls and her refusal to bow to society's convention. Madonna has said herself that she was influenced by Deborah Harry, and then, without Madonna where would we be? Madonna has also flaunted convention and broken rules, portraying women in a different light. I think if we hadn't had role models like that, who would have pioneered the way for a lot of artists like myself, we'd still be in a state of arrested development in terms of women's forays into the music world.'

Manson also speaks eloquently and optimistically about the state of the future of women in music. 'There are more women in general finding the confidence in themselves to get their music heard. There are no longer two-dimensional, stereotypical examples of a female artist out there. There's a huge gamut of different types of talent and different types of personalities out there, that never existed when I was growing up. It's fantastic not only for young women but for young men, to be receiving all these varied messages about what being a woman is about.'

Kate Schellenbach & Theo Kogan

Kate Schellenbach, drummer of the New York pop band Luscious Jackson, and Theo Kogan lead singer of the New York punk band, The Lunachicks, are both products of the post-Blondie New York music scene.

Schellenbach, a native New Yorker, became obsessed with Blondie at the tender age of thirteen. 'I think the first song of theirs I heard was 'Heart of Glass.' I don't remember exactly, but Blondie quickly became my favorite band and an obsession. I discovered them at summer camp in Connecticut – there was this older counselor who was like 18 and he was listening to punk. All of that stuff made me really excited and made me realize there was a whole other world out there – Max's and CBGB's.'

A year later, Schellenbach started going out to music clubs where she encountered a band called the Student

Teachers. 'They were kind of Blondie-esque, and I think Jimmy Destri produced their first single and use to go out with their drummer, this woman Laura Evans. She was one of the main reasons I started playing drums, and it was by going to these clubs that I eventually met my peers, the other members of Luscious Jackson. Their garage band sound is all about the empowerment of the average woman, in everyday life, to go out and make her own fucking music. Like Blondie, LJ also incorporates street sounds, most notably hip hop and 70s R&B influences, in an assortment of very clever, foot-tapping songs.'

Kogan, who is also a native New Yorker, was too young to benefit directly from hanging out at CBGB's, but she remembers how Deborah Harry first got her hooked on being a bad girl. 'When I was eight or nine, my friend and I made a tape of the song "Heart of Glass" over and over and over, and every time Debbie sang "ass", which was one of those bad words we weren't suppose to say, we'd like burst into laughter – Heeheeheehee!' During her senior year of high school, Kogan and her girlfriends, Gina and Squid, started The Lunachicks. Their sound is much harder and faster than Blondie's, but there is a striking resemblance between The Lunachicks and Blondie; the visual similarity between Kogan and Harry.

Besides being blonde with roots, beautiful and sexy, Kogan exudes an almost drag queen like glamour on stage and an absolutely transfixing charisma. Her clothes are circus-like costumes in bright candy colors that play in contrast to the music's loud raging. But, like Harry, Kogan is about deconstructing femininity. If Harry did it by wearing ripped clothes and having roots, Kogan does it by going on stage with perfect movie make-up and letting it melt over the course of the night into a fright mask, while she repeatedly makes herself fall and roll around on the dirty floor.

Schellenbach thinks Harry's appeal to her was twofold. 'Being able to analyze it years later, what first attracted me to Debbie Harry was she sang perfect pop songs with the sing-along chorus and the whoa-whoa-whoas and all that stuff. That stuff captures me – I'm a pop lover at heart, and her voice was so compelling. Something about it – it was syrupy and sexy. And of course, little did I know at the time, as this was before my sexuality became an issue, but I was totally crushed out on her. Lyrically the songs were very strong and sexy, and like "Pretty Baby", they had ambiguous lyrics. I was like, She could be singing that to me! With rock stars, you want to be them or you want to sleep with them and she fulfilled both roles.'

Kogan's affinity with Harry comes from really identifying with her: 'There's something that's really hard about believing in yourself as a performer. You're always insecure and you're always trying to do better and you're really self-critical. But I look at her, the most incredible woman in the world in every way, and if she has doubts too, well, then it must be really fucked up out there! MTV has really changed the way bands are. You have to have a look. For women it's even harder because there's a body type we're supposed to have which is basically a man's body with tits. There are so many things in the media that can throw you into a spiraling pit of doom. No matter how talented, or smart you are you can't be immune to it, not even Debbie.'

Kogan says that after eleven years in the music business, a lot has changed and yet nothing has. What's still acceptable are really clean-cut, non-threatening women with the right sound like Sheryl Crow, Jewel or Celine Dion. Only men like Marilyn Manson get to be overtly transgressive and scary. Still, without Harry, Kogan feels like there would be no original sinner: 'I mean, I can't imagine the world without her, so many people have been inspired by her, like me – I don't walk around thinking I have Debbie Harry's hair, but I do. We might not have Madonna if it wasn't for Debbie, but the thing about Debbie is, that unlike Madonna, when she was first starting out, she was clearly uncomfortable on stage and struggling against it. That was really endearing and really real. At the same time, you wouldn't fuck with her.'

Of her evolution from fan to peer Schellenbach says, 'It's definitely a juxtaposition of nerves. On the one hand I'm feeling like a peer, having worked really hard all my adult life to be a good musician and be respected by other musicians to become a peer. But on the other hand there's a big part of me that's a fan. At some point, during the show I did with Blondie [at Tramps in May 1998] I asked, "Can I take a picture with you?" That was the fan coming out'. For Kogan, although she's technically also a peer, she feels like the evolution has been more from fan to more intimate fan. After years of taking inspiration from Harry's public persona, she now feels lucky to know Harry personally.

THE MEN

Fred Schneider

Fred Schneider of the Atlanta new wave band, the B-52's has a secret that undermines his gentle southern accent – like Deborah Harry, he also grew up in New Jersey. He says with a laugh, 'Yeah, Southern Orange.' But unfortunately for both of them, Harry and Schneider didn't cross paths until 1978, the year the B-52's first released their classic single, 'Rock Lobster'. He says, 'We saw them open for The Kinks in Atlanta and then came backstage after the show. We were always real excited when New York bands came down to play.' Stein, who was doing photos for *Punk* magazine during this time, took pictures of the colorful B-52's and they bonded. When the band relocated to New York in 1979, Schneider recalls, 'We went to [Harry and Stein's] penthouse – it was after "Heart of Glass" hit, and you had to step over gold and platinum records everywhere. They were also just starting to collect Giger, but they made us super-charged margaritas and we just hung-out. We couldn't get over how friendly and real they were.'

Perhaps some of the bond between them stemmed from that fact the both the B-52's and Blondie were on the dance pop end of the spectrum of punk. Schneider says that whenever the B-52's played CBGB's, they felt a really good vibe in the room. He says, 'I mean, there were some nasty people who I won't mention, but in general, everyone was so supportive. Gosh, it's hard to believe that was seventeen years ago.'

Well, actually Fred, it was like twenty years ago, but Deborah Harry remains a presence in popular culture and in the B-52's music. The band's 1998 album, *Time Capsule*, contained a new song called 'Debbie', which was inspired by Harry. Schneider says, 'We were jamming and we [Kate Pierson, Cindy Wilson, Keith Strickland and I] came up with some basic ideas for some lyrics. Keith suggested we call it "Debbie" because we wanted to evoke the emotions and feelings of sitting in a club and hearing a new wave band in 1977 – and Debbie was a perfect jumping off point.'

'Debbie', like most of the B-52's music, has a driving, up-beat rhythm, but unlike the band's more anxious, slightly menacing songs like 'Rock Lobster' and 'Private Idaho', 'Debbie' is purely celebratory, in the vein of the band's hits 'Roam' and 'Love Shack'. The song's chorus exalts a 'shell-shocked supersonic blonde, hyperphonic female, dark sunglasses on', which clearly evokes an image of Harry, but the heroine of the song is described as a guitar player in an all-female band. Not quite Harry, but quite possibly a reference to the legions of young women she inspired. The song also evokes the feeling of the audience, watching this 'queen of the underground' – 'we witness the ultrasonic imploding excitation, bodies exhausted in total elation'.

It's a tribute to the time – Schneider admits he prefers the music of his contemporaries to new music: 'Stuff now isn't wild enough, it doesn't have enough edge.' Schneider can't say enough about Harry, it's clear that to him she represents the most inspiring and most progressive female of her time: 'She was the first. She set the stage for everyone – from Madonna to Alanis Morrisette to whoever – and she still writes the best songs. She's just a totally self-assured, sex bomb. Also, I love her NJ accent – it always gets me. It's sort of incongruous with her looks, but she never took all of it too seriously. Like you could almost see her rolling her eyes when Dick Clark [from *American Bandstand*] interviewed her or something. She was never one to fall for the hype. She's a goddess, in your face and in your ears.'

Mark Mothersbaugh

Founding member of new wave band Devo, Mark Mothersbaugh, recalls how Devo and Blondie first crossed paths: 'We were playing Max's and CBGB's in the late 70s. Chris Stein invited us over to their apartment on 58th Street and we took pictures on the roof for one of those cool, rags [*Punk* magazine]. Devo had our yellow suits on and then Debbie took my shirt and put it on.' The group hit it off with Stein and Harry. In fact, Harry and Stein were so impressed by Devo, they scared them. 'Before we had a record deal, Blondie were so enthusiastic about us, they performed one of our songs on stage, and wanted to record it before we did. At the time, I was like, "Yikes! We can't give away our songs", but in retrospect I wish we had,' says Mothersbaugh. 'They were the best of what New York had to offer at that time. In some ways, we shared aesthetics, we were influenced by Andy Warhol and ideas about art and commerce connecting up. We thought anyone who could do something true to their own vision and be pop was just great. We felt like kindred spirits.'

Although Blondie didn't record any Devo songs, Devo did end up adding some robotic back-up vocals to Harry's first solo album, *Koo Koo*. However, Mothersbaugh now has a much more significant connection to Harry's legacy. With his LA-based company Mutato Muzika, Mothersbaugh and the other members of Devo produce film scores, and two of their recent projects, *The Rugrats Movie* (1998) and *200 Cigarettes* (1999), include Blondie songs. He says the reason Blondie's music works so well today is that it has really good energy. 'It was very positive for the most part, and after the gloom and doom of grunge for the past ten years, I can see why kids would want to take a step back to Blondie and say, Hey, this feels really great!'

200 Cigarettes includes two songs from Blondie's reunion album, *No Exit* – the title track, 'No Exit' and the hit single, 'Maria', as well as 'Rapture'. *The Rugrats Movie* actually includes a rewritten cover of 'One Way or Another'. Mothersbaugh says, 'That was really fun. We wrote parody lyrics for Angelica, the character who is like the bad seed that is always either terrorizing them or leading them astray.' It's the fantasy of a child with the tough demeanor of Harry, although Mothersbaugh says that the song, which was originally written about Harry's stalker, takes on another meaning in the film. He says, 'Angelica uses it [as an anthem] to go chasing down her lost doll.'

Mothersbaugh has no problem identifying with bad girls. His first band, SAT/SUN MAT, was fronted by Pretenders' Chrissie Hynde. He says, '[Chrissie] was the only girl I'd ever been in a band with, so when I met Debbie I was like, "How cool a girl in a punk band", as punk was the primarily the domain of males. Plus she was so beautiful. A lot of girls in punk made themselves look ugly because they were angry and revolting against the tyranny of glamour and beauty in their lives. So here Debbie was, straddling both worlds, yet she seemed amused by her own glamour and beauty, like she could take it or leave it.' To sum it up, Mothersbaugh says of Harry, 'I'm a big fan, OK?'

Ru-Paul, the seven-foot tall, platinum blonde gender-bending host of his own VH1 talkshow, *The RuPaul Show*, and Miss Guy, the sexy, androgynous lead singer of the New York rock band The Toilet Boys, have radically different memories about their first bonding experiences with Deborah Harry.

RuPaul, whose own rags to riches story includes a time when the singer/actor/talkshow host was homeless, particularly appreciates inspiration and the kindness of others, so his encounter with Harry in 1989 earned her a permanent place in his heart. 'A guy I knew who was working at a Fresh restaurant [in Greenwich Village] called me and said, *"Quick, Debbie Harry is here having dinner, come down and see her!"* So I grabbed my latest Debbie Harry album and I ran down there, sneaked into the restaurant and I asked her if she would please sign it. She was so gracious and of course, she did it. I'll never, ever forget that. When you finally meet your idols, and I've met almost all of them now, you're almost always disappointed, except I was never disappointed with Deborah Harry.'

Meanwhile, around the same time, Guy, who as a pre-teen tried both to go to Halloween as Harry and do a lip sync as her in his drama class, remembers, 'I had been doing make-up professionally for two years and my friend Michael Schmidt was asked to design an anti-Gulf War t-shirt for Debbie for *SPIN* magazine, and he got me a job doing her face. It was winter and snowing and I didn't really know where I was going, so I was late getting to the shoot. We started right away, but I was freaking out because she was my dream person to do make-up on and it wasn't going the way I wanted it to at all. Like people have always told me that when I'm doing their foundation that I have a really gentle touch and they say stuff like, "That feels so good, I could fall asleep." But when I started doing Debbie, she was like, "Watch it – you're tearing my fucking face off!" I thought she must be kidding, but she like leaned forward in the chair and glared at me and said, "And I don't like it".'

While Guy wanted to run out of the studio screaming and crying, he says he decided to give back attitude as good as she gave it. In an odd turn of events, it was the beginning of a friendship which still continues, twelve years later. He now says affectionately, 'Anyone who has ever met her has said she's so intimidating at first, but then they can't believe how sweet she is. She really likes to say yes to people. In fact,' he says with a sly smile, 'maybe I should ask her to start cleaning my apartment?'

Guy jokes, but he remains so loyal to Harry, he once even nipped a promising relationship in the bud over her. He says, 'A few years ago I had a crush on this kid who supposedly had a crush on me too, and we went out and somehow we got on the subject of Debbie Harry. I told him I thought she was one of the most beautiful people in the world and he was like, *Are you kidding!* And he started going off on why he didn't think she was pretty and I was like, that's it – you're out!'

Ultimately, Guy derailed his own career as a make-up artist for his love of rock 'n' roll. He started his own band the Toilet Boys in 1996 and of course, Harry was a big influence in developing his stage persona. He says, 'Debbie Harry has the best style out of any woman. I don't look like her – I wish I did, but what I do is an exaggerated version of her.' RuPaul, who also ended up following his own star to fame, landing a record deal and later his own TV show, says Harry influenced his look too. 'Oh yeah, when I decided to make a go of it myself, I wanted to take the blonde goddess archetype and really do a send up of it. To have this *black man* doing the blonde goddess look that Debbie did and Marilyn did and on down the line, I knew that would really turn some heads and it worked.'

By realizing more of themselves, both RuPaul and Guy got closer to their idol. The first time Guy and The Toilet Boys performed, they opened for Deborah Harry at SqueezeBox. Since then Harry has been spotted at several of the Toilet Boys' shows. Guy says, 'I remember seeing her in the audience and feeling so excited! I thought she'd just stay for a couple of songs, but she stood right in the front and stayed for the whole show. She's come to our shows three times, so she must like us. In one of our write-ups, it even mentioned that she was in the audience rocking out. I can't think of anyone else I'd rather have see us. It's cool and exciting and weird. In fact, someone said to me recently, "Debbie Harry is a big fan of yours now!".'

Meanwhile, RuPaul, who following the success of his album *Supermodel*, landed a contract with VH1 television and got the opportunity to invite Harry on as a guest. She appeared as a panelist on an episode of his talkshow, chatting along with filmmaker John Waters, about the concept of 'camp'. He says, 'I asked her to do the show because if anyone knew what camp was, she would, you know? Having the name Blondie and then being Blondie, she was doing a send-up. I mean, the punk generation was really about taking the piss out of everything our culture thinks of as real and sacred. Plus, her acting jobs in *Hairspray*, *Videodrome* and *Tales From The Darkside* – I knew she really got it.'

But what Ru thinks is most worthy of Harry's wannabes, is not that she is a great pop star, but that she is also a great human being. 'I love everything Blondie and Debbie did because that's what an artist exploring herself is all about, and that makes her so cool. Even the personal stuff, like she put her career on the shelf to help a friend – that's fucking cool. Fuck who's on the top of the charts – people will remember that she wasn't some calculating cow, but that she was a real human being. It's not about the gold records and the Grammys baby, it's about the love you shared with people along the way.'

FANATICS

Although almost everyone who was interviewed for this book could be characterized as a fan, it's Harry's so-called 'fanatic' fans who have kept her legacy alive through the creation of fan clubs, collectors' societies and websites, and who pay tribute to her through the creation of fanzines, cable TV shows, artworks and dolls. Some of them even wear her on their skin, others have created their own rock star personas in her image.

This kind of devotion is something Harry appreciates, but ironically, it is not something to which she can really relate. 'I don't think I've ever felt that way about anyone except maybe once when I was a kid. I always wonder if it's real?' Harry offers some pop psychology: 'I know this woman who does manicures and she's a fanatic for this South American singer. Initially, something in the music moved her and she would go and always sit in the first row at his shows. Then somehow or other she gave him a present and she got to meet this person and then suddenly, he had a disproportionate meaning in her life. I think it's a little bit of ego displacement.' And maybe something to do with popular culture nowadays, which tends to exalt celebrities, giving their lives a mythological or fairy-tale quality. The cult of celebrity requires followers and believers, who can then turn celebrities into twentieth century gods and goddesses.

While Harry balks at the idea that she's a goddess of any kind, she embraces her fans' devotion as part of 'human nature' and unlike other celebrities, she truly regards them as more of a pleasure than a pain. Over the years, Harry has held on to many letters and presents fans have given her. She has a reputation for indulging her fans. 'The best thing I ever signed was a dick.' She recalls gleefully. 'It was at a birthday party for . . . what's her name? Oh, my mind's gone blank . . . [she sings, Ride up to the bumper baby . . .]' Grace Jones? 'Grace! Yeah.' Hold on – Grace Jones has a dick? This comment makes Harry laugh. 'Well, if any woman could and wear it well, it's Grace. But no, it was at a dinner for Grace's birthday. I just trotted on in and there was this guy standing at the door in a g-string and he wanted an autograph. So I said, "Only if I can sign your dick." I don't know what kind of mood I was in or why I'd want to do that, but I did it.'

Signing a dick, letting a fan suck her toes, showing up at a tattoo parlor so a fan could have her autograph inked on his arm – these are the lengths to which Deborah Harry will go for her devoted admirers. And if you're a little kooky, so be it. Harry doesn't mind. 'I try not to be judgemental about my fans. I just try to be cordial and respect their requests.' Harry says generously. 'If they want an autograph, I try to give it to them. And, I try to listen to them a little bit, because a lot of the time, people just don't get listened to enough.'

JOHN CANTWELL

'If you came over to my apartment you'd think I was a psychotic stalker or something,' says LA based actor, John Cantwell, whose entire apartment is wallpapered with images of Deborah Harry. The obsession started in 1979, when Cantwell was eleven and living in the sexually repressed Southern town of Tallulah, Louisiana. As a teenager, Cantwell says Harry was his only link to sexual freedom: 'I think because I knew I was gay, I was never really involved with things at school. Most of the time, I would lock myself in my room and read books like *The Year In Rock*, Lester Bangs' book *Blondie* and *Making Tracks: The Rise of Blondie*. So I also started learning about Studio 54 and Andy Warhol and CBGB's and Max's Kansas City and the history behind Blondie. I really started to feel like, Wow, things are going to be okay. I had somewhere to go. No one in my family had ever left the South, but in 1993, I moved to New York.'

Cantwell saw Harry perform in a New York nightclub a few months after moving to New York. A few months after that, he found himself teaching aerobics classes at a gym where Harry worked out with a personal trainer named Brian Moss. Moss introduced Harry to Cantwell, and then for Cantwell's birthday in 1995, Moss brought Harry to a Manhattan tattoo parlor so that Cantwell could have her signature tattooed on his arm. Cantwell recalls, 'Brian just breezed in with her and there she was – smelling like cigarettes with her hair all messed up, in denim jeans and a flannel shirt – not a stitch of make-up. She's 50 years old and there's not a line on her face – the camera doesn't even do her justice anymore – she's so beautiful. I didn't really think she would show up. She kept saying to me, "Are you sure you want to do this?" Then she said, "Are you sure you don't want a picture or something?" And I was like, "A picture of you?" So she's shaking her head at me, but then she started signing her name on a piece of paper for the tattoo, and she totally turned into this school teacher. She goes, "Okay, this is Debbie Harry. This is Deborah Harry. And this is just D Harry." I got tons of autographs from her that day, I just kept saying, "More!" She stayed for about 10 or 15 minutes, but it seemed like forever.'

Cantwell, who currently performs with the Los Angeles-based comedy troupe, The Nellie Oslens, still treasures the tattoo as a mark of his devotion to Harry, who he says has an almost spiritual place in his life. 'I think I could literally talk about her 24 hours a day, seven days a week. I was raised religiously and I've always been into inspiration and what motivates you to do stuff, and I think it's great that another person can inspire you like she has. It doesn't have to be Allah or Buddha or God, but someone who just did her thing and had no idea she was going to touch people so deeply.'

SARAH CONLEY

Sarah Conley, from Warrington, England, is one of Deborah Harry's most dedicated fans. She was actually born the year Blondie's *Parallel Lines* was released – 1978. Her mother, who is five years Harry's junior, could have been a Blondie fan and introduced her daughter to Blondie, but that's not how Conley first became entranced. She explains, 'It was 1989 when she came back with "I Want That Man". I was eleven years old and I was walking past the TV one day and saw the video. I just thought, Oh God, she's so cool!' After that, Conley was hooked and started collecting all of Blondie's and Harry's old albums and memorabilia. Conley recalls, 'I was the only person who liked her. I didn't even find older people who liked her. I don't think a lot of people knew she was still working, and that's part of why I started the Deborah Harry fanzine in 1996. I thought, there must be other fans out there!' Conley decided to call the 'zine *Underground Girl* after the Blondie song of the same title.

Through word of mouth and some advertising in music magazines, Conley was amazed by the response she got to *Underground Girl* in the UK. She says, 'It was hard at first, because at the time I started it, it wasn't like it is now [with the Blondie reunion]. You really had to scour the press to find anything about Debbie.' Conley supplemented whatever information she got from the internet and other fans by calling record companies. The rest of *UG* was filled with reprinted interviews and articles by readers about why they like Debbie, reader reviews, readers accounts of meeting Harry, original artworks, poems and a pen pal section.

Conley got a big break when she met the Jazz Passengers in 1997. Conley, who was just eighteen at the time, planned to attend the Jazz Passengers show, and by chance ended up staying in the same hotel as the band, which was of course, traveling with Harry. 'I saw Debbie in the lobby and just started chatting with her. I didn't tell her about the fanzine. Then after the show I met the Jazz Passengers and I told them about it and they were like, "Why didn't you tell her?" I think they really helped me, because then I sent them some issues and they must have shown them to her.' At a second JP gig in London later that year, Conley had drinks with the JPs after the gig. She says, 'That's when Debbie came over and said, "I know what you're doing and I think it's great. You've made me feel very special." She said she liked my writing and I asked her if I could do the fanzine officially and she said she'd love it.'

Conley says she currently has 350 subscribers from England, Germany, France and America whose ages range from 14 to 67. Conley says that young women, like herself, have no problem identifying with Harry even now that she's 53. 'One of my readers is 16 and she just adores Debbie, but she likes the Debbie of now more than she likes the old Blondie stuff.'

Conley says her own mum has come to accept her daughter's devotion to Harry. 'At first she was like, "Oh no, she was well-adjusted and normal and now she's like a 12-year-old Debbie Harry fan!" She thought it was a phase, but she likes what Debbie does now and she likes that I'm doing something creative with it, doing the fanzine.' There's only one downside to it for Conley, who still lives at home. 'My phone rang from 6 a.m. to midnight with fans who just wanted to talk about Debbie. I tried to be nice about it at first because some of these fans are just so isolated, but I finally had to change my number.'

BOONE, BRIAN & TERENCE

Deborah Harry worship is a family affair for native New Yorkers Boone, Brian and Terence. Boone and Brian are a married couple who have been girlfriend and boyfriend since high school. Terence is Brian's brother, and Boone's best friend, and the trio has grown up literally 'following' Deborah Harry. In fact, in 1986 they heard that Harry was living in the area of Manhattan called Chelsea and walked up and down the streets of that neighborhood, ringing every doorbell that didn't have a name on it. Boone says, 'We'd buzz and say, "Hi, is Debbie there?" The craziest thing is when we got to Ninth Avenue, we actually found Chris Stein. We rang and he just popped out. What we didn't know at the time was Debbie was living in an apartment right above his.' After that the trio began hanging out in Chelsea and they actually spotted Harry a number of times. Terence recalls, 'Even when we weren't looking for her, we'd run into her. I remember when the *Vanity Fair* article came out in 1989, we were eating in the Chelsea Square Diner. I was being retarded and holding up the pictures of her in the window to anyone passing by, and then, I held it up to her. She didn't notice, she was just walking by, but we ran out after her. I'm standing on the corner next to her and I'm like, "Oh, Hi." I was so excited, I almost got hit by a cab.'

Eventually the trio actually moved to Chelsea themselves, and although they are now in their late 20s and no longer as crazy as they were when they were younger, they are still infamous Blondie fanatics. They estimate that they have seen Harry perform over 50 times. Brian recalls one of those magical nights, a Deborah Harry show in 1989 at a New York nightclub called The World, when he collected some of his most precious memorabilia: 'Debbie took a rose on stage and bit the head off and spat out the petals and I was able to catch a handful. I still have those. I also have a small piece of the towel she used to wipe herself on stage. When she threw it into the audience, people tore it apart in a frenzy. All I got was this one little corner. And we smoked a joint with Chris Stein backstage after the show, and after he left, I put it out and kept the stub.' Stein and Harry have acknowledged the trio many times, and Stein once thanked the trio personally for being such loyal fans.

About three years ago, they decided to broadcast their point of view to the world, including their devotion to Harry, through the production of *The Boone Show*, a weekly cable access TV show which features rare footage of Harry in every episode. Boone says proudly, 'We show Debbie clips that no one but Debbie's diehard fans have ever seen.' Brian adds, 'Someone gave us this video called "At Home With Debbie and Chris", which has them walking around their penthouse and showing people stuff like this yellow Hitler piggy bank. Then it has video footage of Andy Warhol taking pictures of Debbie for her portrait. It's incredible.' Brian also plays in his own alternative rock band called The Dopes, and the band literally owes Deborah Harry for some of the band's equipment. He explains, 'One of the best moments I ever had with Debbie was, well, my band use to have this rehearsal space in Queens and one night the whole building caught on fire. So we lost all of our equipment and [SqueezeBox promoter] Michael Schmidt wanted to do a benefit for us. This was in 1995, and Debbie was one of the first people there. She was talking to me and she said, "That really sucks that you lost all your equipment. At least you're on the track to getting your stuff back." After she left, Schmidt came over and said, "Did you know that Debbie donated a $150 dollars tonight?" And I was just overwhelmed – that was the coolest thing.'

SAM HILL

There are a lot of Deborah Harry fans in the world, many of whom have been inspired by her personal style and her music over the years, but very few would dare go as far as to impersonate her on stage. It's something even drag queens like RuPaul are scared to do, never mind ordinary fans with no background in music or performance. But Sam Hill is now no ordinary fan, she's the lead singer of the three-year-old English Blondie cover band, Once More Into The Bleach. Hill says, 'I've been a fan of Blondie since I was about eight, so I knew all of the songs by heart and I've always wanted to be in a band too, so I thought it was worth a try.' Hill's first step in getting the band together was placing an advertisement in the music magazine, *NME*. She says she was surprised by the response. 'All these friends of mine answered the ads. Literally, I knew just about everyone who called – it was so funny.'

After a couple of line-up changes, OMITB finalized its line-up with four musicians, including a drummer who by coincidence learned to play listening to Clem on *Parallel Lines*. The band researched Blondie by listening to the albums together and watching all the videos they could find. Next, Hill had to get her look together: 'The look I have is Debbie circa 1979, the "Heart of Glass" period. I've got the hair done properly – blonde with black at the back.' But can anyone really look like Deborah Harry? Hill says, 'Well, I've been told I look like her, but I think I just get away with it, because who could be as gorgeous as our Debbie?'

OMITB started playing at pubs and clubs around England and their popularity has grown due in part to Blondie's comeback. Hill says, 'We're well known around the country now, and with Blondie coming back, we've been doing sold out shows. For Christmas [1998] we played a show at the Wolverhampton Civic with a bunch of other tribute bands a month after Blondie played there. That was really special – to play the same stage they did.'

OMITB also headlined the first annual UK Blondie Convention, which was held on February 27, 1999 in the West Midlands. Hill says she was nervous about playing in front of 400 dedicated Blondie fans, especially as OMITB was the sole entertainment scheduled for the evening of the conference, which during the day featured booths selling merchandise, records and memorabilia stuff.

So how do Blondie fans respond to Hill? She says, 'People tell me why they love Blondie so much and it's like they think I'm some sort of messenger to Debbie in a funny kind of way. They always say, tell Debbie this or that.' Hill also says that in her experience, there is no typical Blondie fan: 'There's no strict age group. There are lots of younger people, I mean, there are actually ten year olds in the audience sometimes.

'I've actually made a lot of friends doing this, because I'm basically just a fan myself. I loved Debbie Harry because she was always this bit of a bad girl who seemed to be having a really good time,' says Hill. 'That's why I do it. I don't do it to make money, I have another job for that. The way I see it, OMITB is just great promotion for Blondie.'

Is that how Blondie themselves see it? Hill says she first met Harry at a Jazz Passengers gig in Birmingham, then again at another gig in London in 1997, but says, 'I never told her I played her in a cover band!' In 1998, Hill attended six Blondie shows in England, and got backstage to chat with the band. '[Bassist] Leigh Foxx finally got it out of me, after asking me all these questions, like what kind of band are you in? What kind of songs do you sing? So I told him and he turns to Jimmy Destri and says, "Sam sings in a Blondie cover band!" and I turned bright red but they were really pleased.'

Hill says she's heard of a few other Blondie tribute bands, most notably one in Florida called Parallel Lines, but

Above: LIMO LIFE: Deborah Harry and Chris Stein decompress on the way to a tour date in Asbury Park, New Jersey, 1979. © ROBERTA BAYLEY

Below: BLONDIE ON TOP: Blondie wins the UK by vamping it up in 1978 on *Top of the Pops.* © PICTORIAL PRESS

Above: IDOL WORSHIP: Deborah Harry meets fan, Billy Idol, New York, 1978. © ROBERTA BAYLEY

Left: DRESS FOR SUCCESS: Deborah Harry's classic white shift dress, armband and slides, New York, 1978.

© ROBERTA BAYLEY

Above: LEADER OF THE PACK: Mike Chapman toasts Deborah Harry and Ronnie Spector at The Record Plant, New York, 1978. © ROBERTA BAYLEY

Below: I'M WITH THE BAND: The Blondie gang get some sun during a recording break outside The Record Plant, New York, 1978. © ROBERTA BAYLEY

WHO NEEDS COCK
ROCK?: Deborah
Harry knows how to
use her equipment,
Alladin Hotel,
Las Vegas, 1979.
© ROBERTA BAYLEY

Above: THE DISCO ROUND: Glamour puss Deborah
Harry and fashion photographer Francesco Scavullo,
New York. © PATRICK MCMULLAN

Right: THAT'S WHAT FRIENDS ARE FOR: Deborah Harry lends a hand to Michael Schmidt at The Dopes Benefit, Squeeze Box, New York, 1995. © TINA PAUL

Below:
QUEEN AND COUNTY: Deborah Harry and Jane County at Wigstock, New York, 1998. © TINA PAUL

Top Right:
FESTIVAL FEVER: Deborah Harry perform at Glastonbury in the UK, June 1999. CORBIS/ RUNE HELLESTED

Bottom Right:
BLONDES TOGETHER Deborah Harry back- stage with David Bowi at his concert in Manchester, 2003. GETT IMAGES / IAN HODGSON

A PASSION FOR FASHION: Deborah Harry attends the Marc Jacobs spring 2003 show during New York fashion week. CORBIS / GREGORY PACE

OMITB is the best known in England. But now that she's proved she can front a band, how long does Hill see herself just doing Blondie covers? 'Well, I don't know how long I'll keep at it. I really enjoy it right now, even though it's hard work,' she says, 'But it's like the guys from Blondie told me – I really should do my own stuff as well.'

CHAPTER NINE
Downtown Now

There's a proliferation of folklore about New York in the 60s, 70s and early 80s – a time when misfits and artists came to the city and didn't have to start making $50,000 a year minimum to afford the privilege of being here. Nowadays it's hard to imagine anything being as significant as the people and the places of the past. Sure there's a lot of new stuff – theme restaurants, cyber bars, trip-hop lounges, gay circuit parties – but will any of these phenomena be as vital and pure as the scenes that developed organically before everything was defined by media hype? No doubt, in some way their charms will prevail when nostalgia makes history of them too. But it is more likely than not that the people and scenes that will really change the world are currently lounging in obscurity somewhere outside of New York City.

But downtown, although it is declared so every six months by some middle-aged media mogul, is not dead. As expensive, exclusive and desperate as Manhattan has become, those who miss or just plain missed-out on The Factory, Max's and CBGB's, are building on the concepts and the spirit of those times and making their own fun. What more proof do you need of that than to hear that Deborah Harry is still hanging out?

WIGSTOCK

Watching Deborah Harry interact with her fans and the press is exhausting. Ooooh, she's drinking water ... She's talking to a young man – who is he? Now, she's holding a cigarette – quick, get her a light! People note her every move, analyzing each gesture for significance. Then, every other moment is punctuated by a camera's flash. But she handles it all like a pro, beaming radiantly, moving slowly and purposefully, greeting people and smiling. While speaking with her, you notice that although you have the impression she's giving you her full attention, she manages to manoeuvre to give each swarming photographer a chance for a good shot. It's a kind of poetry in motion.

Harry is backstage at Wigstock '98, the annual festival of peace, love and good hair (aka wigs), held for the past dozen years or so in New York City during Labor Day weekend. Like Harry, Wigstock has kind of outgrown its bohemian roots. It started as a very loosely structured free music event in Tompkins Square Park in the East Village when a dozen or so club denizens (including the now deceased Wendy Wilde), decided to take over the park's bombshell stage and show themselves in the light of day. Now it's a major production with corporate sponsorships and a $20 admission fee, which takes place on the Westside Highway piers and attracts an audience upwards of 10,000 people. But also like Harry, despite its high profile, Wigstock remains true to the spirit that inspired it.

Most of the performers who will take the stage today and who really comprise the heart of Wigstock are local drag queens – regulars on the club circuit and at this event – whose job it is to try and top their number from last year. They'll pull out all the stops – costumes, back-up dancers, props – all is fair in love, war and Wigstock. Others are downtown legends like transsexual punk rocker, Jayne County (the artist formerly known as Wayne County), and blues chanteuse and former Mudd Club door person, Joey Arias. New recruits to the line-up are the dance anthem divas, like Kristine W and Ultra Nate, with hits on heavy rotation in gay discos all over the world. Deborah Harry, who has appeared at Wigstock three times, qualifies in all three categories.

This year, Harry's wearing a floor-length platinum blonde wig that makes her look like the love child of Marilyn Monroe and Cousin It from *The Addams Family*. Harry explains the wig's genesis: 'When I first started thinking about pulling [the character of] Blondie out of the closet, I thought, Oh God, what would she look like after all this time? Well, her hair would be down to the floor, and she'd have a little walker!' When Harry shared this idea with friends, they advised her against the walker. 'They said, just wear the hair.'

Shortly after Wigstock, Harry will depart for Europe with the band Blondie on the first leg of their 1998 reunion tour. But audiences at these shows will not see Harry in this platinum Rapunzel wig. Only audiences at Wigstock have the pleasure of witnessing Harry's good-natured poke at herself, although no one was really in on the joke. People just assumed it was an extremely fabulous outfit. They watched rapt as Harry did a dreamy rendition of her *Debravation* album ballad, 'Strike Me Pink'. As usual, her performance was one of the highlights of the eight-hour musical marathon.

Harry doesn't recall how she first got involved with Wigstock, but she's been playing at gay-oriented events long before Blondie remixes, like Diddy's 12" mix of 'Atomic', hit the gay dance floors of the world with a fury. In fact, her history of playing at gay events even predates the music industry credo identifying the gay audience as a 'desirable niche market'. Harry reveals, '[Blondie] played at the very first Gay Day festival in New York.' She's a little fuzzy on the year: '1944?' she jokes. 'No, it was probably

1975 or 1976.' She's a little baffled and insulted to be asked why she decided to play at Gay Day. 'Why? Why not? All my friends would be there and it would be a fucking great time.' And likewise with Wigstock, Harry says, 'Again, it's my friends and a fabulous time. Plus, I get to show a slightly different, more creative, artistic side of what I do.'

Wigstock's drag queen founder and MC, the Lady Bunny, doesn't remember how Deborah Harry first got involved with Wigstock either. Apparently one thing that hasn't changed about downtown from the 70s is everyone is still having so much fun, they make for very unreliable historians.

A downtown legend herself, the Lady racks her Bunny brain, 'I don't think I asked her to do it, but somehow there was a hint in the air that it might happen. I knew she did downtown stuff, but I thought if she shows up, then I'll believe it.' So as haphazard Wigstock history goes, Harry did show up for the first time in 1993, the last year the festival was held at Tompkins Square Park. With no sound-check, rehearsal or fuss, Harry made her Wigstock debut. 'I was just delighted to have her on stage doing anything,' says Bunny, 'But, of course with someone that well-known, the audience expects the hits.' What's interesting is that instead, Harry, dressed in religious robes, sang a reggae version of 'Love to Love Ya Baby' followed by a new song off her *Debravation* album called 'Communion'. Bunny recalls, 'She didn't have a recognizable Blondie look, but I thought it was a hoot because she was willing to get up there and just have a good time.'

It was a coincidence that the year that Harry first appeared at Wigstock, Miramax Films started shooting footage for *Wigstock: The Movie* (1995), a documentary about the festival. In Bunny's opinion, the film failed to capture the celebration at its best. 'The filmmakers decided not to use any footage from her performance because they thought it wasn't one of the strongest, but we begged them to include her,' says Bunny. 'For marquee value alone she would have been the biggest name attached to it. They ended up cutting out footage of her backstage too, saying they thought it would be weird to show her when she wasn't doing a number.' Ironically, Deborah Harry's name appears in *Wigstock: The Movie*'s credits. Bunny quips, 'To show how tacky they are, they cut her completely from the movie, but put her picture on the video rental box. That's a tacky Hollywood trick.'

Almost being in *Wigstock: The Movie* isn't the only notoriety Wigstock has brought Harry over the years. Bunny recalls, 'I think it was Wigstock 1994. Drag duo, the Dueling Bankheads covered "Rapture", and afterwards, Debbie, wearing a lavender Cleopatra wig, checkerboard glasses and chunky platform shoes, ran out on stage and attacked them. Then, a few weeks later, I saw something about it in a national newspaper saying she was such a mess she was attacking drag queens.' The press was particularly hurtful as Harry had been keeping a pretty low profile, leading some tabloids to speculate in fantastical terms about what had really been going on in the life of the world famous pop icon.

Of course, the fight was a planned hoax. David Ilku, the actor behind one half of the brilliantly funny Dueling Bankheads (imagine twin Tallulah Bankheads at 60), refers to the incident as the 'Slap Heard Around The World'. Ilku explains, 'I first suggested we do the fight with a bloody axe. We just wanted to make it real, so I told her, really slap me – I don't care. Nobody was expecting it – we didn't tell a soul.' The fight was a glorious crowd-pleaser, a moment in Wigstock history people still talk about. But people who weren't there that day got a very different account of what happened and why. 'Right afterwards, Debbie went on tour in Europe,' says Ilku. 'I was lying in bed one morning and she called me. She doesn't call me often so I was a little surprised. She said, "How are things with you?", and I'm like, "Fine.

How are things with you?" and she says, "Well, I'm in Europe and apparently, I'm some kind of international fag basher and my management is giving me hell for it."' Bunny laughs, recalling that the mock-fight was, 'Hilarious. Debbie threw herself into it with gusto.'

It's really high shenanigans like these that make Wigstock worthwhile for everyone who participates in the festival, none of whom are paid to appear. Bitter, scathing jabs and crude, pathetic pleas are the stock and trade of Wigstock, where they are exchanged with wit, regularity and affection. Bunny, who has been a fan of Harry's since being a wayward teen in an English Quaker boarding school, knows that Harry understands it for what it is. 'She is a gorgeous goddess and will always be, but she's also a kook and a nut. I've never felt like I had to temper my own ill humor around her.'

Bunny has a few good Deborah Harry stories up her sleeve. 'I run into her at the strangest times, like two years ago in a Dallas airport at 7 a.m.' Bunny remembers this surreal meeting well, as Harry was nice enough to have her bumped up to First Class. 'Another time I ran into her out in front of my house. I saw her coming, so I put a very puzzled look on my face and started digging through the garbage as if for food. She just looked at me and kept walking. So I said, "Debbie!", and she was like, "Oh, I didn't see anything out of the ordinary."' Bunny squeals and continues: 'And another time I saw her in that gorgeous vintage car she drives – to see her in it is very much like seeing a fantasy of a living legend's lifestyle. Anyway, I saw her stopped at a red light, so I limped very sadly across the street in front of her and she cracked up. I never feel like I have to say "Oh, Miss Harry!" or anything. I can just be my true sick self.'

When Bunny's not organizing Wigstock, she works as a DJ in popular gay clubs around Manhattan. ' "Heart of Glass" and "Rapture" are a sure thing with everyone, anywhere. Like Diana Ross, Debbie Harry has a way of vocalizing that's uniquely her and all of her songs have it. It's not off, it's just odd, ethereal and breathy. It's just the kind of voice you expect to come out of a heavily glossed lip and alpine cheekbone. I watched the "Rapture" video again recently and her moves are insane! It's like a little bit off but very sexy, very provocative and yet somehow, effortless.'

Like the many gay men in this scene, Bunny's favorites are definitely Blondie's disco numbers. 'I'm more into dance music, so I'm glad she went into that.' Likewise, she thinks that because Deborah Harry's roots are in punk and rock, that she's not necessarily thought of as a gay icon. 'Not an icon for mainstream gays – maybe in England, but not in this country. But is she an icon for alternative gays, like gays into rock and New York gays? Yes. Maybe even *the* icon.'

SQUEEZEBOX

Michael Schmidt, Deborah Harry's friend, designer and ex-roommate, would agree – Deborah Harry is certainly the icon of his scene. As the promoter of the queer rock club SqueezeBox, Schmidt has filled a gap in the 90s by bringing back a little bit of the rock 'n' roll downtown of old. After being nominated for an Emmy Award for designing clothes for Cher's CBS concert broadcast in 1992, Schmidt started to tire of Hollywood and of fashion. 'I could have easily stayed in LA and got into doing clothes for movies – that would have been the next step, but I just hated LA and wanted to come back to NY.'

A former boyfriend of Schmidt's, Patrick Briggs, lead singer of the band Psychotica, was managing a nightclub called Don Hill's. Briggs asked Schmidt if, with all his connections, he'd be interested in promoting a gay night there. Schmidt recalls, 'I said no right away – I wasn't interested in doing a gay night. But I told him I might consider doing a night if I could bridge the gap between the straight and gay scenes with rock 'n' roll.' Schmidt knew there was a lot of homophobia in the rock scene and that gays into rock were often uncomfortable attending shows at mainstream venues. He also knew that there were queer and queer-friendly rock bands and performers who didn't fit into the scene and needed a place to play. 'I could never understand that mindset because rockers are just as put upon and just as much social outcasts as gays. For one subgroup to harangue another just didn't make any sense to me.' So Schmidt, inspired by the sexual fluidity of scenes like Max's Kansas City and the Mudd Club, decided to attempt to bring it back for everyone who wasn't there to experience it the first time around.

SqueezeBox opened its glitter-glam rock doors in April of 1993 and caught on like a brush fire among a select but very vibrant crowd. The scene there brought everyone out of the closet – gay boys who'd been in the closet about liking rock, straight boys who been in the closet about wearing make-up, and girls who liked them both. And there in the mix was Deborah Harry. Schmidt says, 'Debbie was a supporter of SqueezeBox right from the beginning.' Schmidt refers to the quote Harry says he'll never let her forget: 'I remember reading this quote of hers from like 1973 where she said, The only people who can do anything new in rock 'n' roll are girls and gays. So she was a big presence at SqueezeBox and I think she liked it because she could be very relaxed. I never let celebrities be photographed or exploited, so like [filmmaker] John Waters always says, the reason he loves SqueezeBox so much is that he can hang out there and he doesn't need to worry that some overheard sentence of his will end up [in the gossip columns].'

And so celebrities came to SqueezeBox in droves – everyone from rock stars like Courtney Love and James Iha from the Smashing Pumpkins to Hollywood actresses like Drew Barrymore and Sandra Bullock. Although it probably had less to do with them feeling protected, and more to do with just having a damn good time. Including Deborah Harry, who found in SqueezeBox both something familiar and something new. John Waters, who directed Harry in his film *Hairspray*, offers this explanation: 'I think Debbie has always wanted to remain in touch with the newest thing all the kids are doing because it's interesting and you can use that in your work in some way. Debbie always was on the edge of the newest thing going on and in fact she helped invent half those edges so, of course she'll still be interested and so am I.'

Harry used SqueezeBox to experiment with new music in front of an intimate and appreciative crowd. According to Schmidt, Harry first played SqueezeBox on New Year's Eve 1995. Then she played again the night SqueezeBox presented the first large scale live internet broadcast in early 1996. 'It's important for Debbie to maintain a closeness with the people who support her music and it's important to her that she's not removed from people, like you are when you play big stadiums.'

It's also important to Harry that she not be removed from the source of her inspiration – New York City itself. Even at the height of her fame, she never opted for a mansion in Beverly Hills where she could hide out and view the world from the other side of an electric fence, or through the lens of a security camera away from the vital funk.

JACKIE 60 & MOTHER

It appears however that Harry's need for funk isn't just about taking energy and inspiration, it's also about giving it. Although Harry happens to be internationally famous, she's also a peer among a community of downtown performers and she wants to actively participate. It's not that the adoration of Blondie fans around the world isn't enough for Harry, but it is possible that the validation she gets from downtown audiences, filled with nameless artists doing very cool things, who will never be famous, means just as much to her, if not more.

It's interesting to consider why, during an exhausting week when Deborah Harry had shot the music video for 'Maria', was being followed around by CNN cameras, interviewed and photographed for *People* magazine and in preparation for a massive Blondie tribute and performance at the American Music Awards, she agreed to appear in a Christmas variety show in a theater with a total of just 60 seats where people paid just $10 a head. The answer is simple enough – it's tradition. Although *A Very Jackie Christmas* itself isn't a traditional take on the holidays – this year it opened with Santa reading a porno magazine and two topless she-elves – it's a four-year-old tradition for Harry to appear in it.

The show is the Christmas spawn of the Jackie Factory – the think-tank behind the nightclub named Mother. Located in the Meat Market district (so named for both local industries – meat-packing and prostitution) of Greenwich Village, Mother isn't by any stretch of the imagination the biggest, richest or most lavish nightclub of the 90s, but it's by far the most original, the smartest and in the tradition of what downtown has always been about, the most New York. Even under the censorship reign of Mayor Rudolph Guiliani, Mother and its brightest child – Jackie 60, have remained kinky to the core, presenting a pansexual hybrid of literate fetish gatherings and dance parties. Mother is perhaps best described as 'art club', also inspired in part by the Mudd Club, where its founders, Johnny Dynell and Chi Chi Valenti both began their careers in the club world.

Valenti speaks very highly of Harry, whom she has known closely since the late 80s: 'She must have the clearest karma of almost any human on earth.' As for why she continues to participate in non-commercial downtown happenings, Valenti says, 'It's like an experience you're giving both yourself and the audience. When her mother died [in February 1998], it was two days before [a Jackie event], and no one expected her to show up but she did. She said that it helped for her to be there – it's that affirmation.' Whatever Harry gets from Mother, it's clear that Harry wants to give back: 'Just by participating, she's saying, I'm giving my weight to this and my stamp to this,' says Valenti. '[With Jackie] she uses her name very generously. It's so above and beyond.'

Harry has appeared in *A Very Jackie Christmas* since its inception in 1992 (that first year, Harry sang and danced on stage in a strait-jacket), but she's been hanging out at Jackie 60 and participating in all kinds of shenanigans since the club opened its doors in 1990. 'I remember Debbie and [her dog] ChiChi coming early and hanging out at Jackie when it was just 150 people and a couple of Hasidic Jews who were cruising the area,' says Valenti, who created the club with her husband Dynell after realizing that if they wanted an environment like it to exist, they had to do it themselves.

The first odd, but ultimately wise move they made was to launch Jackie 60 on Tuesday nights, a night on the club scene when there was nothing else. Tuesday was also a day off for other people who worked in clubs, and in Jackie 60, even they found a place in which they could indulge. 'Debbie had nothing to fear from that crowd,' says Valenti. Harry was so comfortable in fact, one night she even gave an impromptu performance as a bartender. 'The first night we got really busy there, we only had one bartender – I mean, we only ever had one bartender, so Debbie said, I used to tend bar and she jumped behind the bar and she bartended there until the rush was over.' Valenti continues, 'So, people were handing Debbie $20 tips at the bar – it was just so major for her to do that, and at the end of the night she left her tips for us and said to put it towards Jackie because at that point we were losing money every week.'

After about nine months of struggling, Jackie 60 earned a reputation for being the only place left to get a slice of this kind of New York nightlife. One of the elements of Jackie 60 which lead to its enormous popularity was that each week, Dynell and Valenti came up with elaborate themes such as The Brown Party (an exotic celebration of all things earth mother, granola and hippy) and the Night of 1000 Stevies (a tribute night to the cult of Stevie Nicks). These were inspired by the kind of hybrid theme nights the Mudd Club originated. Valenti explains, 'Mudd didn't have a theme every night but they took the idea of the theme party from gay color parties, like the Black Party, and they'd do theme parties like the Dead Rock Star Party or the Combat Love Party. And everyone dressed up because it was creative expression.' Besides themes and suggested dress, Jackie 60 featured nightly performances which allowed individuals to creatively express their own particular relationship to the theme. A number of local performers became regulars on stage and soon became known as part of the 'Jackie family'. After a number of infamous performances you also became a 'Jackie legend'. Deborah Harry distinguished herself in both of these capacities.

Valenti recalls, 'She's appeared through the years in several performances at Jackie 60, including the Patti Smith night in 1992. It's so Debbie that once she found out we were doing a Patti Smith night – she was probably just at the club the week before – she said she wanted to do something.' Dressed in black Patti wig, Harry performed a rendition of 'Pissing in the River'. In spite of all the legendary malice Smith directed towards Harry, Harry's performance was a tribute. Valenti says, 'We love Patti's music and give her total pointage as a performer, but she's just so pretentious. Debbie is always so diplomatic, but once I asked her about Patti. Because she'll never dish anyone, all she said was, "She can't love me". Friends of ours, The Crass, totally amazing people, once went all over town stenciling "Patti Smith is Dead". When you look at all these people who are flawless having a problem with the same person, it must mean something.'

According to Valenti, Harry also predates the current rage in Bindi chic: 'Another time Debbie performed at our Indian night with Joey Arias. She was Shiva and she had all these girls from the House of Domination [Jackie's in-house go-go dancers] doing all these arms behind her. They looked so amazing.'

But perhaps Harry's most infamous number took place off stage. One of Jackie 60's most popular theme nights of the year is their annual A Night of 1000 Stevies. Nicks fans from all over the world now fly in to be a part of it, but the very first year, Harry paid her tribute on stage and off. On stage, Harry, dressed in signature Stevie shawls, accompanied a local drag queen in doing some dramatic twirls. But she put in a better performance later that same night. Valenti recalls: 'It was late April 1991. It was the first night that we were packed out and the bathroom line had just become untenable. Debbie needed the bathroom and Johnny said to her, "I'll take you to the front of the line", and she says, "Oh no, I'll go right here", and she squats down right in the hallway and pees on a Stevie flyer that had fallen off the wall.' That first year, Valenti and Dynell created the annual tradition of the Jackie Awards to honor the best of the best Jackie performances. For her ultimate punk goddess hallway stunt, Harry was nominated for Best X-rated Performance and won. Valenti recalls, 'When Debs accepted the award [in front of a cheering crowd of her Jackie peers], she said, "This means more to me than a good bowel movement."'

Over the years, as Jackie 60 outgrew its original intimate audience, Valenti and Dynell bought the space that housed the club, renamed it Mother and expanded their efforts to six nights a week. Harry is still a regular visitor, although she no longer hangs out late. Mother's growing popularity, even with a dress code to weed out the uninitiated, still attracts many Harry fans. Valenti says, 'She's never been a hide out in the office type person, so now she seems to come early and see the [go-go] girls [the House of Domination] and leaves around 12:30 a.m. She'll have a real fun time before the crowds set in.' Valenti has also observed that when Harry does come out in the prime-time hours she often comes alone. 'I think sometimes, even for the people she's with it's uncomfortable to have fans barraging her and she knows that. So, almost to spare her friends from torture, she just goes out alone. And in the end, if you can't handle it alone, you just can't handle it. That bodyguard stuff is total bullshit – it's about the way you handle it.'

Valenti is protective, not just of the celebrities who frequent Mother, but of the atmosphere they create, which, like Max's Kansas City and the Mudd Club, aims to be a cradle of downtown civilization. 'We're not like – DON'T BOTHER OUR CELEBRITIES – but let them also just experience Jackie,' emphasizes Valenti. 'Like when the Spice Girls came to Click & Drag [Mother's Saturday night party], then we had Spice Girls' fans coming who really didn't care about what we are trying to accomplish.'

Fans should also be aware that if they go to Mother to see Deborah Harry, it's unlikely that they'll find her doing whatever it is that they most expect. If you do make the trip, you'll definitely get a taste of her downtown roots, but it's unlikely you'll ever see her belting out any of her old Blondie numbers.

THE JAZZ PASSENGERS

Roy Nathanson, founder of the Jazz Passengers, knows what it's like to deal with Deborah Harry fans who are expecting something they don't get. 'I knew with Debbie involved we'd get bigger audiences, but I didn't really know what that meant,' he says with a laugh. 'What was confusing was that a ton of people would come to the gigs – like fanatic fans – and they weren't really there to listen to the Jazz Passengers at all. So that was difficult, but she was so great with us and she was so cool, we kept doing it.'

When Deborah Harry first joined forces with the New York nouveau jazz ensemble in 1994, there was definitely an adjustment period. Although she had been doing solo work and touring throughout the late 80s and 90s, the Jazz Passengers marked a dramatic shift in Harry's singing style. Even just playing gigs in New York in alternative music spaces like The Knitting Factory, Harry got a lot of attention, which brought unexpected benefits for her and for the JPs. Nathanson says, 'They took the combination of her and us more seriously. Her thing was already good, but she got another kind of respect with us, you know – artsy, cultural. Then we kept getting bigger and bigger gigs.'

One of those big gigs was the opportunity to play at the Meltdown Festival in London in 1995 and to work with Elvis Costello. Nathanson recalls, 'Costello heard our record and he really loved it. He was putting the Meltdown Festival together that year and he invited us and then he wanted to involve himself with each artist so he did a song – "Aubergine" with Debbie and us.'

Not surprisingly, the collaboration between the Jazz Passengers and Harry also has its roots in the downtown scene. Nathanson, whom Harry refers to as 'very similar to Chris [Stein] – a real Brooklyn guy', also has his own down-town pedigree. 'I was in the Lounge Lizards with John Lurie, and I was in the CBGB's scene even though I didn't like that music. But I always liked Debbie because I like people with attitude, and she was obviously smart and funny.'

Over the years, Nathanson and Harry had mutual friends but it wasn't until one of them, producer Hal

Wilmour, suggested Harry sing a song on the JPs' album *Jazz Passengers In Love*, that a collaboration was born. 'I had written this song called "Dog and Sand" and she sang it great. After that, I thought well, maybe she wants to work with us, so I just asked her.'

Harry enthusiastically agreed to join the JPs for tour dates in support of the album on the West Coast, East Coast and some of the Midwest. Nathanson was amazed by how easily the pop star traveled, 'You know she just drove around in the van with us and that was kind of impressive. She's a really considerate person – she thinks deeply about things. When we're together she reads and she sleeps and she plays and she tries to eat salads,' he laughs.

Nathanson was also impressed by the way Harry handled her fans. 'She's really respectful of her fans. Like there will be ten Blondie nerds standing around, waiting for her autograph, and they'll bring out some 90-year-old pictures and she'll sign them even though she's exhausted.' Nathanson says, however, that part of the reason she handles it well is it isn't as overwhelming as it once was. 'I didn't know her at the height of her fame with Blondie, but she says she's more comfortable now where some people know her but not everyone. But when she's with us, she flies coach and very rarely do people make a big deal out of it.'

It was Harry's no-nonsense quality and sense of humor that helped her click with the Jazz Passengers, who include members Curtis Fowlkes, Brad Jones, Rob Thomas, Bill Ward, E. J. Rodriguez and Curtis Hasselbring. Nathanson speculates that the chemistry between them is so good because even though they play jazz, the band's attitude is very experimental, very downtown and in some senses, very punk. The Jazz Passengers are often cited for trans-gressing the boundaries of traditional jazz, both offending old school listeners and recruiting new ones. 'Our band is really a band – we've been together like eleven years, in a funny way we were closer to the *idea* of a rock band, than a rock band. She seemed to really like us and the guys loved her – she's the greatest – who doesn't love her?'

Who indeed, Even sceptical critics have had to admit, Harry has grown into her jazz vocals. 'When we first did *Jazz Passengers In Love*, I remember people saying Debbie Harry can't sing this stuff, but they didn't know shit. Something about Blondie transmitted the idea that the charm was that it didn't have much technique. But Debbie has gotten so good. Her voice is like etched in stone. She's been working on it, taking a lot of voice training and she's very serious,' says Nathanson. 'Now compared to four years ago, it's like she went to conservatory. She can do the Blondie thing, she can do whatever she wants – she's never going to sing anything the same as she did before.'

The difference is apparent on Blondie's reunion album, *No Exit*. There's even a jazz song on the album – 'Boom in the Zoom Zoom Room'. Harry laughed when it was suggested that she appeared to really enjoy singing jazz songs as opposed to performing the repertoire of Blondie hits. She replied, 'That's because I really get to sing the jazz songs, on the other ones, I realize now that I'm just screaming.'

Even though Harry has no plans to stop screaming pop songs, Nathanson has further insight as to why Harry may enjoy singing jazz even more than rock 'n' roll. 'Jazz songs are structures to be played with, it's a jumping-off point for the moment. She's such a good actress and performer, there are so many qualities she can do, so it's more of a challenge for her. And you can do a song 90 times but it can be different every time, you can see her making decisions,' he adds. 'She plays herself down, but she's a remarkable person, deeply bright. As an artist, she's always looking to find an honest thing.'

Just when critics have been praising Harry for settling into a grown-up persona with the JPs, she turns around and shows them she still hasn't lost touch with her Blondie roots. While the Blondie reunion has made Harry less available for the JPs, according to Nathanson, her involvement is a standing thing. 'I plan on doing this with Debbie forever. As far as I'm concerned, whenever she says she can do it, that's it – we'll do it.'

This is an open door policy that's echoed by the Lady Bunny, by Michael Schmidt and by Chi Chi Valenti and Johnny Dynell. Even with the Blondie reunion threatening to launch Harry back into the limelight as an international pop star, at Wigstock, at Squeezebox, at Mother, as well as with the Jazz Passengers, Deborah Harry is family and she's welcome anytime.

CHAPTER TEN
The Deborah Harry Interview

PART 3

THE XX FACTOR

Unlike a lot of women of her generation, Deborah Harry does not balk at being called a feminist, nor does she roll her eyes when discussing the sometimes tedious, but important, subject of women in rock. She's also aware of what it has meant for her to be a woman in rock and a woman of her time. Although her Blondie persona was bigger than life and acted like the world was her playground, Harry never tried to pretend that she, as a person, was immune to the issues and insecurities regular women face. Part of the reason other women like Deborah Harry is it's clear that she likes other women, and being a woman herself.

So it seems like it was okay to refer to you as Debbie in the 70s and now it's not?

Oh, I don't care what people call me. I was just trying to make a change after I went solo and it was good to force it a little. It was also good not to be so teenage. Plus, Debbie was Blondie. Deborah was new territory.

By the time you had top ten singles, you were already in your 30s.

Yeah, I started late. I got into pop and rock late, when I got into The Stilettos I was already 27 or 28. You don't usually start in a rock band in your 30s, you do it in your 20s.

But was it a blessing in a way, in the sense that when fame and success came, you were better prepared to handle it and keep it in perspective?

Well, I can only judge for myself. For my emotional make-up, that was the way I had to do it.

It seems that in the 70s, most of the women in the punk scene were groupies. Women who wanted to be a part of rock had to sublimate their desires and sleep with the men in it.

Yeah, that was pretty much it. Like in the late 60s and early 70s, I would go to jam sessions – jam sessions were a thing, like happenings were – people would just get together and play or do some kind of acting out or chanting or God knows whatever. So musicians from the lower east side who knew each other would hear about it and we'd all get together at someone's loft and just play. And it wouldn't have to do with any after-performance or [forming a band], it was just that and that alone. So, I went to one and I wanted to play bass, which I could play feebly but just as well as some of the guys who were there, and I was told in no uncertain terms that men played bass and you needed balls to play bass and that was that.

It was very brave and bold to be a woman in rock when you first started out.

There were women I admired in music all along, there just weren't that many. The industry wasn't really working it at the time – it was a macho industry and a macho art form. I mean, there were clearly some women rockers who broke through but it wasn't like it is now. At some point, they just sort of said, Boing! Oh, women – this is a whole new area to exploit! Thus my quote [friend, designer and rock 'n' roll promoter] Michael Schmidt always reminds me of.

Someone in the 70s interviewed me and asked, 'What's going to be the next new thing?', and I said, 'The only people who can do anything new [in rock 'n' roll] are girls and gays.'

What's this legendary competition between you and Patti Smith? The only quote you have about Patti in Please Kill Me *is that you thought she didn't like you much.*

Right, well, she didn't. She was completely tough and really very competitive.

Do you think we should resist the urge to be competitive?

No, it has to do with how confident you are doing what you're doing and where it's going to take you. I certainly had a mission in life and I felt I was already there in some respects, I knew that there were certain things I would do and that was that. So my competitiveness expressed itself in different ways.

I guess I mean competitive in the sense of actively trying to discourage or limit other people.

I may be quivering inside and squirming with jealousy and fear but I would never try to eliminate someone else's chances, I would just fight harder for my own. That's just the way I was brought up.

You've helped a lot of people since you got successful.

Have I?

Yeah, by giving them a word of encouragement, by coming to see their shows, by asking them to collaborate with you or saying yes when asked to collaborate. People like Joan Jett, Shirley Manson, Kate Schellenbach . . .

Oh God – Kate's a genius. I'm going to sing on their record – it's so exciting. I'm very happy about that. Luscious Jackson is a great band – one of my all-time favorites.

People make a big deal out of the fact that you took a break during the height of your career, from 1983 to 1985, but what was the big deal, it was only two years?

I think the obvious thing, and what most people would have done if they had been in my position, was to have moved on into real commercial overdrive – kill, smash, swat and beat the consciousness of the world into shape and grab that fucking carrot. I don't know if I couldn't do it, or I wouldn't do it, or if it wasn't in the cards at that particular time, maybe a combination of all three. Let me check in with the shrink and get back to you on that one, okay? [laughs]

Have you ever been the subject of any interesting tabloid stories?

No, not really. I feel like I should do something interesting [for them] now but I can't figure out what that would be.

What could possibly be shocking now? Being nice or being honest was shocking for a while, but that's lost its impact.

Nothing. Maybe I should become a militant Muslim and move to Iraq – that would make headlines wouldn't it!!?

Why is there so much resonance with you and gay men?

I don't know, maybe it's what I was saying before, the sexuality thing changing when I was being the narrator and switching back and forth. Even as a child I regretted being locked into just being a woman. I really regretted the restrictions on power and exercising power, in a nonsexual way. We can always be sexual and seduce and play those games, but the bigger roles in society and allocating power – I always felt like, Gee, I got stuck in this thing and here I am inside, this other thing. It's all been a part of our evolution I guess.

As we approach the millennium, I hope people are thinking about that word – evolution.

Oh fuck that! It will be exciting to write 2000 – Oh, look at this, this is cool and good graphics. That's what it will amount to – good graphics.

As a strong female vocalist, what have your unique contributions to pop music been?

Well, in Blondie I found myself singing a lot in the third person, as the objective camera or eye. As an observer. It didn't always come off, but I also switched between narrating from the female and male points of view. The other thing I tried not to do was sing as a victim because I think there has been enough of that, but I wasn't the only female vocalist or the first to figure that out. I mean, Nancy Sinatra had her boots.

When people ask you what it's like to be so beautiful or what it's been like to be a sex symbol, what do they really want to know?

I don't know, some kind of mantra perhaps, some kind of formula?

Why do you think women obsess about being beautiful? Naively, do we think being beautiful would solve all our problems?

I think it's because of the emphasis on appearance and the value of it as a trade-off in success or survival is heavy. I think I have a certain amount of talent, but had I not been unusual looking or strong looking, I don't think I would have gotten as famous. Certainly, 50 per cent of my success is based on my looks, maybe more, and that's a bitter pill to swallow at this stage in my life. I think, Oh God, I really want to be good at what I do.

Oh, please! There are a lot of beautiful women in the world, very few are as famous or accomplished as you are. Also, the same could be said about Mick Jagger, but like you, it's clear that he's got a look and he's good at what he does.

Yeah, well, everybody has moments of doubt. Don't you?

Of course, but never having been called one of the most beautiful women in the world, I can't imagine how much pressure that must put on you. But I wonder, did you get to use being a sex symbol to fulfil all your own desires?

No, and I didn't think it would give me that power. There are limitations to everything and once you get set up in a particular formula, you have to approach life in that way. It doesn't give you more freedom, it may give you more power and a more focused approach, but then that becomes restrictive in itself. Maybe that teaches you something, but I found it a little prohibitive. Things were a little more complicated than that for me because I was on a search. I wanted to know more and sample more, I wasn't interested in focusing in. I think now I feel more attuned to what I can really do and all the things I've experienced. I feel so organized and I feel totally different than I've ever felt before. I feel great on stage and more at ease than I ever have before – totally different from when I was doing Blondie before, but who knows – probably everybody will HATE it now [laughs].

REUNION

What inspired the Blondie reunion?

The question should be who inspired the reunion. This man named Harry Sandler, a managerial type person was introduced to Chris and they started talking about the past and he was like, Why don't you guys make another record?

And you guys were like, Why not?

[laughs] No it wasn't quite that simple or easy. It took us like a year to get together. We did some shows last summer and now we're doing a record and some touring.

Are you enjoying being together again?

Yeah, it's nice. We have different priorities now, I know I've had a chance to experiment a lot with music, singing with the Jazz Passengers and acting, Clem has experimented a lot with new music, Jimmy has raised a family and Chris has done sculpture and a lot of different types of writing – it's like we're all different people now and we're in different places. It will be interesting to see how people react to the new album because a lot of the music will be the same but the message and the emotional impact of the music will be very different.

That was a great review you got in the Voice for your sneak May '98 Blondie shows at Tramps here in New York.

Yeah, I felt I should retire after that. [Robert] Christgau is never really that effusive. I was like, Oh God, quit while you're ahead.

Has it been a little bit scary, with Blondie being back together? There must just be this flood of attention reminiscent of 1979.

It's very rewarding and gratifying, but the downside is the backlash that must be expected – momentarily. That probably won't be so much fun. We've all played the game before so we know what to expect. It's very satisfying in some ways and not in others, like with everything in life. You just have to enjoy it while you can.

Can people relate to you as you are now, or are you stuck in some time warp for them from 1979?

I don't know. Time warp? It's a dance. Seems like a good place to be stuck. I don't know. Fortunately, there's a lot to choose from.

Is there the possibility of a film about you and Blondie?

I don't know if we should talk about that yet, but yeah, it's a consideration of course, because we have quite a story to tell and one that really hasn't been told.

Did you wear your 'Blondie Comes Out Of The Closet' wig from Wigstock on the Blondie Fall 1998 European Tour?

No, I'm not satisfied with it yet. I sort of pinned it up myself to make it wearable but I want to do some radical work on that. Plus, it's too hard to wear on stage. I can't move around in it and it's very hot.

You can't kick up your heels which I heard you were doing in London. You have such a strong following in the UK.

I can't complain actually, it went very well. It's obviously such a stronghold for Blondie. I don't know why they decided to tour there first. The record company and the management company have their master plan, although we have ultimate control. I don't really want to have to plan that stuff and do all that marketing business – it's just not that interesting. Plus, it's their thing, so just let them do it and do it well.

Were there times when you were on stage, singing Blondie songs when you were just like – this is so familiar yet so strange?

I think that during that first show, I felt a little out of space, out of time. But I had done three world tours with my solo albums and I played the exact same venues. I didn't get as much press or attention or flash as Blondie does. But I played the same halls all over and it wasn't that long ago. Plus, I've been touring with the Jazz Passengers. It's not a big gap for me because I'd been doing it steadily. I think it might have been a little stranger for the guys. Chris came with me on some of my tours, but Jimmy was totally gassed by it.

Isn't Blondie the first band to have number one songs in three consecutive decades – 70s, 80s and 90s?

I don't know if that's true. I mean, what about Cher?

I don't know but it's great that she's taken back her music. Apparently the dance remix of one of her songs on her last album did much better than the album, so this time around she wanted to make the dance mix of her own song. And 'Believe' has been number one in Europe and now it bounced back to the US and is in the top ten. Maybe that will happen with 'Maria'?

I don't know if 'Maria' is right for the States right now. We'll see soon enough. 'Maria' wasn't my choice for the first single off the new album. I would have chosen a much bigger song, not such a simple pop song. Now, we're just going to let the album go out and do what it does and see where the interest lies. I think the rap song might do something in clubland, whether it actually does something as a single. But I don't know, I can't pretend to know what will or will not happen because I don't know how to play the game, I'm not in it. I mean, I'm making music but I'm not totally educated about the ins and outs of what makes a hit these days. The balance of power lies with the rule players, and they are the ones who run the game now, it's not the artists. It's clearly merchandisers and radio programmers who do. I'm not condemning them, but it's so firmly entrenched and it's just not that interesting to me.

Are you prepared for all the press, the drudging up of the past and everything else a Blondie reunion will bring?

Am I prepared for that? Not really. We'll see how we're going to approach it. We've never had anything iron clad. One of the ways we've always sort of maintained our sanity was by doing a certain amount on the spur of the moment and having a certain frivolity. Sometimes it works, and sometimes it's horrible, but it gives us some kind of credibility and artistic freedom.

AT HOME

I've seen you a number of times performing or just hanging out at Jackie 60, SqueezeBox and Wigstock. You've remained a part of downtown culture. What do you make of claims that downtown is dead?

Well, it's difficult. It's so expensive to live here, it's a wonder that downtown hasn't been knocked down. It's difficult to have an art scene with young people who are excited about new things when it's so expensive to live here. NYC is a cultural mecca but it's driving the people who create the culture away. So if [newspapers and editors who say downtown is dead] want to contribute to that, then fuck them. It's discouraging. All this and cutting endowments for the arts. The woman who ran the NEA (National Endowment of Art) is a saint, and I say that even though I don't really believe in grants because I think the people who apply for grants and get them are just professional appliers. There are some good things that come out of them, but the people who apply for them are very organized and do a different kind of work than people who are really crazed and should be reached out to in a different way. People have to realize that throwing money at artists isn't going to be an investment in the same way that you buy a painting. It's going to look like money being thrown down the toilet and actually, that's what it should be called – 'toilet money'. It pays off after a period of time, like educating a child.

People say perhaps one of the reasons you still do new things today is you never moved away from the source of your inspiration – downtown NY?

No, I definitely could not do that although I did have the opportunity. When I went away I felt disconnected from my soul – I sort of hate that expression – soul, but I certainly didn't feel comfortable and I didn't want to be away from my funk. I needed it. At my core, I want to be an artist, I really do. And I do want other things – I want to be successful, I want fame, and all that other stuff – that doesn't necessarily go with being an artist, but at my core

I'm very happy to be an artist and see things and feel things that way.

Did you know that *Rear Window* was written about my apartment building? There are about 500 or 600 apartments I can look into – it's a massive complex with like 4,000 apartments. I'm going to have to move soon and I'm kind of looking forward to it. I'm getting tired of the massiveness of it. There was a time when you could really see some good fuck-fuck action here, but now it's turned into this yuppie ghetto and it's so boring. I don't think these people have sex – they just toss salad and make pasta [laughs].

On the new Blondie album, No Exit, you're playing with the theme of surveillance. What do you think of Guiliani's [Mayor of New York] threat to put a camera up at every street corner?

There are already a few cameras up at major intersections. You know, in Belgium, they don't even have traffic cops, the cameras and radar are set up along the roads and based on that they just book you and dock you. They've got you, they've got you on film and they've got you on radar. The next thing to do is get some device that blocks the camera and radar signals.

Yeah, like how you can block caller ID.

I'd like to know how to do all that stuff. If I were just starting out now, I don't think I'd even be a musician, I think I'd be a [computer] hacker.

DOG TALK

Deborah Harry, for all the spectacular details of her life, is not immune to simple creature comforts. She lives now with a much beloved, furry, four-legged female companion – a tiny Japanese Chin named Chi Chi. This toy breed has the flat-faced pout of a Pug coupled with long, spindly tufts of white hair best associated with characters from the books of Dr Seuss. Chi Chi is even more otherworldly than most of her kind, as she carries herself with a regal aloofness betrayed only by her penchant to be, at times, quite vicious. Rumor has it that she once killed two rabbits when left unattended in a room with an Easter display.

Dog people say that a pooch's personality reflects an aspect of its owner's. Could Chi Chi in fact be Harry's 'id' raging, off the leash, in canine form? She certainly likes to snip at people who get too close, a luxury Harry doesn't allow herself. Whatever the truth, like any loyal canine, Chi Chi simply sees it as her job to be guard dog. Although Harry never has a bodyguard in tow, it wouldn't be an easy job even for a six-foot-tall muscle-man much less a 12-pound chien. But oddly enough, Chi Chi has grown into her role and is all the protection Harry feels she needs.

Deborah Harry is sleeping at her modest summer house at the beach when the time comes to do this interview. I wake her and our subsequent chat has a sort of floating quality to it, untethered to any urgency or structure. The success of the Blondie reunion is ahead of Harry, and at this point, in the Summer of 1998, it's just a nice idea with unknown results. She seems to me to be happiest at this moment.

Sorry I woke you from your nap.

I don't take naps, I take siestas, there's a big difference [laughs]. I get real sleepy out here. I haven't been so unwound in years. I can keep pushing myself and pushing myself until my judgement is completely impaired. This other mentality takes over and it's not a healthy one [she growls] – I get real nasty. [laughs] I'm glad I did this. We were fortunate, we got our money's worth from this place. And we've been able to have people out here. It's kinda straight around here – it's like being in suburbia, which kinda sucks, but it's really, really beautiful.

I bet Chi Chi loves it. Does she go in the water?

Chi Chi is a real lady, she runs up and down and sometimes she likes to get her feet wet but she loves sunbathing. It's great to see her out here, off the leash, they turn into real animals.

Is Chi Chi named after anyone in particular?

No. Her real name is Chi Chan, which I looked up in a dictionary and thought meant 'ferocious blood'. I wanted her to have a strong name because when I first got her she was so little. I picked her from a woman whose own two dogs had produced a couple of litters. When I saw her I thought, Wow, that's the perfect dog for me. She had such an amazing temperament and was the right size, and I thought, Gee, I'd like to have a dog that I can take with me whenever I have to travel.

Was it in some way symbolic that your life had settled down enough that you could finally be responsible for something beyond yourself?

Yeah, and it was very beneficial for me to be on a schedule. I think working is a very necessary part of my life, but what it really provides is the idea of a routine and some discipline and a way of organizing time. Usually when I'm not working I'm like . . . [head lolls] da, da, da, da . . . and having to feed the dog and walk the dog is really a good thing.

Yeah, I think you fantasize about having a life where you get to sleep in every day, but when you actually can get to do that, it becomes very unmotivating.

Yeah, and I hate when I get into the house and just turn on the TV and start pushing those buttons. I'm like, Here I am again . . .

Do you ever sing to your dog?

Well, I always take her with me to the studio and she insists on going into the room with me and she curls up on the floor and goes to sleep. It's very inspiring. I was just having this conversation with a friend about how much better our lives are since we got dogs. They have some kind of curative quality.

FUTURE

What are your plans for the Fall?

We're going to do some touring. As far as doing something in New York, we don't have a sound man, so we may just do an open house when we're rehearsing, or perhaps sneak into a club late. It would be relatively easy to sneak into Lust For Life or SqueezeBox. It would be really good for the band to play in public, but it has to be unannounced for everyone to be really at ease and just get their feet wet. We're really under such a spotlight at this point, so we can't do without a sound man. We'll figure it out, and in the next month we'll have some time to actually freak out and play. That will be fun.

Is this the worst time for you, before a new album comes out?

I have anxiety but I don't know if it has to do with the new album coming out as much as wanting it to encompass so many things, when you know you can only do so much with it. But that's very, very personal and something that has nothing to do with the performances and with the band. All in all, I think it will be a good experience. As with most rock bands – recording, doing shows – all of that stuff isn't a real musical experience. I mean, I've had times performing live with the Jazz Passengers that were real vibrant musical experiences, but in rock 'n' roll, it's more memorized and you pull it off and you pull it off well, but there are very few rock 'n'roll musicians like Hendrix that go up on stage and really play.

You mean, who have that freedom to improvise?

Exactly, it's not like an acting experience or a musical experience that is really in the moment and fantastic. It will be a musical experience of a really high calibre but it's not going to have those inspired moments, you know? I mean, I've gotten to know a lot of different stuff working in all these different areas and these are really personal thoughts and they aren't put-downs of Blondie or the efforts that anyone is putting into it, it's just what I've gained from my experience. I've gotten to do some really interpretative work. It doesn't mean I'm not going to put everything I have into it, but it's just going to come out a certain way and it's much more calculated, like the edited version of a film.

What are you writing songs about now?

Same old shit! I don't know. It's the same old angst. I wrote a few songs with Romy Ashby. We started writing in late January and then we started working on lyrics in February and March. My mother had just died and I wasn't really with it, but Romy was great to work with, so this is a little bit different. I think she's a really incredible writer, so it's like my ideas and her tremendous ability with language.

How long have you and Romy Ashby known each other?

A couple of years off and on. This year we've gotten to know each other much better as we've been working together.

How do you choose your collaborators?

I guess it just happens socially, you meet someone you admire them, or you start talking – any number of ways. When we worked with the guys from Chic, I think it was mutual admiration. And it seemed like good business at the time. I guess something I learned from Chris was to burn through things quickly and always look for what's new.

Is that to suit the music business or your attention span?

I certainly hold on to some things but you also want to make discoveries, you want to own things. It certainly had something to do with the whole mentality behind the punk movement.

You mean making new discoveries and not accepting what was being sold to you?

Yeah, I mean what's going on today. Everything is just so controlled and force fed that everyone just accepts it.

You and Romy wrote 'The Dream's Lost On Me' together right?

Yeah, and it's so sweet. She said, I wrote these words and I don't know if you'll like them. We could write something else . . . And I looked at them and I said, Are you crazy? This is so beautiful, so perfect – I just love it. I want to do that one in Spanish also.

Have you done Spanish translations before?

Just one song, 'Call Me'.

Let's talk about other songs on the new album. How about 'Nothing Is Real But The Girl' – is that a Jimmy song?

Yeah, it's about his daughter. It's about the hard times he went through and watching his little girl. Nothing mattered but her. It's very sweet too.

How did the song 'No Exit' come together?

That's a real combo effort – it was Jimmy and Chris and Romy and me. Jimmy wrote a couple of verses of a gangsta rap and I said Jimmy, I can't be a gangsta rapper! That would really be tasteless and unethical. So he says, Okay, let's make it a Gothic rap about a vampire on the scene. That worked a lot better. Then we made it like, the monster ain't doing too well. He gets fat, he's gluttonous. That reminds me, I saw these silent vampire movies from France on TV that pre-date Hollywood. Bela Lugosi copied this French movie – the characters are all the same.

Poor Lugosi, he had no idea we'd be able to track information the way we do today and uncover his source. A colleague of mine interviewed these modern-day vampires who live in New York. It's a big fetish scene here.

Yeah, and they really cut each other and drink blood.

Yes! This couple video themselves doing it so they could relive it without having to do it every time. Some of the modern-day vampires get fangs bonded to their real teeth. What do you think about that, about plastic surgery that defies societal beauty norms?

I think that's the way to go, absolutely, because some of the things people think are normal are just horrific. We see these cheek implants and nose jobs that are ghoulish. I'd rather see something that's stunning and creative and individual than these template faces that people are wearing that don't fit.

They don't look human.

And one wonders if they are.

Maybe they shouldn't look human. Maybe it's sort of like male to female transsexuals who say they don't want to look real and pass as women, they want to look like transsexuals. Maybe some people want to have surgery and look like they've had surgery?

Exactly.

I wrote an article once about this woman who was looking for a doctor to help her do something unusual. She wanted to have three breasts.

Wow, did she get them?

I don't know. At the time, she had finally found a doctor who would do it for her, but she couldn't afford it, it was like $40,000. Do you think women have taken pictures of you into the plastic surgeon and said I want a face like Debbie Harry?

Uh, yeah. I know this person, and I can't really talk about it because she's very present in our world, but I know for a fact that she was inspired by my face. Also, Andy [Warhol] said in his diaries that if he wanted to have plastic surgery to look like anyone, he would get my face. I was really flattered by that.

Someone said that besides the obvious things – both of you being smart and funny and interested in particular points of popular culture – the bond between you and Andy was that you were both unpretentious. What do you think was the connection between you?

When I was hanging around Andy, I was a little bit more searching than I am now. Had he lived, we possibly would have become better friends. I looked up to him tremendously. I thought he could do no wrong – he was wonderful, outstanding, a genius. But if there was a relationship between us, I don't think I really understood it. I guess he could count on me for being straight with him because I was too fractured in my own mind to possibly be devious with him, and he liked that.

People have said that you are very honest, and they thought it was a liability to you at times in the entertainment industry.

Yeah, but I never wanted to be an entertainer. I mean, I like being an entertainer but I wanted to be an artist and have artist sensibilities, and I think to have artist sensibilities, you have to have a great deal of honesty. Or clarity. As I get older, if I get much older, I'll probably get much more dishonest.

Epilogue

October 4, 2013,
Roseland Ballroom, New York City
Blondie No Principals *Tour*

In 2014, it will be forty years since Deborah Harry and her artistic soul mate, Chris Stein, founded the punk-pop band Blondie. Tonight they are on stage inside the legendary Roseland Ballroom, a performance hall that was founded in 1917 and which has featured artists as diverse as Count Basie and Louis Armstrong, Bjork and Beyoncé. The scene is akin to a rock and roll family reunion. Joan Jett is in the house, and so is the *Sex and The City* costume designer Patricia Field, along with other fans who have been coming to see Blondie since the CBGB era. But one might ask – who are these kids? Literally, there are several seven-year-olds in party dresses and dozens of seventeen-year-olds in skinny jeans. Though I suppose it makes sense that Blondie's infectious music is familiar to those born after 1974 from popular soundtracks like the movie *Bridesmaids* or the hit TV show *Glee*, and commercial jingles for products as pedestrian as Swifter – especially if their parents are fans.

Just like the rest of the world, the band has gone through some changes over the past four decades. Original keyboard player Jimmy Destri was part of Blondie's reunion album and tour in 1999, but left the band in 2003. Bass player Leigh Foxx, who began as a session musician in 1997, has officially been part of the band since 2004. Though he's not an original member

231

of Blondie, Foxx has played with Blondie longer than early members Gary Valentine, Frank Infante or Nigel Harrison. And then there are two current players who bring some younger energy to Blondie's beats – Matt Katz-Bohen on keyboards and Tommy Kessler on guitar. Both of them joined in on the fun in the past five years.

Then there are the three original members of Blondie who continue to anchor the band. Clem Burke on drums has his signature full head of Beatles-style hair, though it's now salt and pepper. He still pounds his drums hard, discarding drumsticks that fly through the air randomly between songs. Chris Stein on lead guitar is entirely silver-haired. One gets the impression, watching him survey the crowd – his arched brows raised over his black Ray-Bans – that though he could play Blondie's set in his sleep, he's still having fun. Stein's special fans – his pre-teen daughters, Akira and Valentina (named after the artist Vali Myers) – are watching his antics from the side of the stage. And of course, there is the luminescent person upon whom all eyes rest – Blondie frontwoman Deborah Harry. Harry is still platinum blonde and brazenly stunning, but gone are her days of being stiff, distant and frosty. She marches out on stage with a dozen members of the What Cheer Brigade, wearing an infectious grin and what appears to be a black wizard's robe and pointy hat. Later in the show, she will peel off the Merlin gear to reveal that workouts with a personal trainer have her back in prime form. Photographs that appeared the September 2013 issue of *Vogue Espana* (shot by Victor Demarchelier) are proof positive that she's still one of the most beautiful women in the world – when she wants to be. But one gets the impression that Deborah Harry, still vital and mysterious at age 68, her sultry vocals dripping with seduction, isn't trying to sell anyone on anything tonight. She doesn't have to. She's here among loyal fans and dear friends, and she's determined to have a bit of fun.

In support of Blondie's upcoming album, *Ghosts of Download*, tonight is the last stop on the *No Principals* tour. The tour's title refers to the fact that Blondie is sharing headline status with the Los Angeles punk band, X, fronted by Exene Cervenka and John Doe. But with Blondie, you can be assured that this title has at least a double (if not triple) meaning. Is the band suggesting they have no principals? After all, they once had buttons made up that stated 'Blondie is a group'. Or perhaps they are making fun of the idea that their success came at the cost of their own principles? Blondie was accused of 'selling out' their punk roots when their hit single 'Heart of Glass', a disco song, shot to number one on the US charts. But history shows that their achievements have hardly been the result of a 'by any means necessary' ruthlessness. Their success was in part good timing and luck, but they also delivered the goods and broke their backs making their music. They were such workaholics that they needed more than a decade off. But what brought Blondie back together, and what the band still revolves around today, is making tracks. Harry said in a recent interview, 'Making new music is really, really important for me and for the rest of the band. When we first got back together in 1997, one of the stipulations I had was that it not be just a review of Blondie's greatest hits. I really felt convinced of and dedicated to the idea that we had to move ahead and do new music.'

Since their 1999 reunion album, *No Exit*, Blondie has released two albums – *The Curse of Blondie* in 2003, which saw a return to the rock arrangements and style of their early 'classic' albums; and *Panic of Girls* in 2011, which explored more contemporary rock, pop and dance styles. *Curse* was by most accounts a solid album but was received tepidly by critics, though a track called 'Good Boys' made it to number twelve in the UK. *Curse* was a disappointment for Blondie, but the band was re-energized by their induction into the Rock and Roll Hall of Fame in 2006, the same year Miles Davis, Lynyrd Skynyrd and Black Sabbath were also honored. Though the ceremony was not without controversy when ex-Blondie band members Nigel Harrison and Frank Infante asked to perform with the band and were denied, Harry was quoted as saying that this recognition was a career highlight

– 'That really legitimized us and made people say, *Okay, those guys really have something.*'

Blondie continued to perform with their new line-up of musicians completing the 2008 *Parallel Lines* tour to celebrate the 30th anniversary of their seminal 1978 album ranked number 149 on the list of *Rolling Stone*'s Top 500 Albums of All Time. Blondie also hit the road with other '80s acts, including Pat Benatar for the 2009 *Call Me Invincible* tour, the Pretenders for the 2010 *Endangered Species* tour and Devo for the 2012 *Whip It To Shreds* tour. But the 'curse of Blondie', which refers to a long-running inside joke between Chris Stein and Deborah Harry that the band can never realize things the way they were originally planned, continued when the release of *Panic of Girls* was delayed for over a year due to a record company mishap. The band finally released the album themselves in 2011 on a label owned by their management company, 10th Street, adapting to the new world order of the music industry by selling it directly on Amazon.com.

One song on *Panic* managed to stir up a bit of a commotion, though not for its musical merits. The press speculated that the lyrics to 'Mother', an ode to the 90s fetish nightclub where I first encountered Harry myself, might be about the adopted Harry's own maternal issues. Harry joked in an interview, 'That was a misunderstanding completely. I don't think my mother was into patent leather, except perhaps on a pair of Easter shoes.'

Harry's long-time friend and collaborator, the artist and director Rob Roth, appears in the music video for 'Mother', where *The Walking Dead*-style zombies attack audiences and then the band. Roth's work and play with Harry keeps evolving and ranges from cooking up midnight performances at Mother to touring as one of her backup dancers 'the fishsticks', appearing with her in an episode of *Absolutely Fabulous*, and designing and directing music videos, album covers and stage show graphics. A short video *Blondie Tour: Behind The Scenes*, which includes interviews with Deborah Harry and tour footage of Roth's graphics for the 2012 Blondie tour with Devo, is posted on Vimeo by the creative editing shop where Roth often works – The Mill.

Roth's graphics included a slot machine from hell, which he says just popped into his head – 'the symbols we came up with were the heart for love, the skull for punk, the anarchy symbol, the peace symbol, the chaos symbol and of course, the radioactive symbol for danger.' These fit perfectly with the overarching theme he conceived of 'Death Vegas' punk glamour. 'I wanted Debbie Harry to be on par with Elvis – that's how she is treated in the UK.' Roth also envisioned the stage show to include elaborate costume changes and professional platinum blonde wigs by NYC nightlife legend, Codie Ravioli – things that turned up the volume on Harry's presentation. 'I knew the fans really wanted to see her like this; I wanted to see her like this.'

Roth says Harry is the ultimate collaborator, 'She's just so fearless and has this immense dramatic capacity. What we created here is something I'm really proud of and it's so satisfying to add something of this caliber to her legacy.'

Unfortunately, the reviews of *Panic* continued to express ambivalence about Blondie's dark side and signature mix of musical styles. Blondie seemed to be praised for their ability to sound so clean and contemporary, while at the same time being accused of sounding more like chart-topping bands like The Killers than themselves. Yet, unlike The Killers, another hit single eluded Blondie. Harry was quoted as saying, 'I'm disappointed now that I can't get my new music into the charts. I don't know if [my music] is completely compatible with the way the charts are today, but before I stop making music, I would like to have another hit song.'

A contender has to be Blondie's latest synth dance single 'A Rose By Any Name' combining the rich, textured vocals of Deborah Harry with powerhouse wails from Beth Ditto of the band, The Gossip. The lyrics – 'if you're a boy or if you're a girl, I love you just the same' – seem to be a progressive chant in support of choosing your gender identity, being able to be masculine or feminine despite your biological sex. This is a powerful sentiment sure to resonate with Harry's progressive fan base, though Harry says the song was really written in anticipation of band member Matt Katz-Bohen's unborn baby. Besides the positive message and earworm chorus, 'A Rose By Any Name' has a wickedly infectious beat, but is any of that enough in the mercurial landscape of how the music industry now functions? The jury is still out. You could certainly never fault Blondie or Deborah Harry for legwork – shooting music videos, doing promotions, giving interviews, hawking merchandise, going on the road and even sleeping on a tour bus all come with the territory. Despite this, Harry says she still enjoys being a working musician, 'Well, it's what I do – what I've trained myself to do. And I still learn things from it – I don't walk out like a zombie or a robot, there are still new moments.'

In fact, there are many, many new Deborah Harry moments as she continues to live like she always has in New York City -- finding friends and collaborators where the realms of music, fashion, acting and the art world cross-pollinate. Even her management team can't keep up with her. For every official project you can read about on her beautifully maintained fan sites, there are about ten unofficial ones she just decides to do on a whim. It's a luxury she has because she can still fly slightly under the radar in the US. As Harry explains it, 'I'm still sort of a cult figure. I'm not J-Lo, I'm not in the gossip mags and *USA Today*. Sometimes, I'm in the *New York Post*.'

Necessary Evil was the name of Deborah Harry's fifth solo album that came out in 2007 during a gap in Blondie's discography. This was Harry's first solo effort since 1993's *Debravation*. *Evil* boasted songs written and produced with Super Buddha, the Brooklyn-based duo of Barb Morrison and Charles Nieland, who have also worked with The Scissor Sisters and Rufus Wainwright. Reviews of *Evil* seemed perplexed by the radically disparate clash of musical styles. And similar to Harry's previous solo records, the collection was deemed too esoteric and 'weird' to appeal to a broad audience. Harry reflected in an interview, 'I've always had strong tastes and I don't think I'm particularly afraid of controversy. From my point of view, that's what rock and roll is all about, coming from the age that I come from, when rock and roll was considered antisocial and clandestine and bad for you – that it was gonna ruin everything.'

Indeed, Deborah Harry's punk roots continue to show. And all the while punk continues to become mainstream, evidenced by the Metropolitan Costume Institute exhibition in 2012, which included several of Harry's outfits and a 2013 movie about the birthplace of the NYC punk scene, *CBGB*, starring Malin Akerman as Harry. John Holmstrom even reports that *Punk* magazine's original artwork was recently purchased by Yale University! But Harry is a reminder that rebellion can take many forms. Harry was quoted as saying, 'What happened is that punk, later on, became identified with a certain style of music because of the Ramones and, originally, the punk scene was about a sensibility, about a point of view, about an attitude. So we fell into that, definitely, because a lot of our songs were sort of antisocial and a different political stance, especially for women. So, in that respect, we were definitely of the punk sensibility.'

Perhaps it's a more interesting question to ponder what antisocial urge caused Harry to title her album *Necessary Evil* in the first place? In this instance, is she referring to being a pop star itself as a necessary evil?

The tension between being popular and being authentic is a classic theme in the struggle of most artists, and while commercial success and critical acclaim need not be mutually exclusive, it's a difficult balance to achieve. Deborah Harry has clearly blazed her own path and ended up – the 'curse' be damned – with both. Sales of an estimated forty million records might be enough proof of her popularity, but in 2010 Mattel, the same company that owns the American Girl doll line, produced a special 'Ladies of the 80s' Deborah Harry *Barbie* doll. It came complete with her signature dark roots and a dress inspired by the one made by Anya Phillips, which she wore on the cover of the Blondie album *Plastic Letters*: Deborah Harry was now officially a role model. Harry was quoted saying gleefully, 'I was completely surprised, but if they did Joan Jett, why not me? It's Barbie but wearing my hair and my dress. Barbie does Debbie!'

Deborah Harry also maintained her status as a living doll and fashion icon by choosing to style herself in the age of fashion stylists, and rejecting designer labels. At the same time, she maintains friendships with several top designers and makes annual appearances at New York Fashion Week. Her fashion insider status earned her a guest spot on the Fashion Week-themed episode of the British television series *Absolutely Fabulous* in 2002, and in 2013, she appeared as a judge on the 'Punk' episode of the US television show, *Project Runway All-Stars*. Harry maintains that she's always played dress-up unequivocally. 'I loved fashion and I wasn't going to hide that,' she says. 'I wanted to look good, I *enjoyed* looking good. I still enjoy looking good, although sometimes I see myself on someone's T-shirt and I wish I still looked like that!'

A highlight in recent fashion history was Harry's 2008 tribute to the late designer, Stephen Sprouse, who created her most iconic looks. The Sprouse tribute launched his second accessories line at Louis Vuitton with designer Marc Jacobs four years after his tragic death from lung cancer, and also raised money for an art charity.

Likewise, Harry's involvement in the art world continues as both muse and upstart. The more tame moments include Harry's 2010 portrait by Shepard Fairey, but of course she tends towards the radical. In 2011, she scandalized the Los Angeles art world with her collaboration with the Serbian artist Marina Abramovic at a benefit gala for the Los Angeles Museum of Contemporary Art. This was a particularly controversial event that asked the fashionable attendees including Gwen Stefani, Will Farrell, Pamela Anderson, David LaChapelle and John Baldessari, to don lab coats and participate in an art 'experiment' that raised

$2.5 million dollars for the museum. The budget was grander but it sounded no more twisted than any number of Harry's fabulous nightclub performances at Mother. First, Harry sang a set of songs while diners ate at tables with live human head centerpieces. For dessert, very realistic naked life-size cakes of both Harry and Abramovic's bodies were carried in on the shoulders of young, scantily-clad virile men. Both 'bodies' were then laid out on a table and Abramovic and Harry triumphantly hacked into them with giant knives.

With her penchant for the macabre, Harry reportedly took a knife and cut her own red velvet heart out. Then, the cakes were served to guests a breast, foot or hand at a time. Marina Abramovic, undoubtedly the most scandalous performance artist of this decade, explained it this way, 'You know [Deborah Harry] and me, we have these life-size cakes that look like us, and we cut them, and this man started screaming about abuse of the woman and cutting the body. Everybody sees what they want. For me . . . we are both public figures, giving our metaphoric body to the public – it's the ultimate gesture.' A video of the night's shenanigans can be found on YouTube – Marina Abramovic: An Artist's Life Manifesto | MOCA Gala 2011. Meanwhile, Harry may top this with her part in the five-hour long art film by Matthew Barney, husband of the musician Bjork, debuting at BAM (The Brooklyn Academy of Music) in 2014.

Unfortunately, though the camera loves the angular planes of her face, making movies has not been a big part of Deborah Harry's past decade. Harry's two major roles were in independent films – the Sarah Polley film *My Life Without Me* (2003), where she played the mother of the main character (Polley) who discovers she is dying of cancer, and an appearance as the wife of Dennis Hopper's dying character in *Elegy* (2008) also starring Ben Kingsley and Penelope Cruz. She also lent her gravitas to a dozen or so other smaller projects, but it seems that music has taken center stage in her life once again.

NEVER OUT OF STYLE

Back at The Roseland Ballroom, Deborah Harry and her long-time friend and collaborator Guy Furrow [AKA DJ Miss Guy] have taken the stage. The stage set and Harry's little black dress are no nonsense tonight – maybe some would describe the pared down look as 'old school'. Blondie is debuting their new song, 'Rave', a duet with Furrow and Harry. Furrow's relationship with Debbie is unique in that he's a long-time fan (check out Chapter 8 for the hysterical story of how they first met), a personal friend and a musical collaborator. His band the Toilet Boys once opened for Blondie at Madison Square Garden and they routinely sing on each other's albums. Furrow was also the DJ at the official party for Blondie's Rock and Roll Hall of Fame induction and in July 2013, he flew out to the UK to join Blondie on tour for Harry's 68th birthday. He observed how British fans respond to Deborah Harry, 'For people in the UK, she can do no wrong. They just adore her and she never goes out of style.'

Furrow has also been a famous NYC DJ since the mid-1990s and he remarks that one of the things that has remained constant during his twenty-year reign over the downtown club scene is Deborah Harry. 'She still loves to go out. She loves nightlife more than I do,' he says, 'I think she gets energy from it – she talks to people, hears new music and gets inspired.' He reminds us with his DJ wisdom that Harry's artistic curiosity changed the course of history. 'Debbie has the same sense of adventure and interest in the underground that she did back when she and Chris were going up to Harlem to hear early rap and hip hop artists. And it's a good thing too since incorporating rap into their music changed the course of music history.'

Furrow reflects on how Deborah Harry keeps up the frenetic pace of her life. 'She's a freak of nature in every way – she can just go-go-go. She really proves that your age is irrelevant and your attitude makes you young or old.' We discuss her recent cover photo of *Fabulous* magazine in the UK, and how beautiful she remains in her seventh decade. 'Women get judged so much more harshly when it comes to age.' Furrow, also a former make-up artist, observes, 'You're either letting yourself go or you get criticized for having surgery and not acting your age. It's like women can't win, and it's not fair.' My observation is simply that Deborah Harry always seems more relaxed and is having more fun when Furrow is around, but he says he thinks she's just the happiest now that he's ever seen her, period. 'I think she's really embracing the character of "Blondie" that she created and having fun with it,' he says. 'She might have felt like it limited her in the past, but now it's obvious that "Blondie" is one of the greatest characters ever in rock history.'

And it's rock history that Deborah Harry continues to upset. In 1999, at age 53, Deborah Harry became the oldest woman to have a number one hit single on the UK pop charts with 'Maria'. Much like she was wayward and made her own rules when she was in her 20s, 30s and 40s, Deborah Harry – along with other trailblazers like Cher, Tina Turner, Stevie Nicks and Madonna – is breaking down barriers for women by showing us how to "rock" our 50s and 60s. For any woman, ageing can be frightening, but gaining wisdom is powerful. As Harry said recently in an interview, 'I thought I'd live to a ripe old age, because I always felt there was a lot to do. I had a driven feeling. I always thought in the present.' She continued in this theme in another interview that tried to get her to drum up her regrets, 'Look, I've had an incredible life so far. I can't complain at all.'

The Official Blondie Website's Barry L. Kramer Shares His Top 10 Highlights in a Decade of Deborah Harry (2003–2013)

10 – December 2009: The Debbie Harry 'Ladies Of The 80s' Barbie doll was released by Mattel. The doll is a gorgeous likeness of Debbie from the *Plastic Letters* album cover, including her pink dress designed by Anya Phillips and trademark two-toned hair.

9 – October 14, 2006: Blondie played the second to last show before CBGB closed its doors forever. Debbie was joined by Chris Stein, Paul Carbonara, and Leigh Foxx at New York's legendary punk/rock venue, CBGB, the birthplace of Blondie. Hilly Kristal, founder of CBGB, passed away at the age of 75 on August 28, 2007. A CBGB movie starring Malin Akerman as Debbie premiered October 8, 2013 at the CBGB Festival in NYC.

8 – Blondie's ambitious tours and collaborations. Debbie toured internationally with Blondie every year from 2003 to 2013. Consistent with her desire not just to play past hits but to have a voice in the present, she continues to write new and innovative material, release new albums, and perform a diverse selection at every show. Blondie has toured with many popular bands, including the B-52s, The Pretenders, Devo, The Stranglers, Pat Benatar, Cheap Trick, and most recently, with the LA punk band X.

7 – Debbie Harry recognizes the importance of technology in the music industry. Blondie was an early adopter of synthesizers in their music amid criticism that they were not real instruments. In 1979, *Eat To The Beat* became one of the first full-length video albums ever released. In 1985, Andy Warhol digitally manipulated an image of Debbie on an Amiga 1000 computer.

More recently, Debbie has recognized the role that technology plays in music, communications, and music distribution by giving away a number of songs and videos free on the internet and using the latest social networking tools to interact with fans. Blondie continues to use the latest technology to create, record, and mix new music.

6 – May 13, 2010: Debbie Harry performed on stage together with Lady Gaga and Elton John to celebrate the Rainforest Fund's 21st birthday at Carnegie Hall in New York City. Rock for the Rainforest is a benefit concert held by the Rainforest Foundation Fund, hosted since 1991 by the organization's founders Sting and his wife Trudie. The event holds the Guinness World Record for the largest environmental fundraising event, funding projects that benefit the indigenous peoples of the world's rainforests.

5 – May 22, 2006: Blondie became a part of Hollywood's RockWalk, the only sidewalk gallery dedicated to honoring those artists who have made a significant impact and lasting contribution to the growth and evolution of Rock 'n' Roll, Blues and R&B. Along with Chris Stein, Clem Burke, and Jimmy Destri, a cast of Debbie's handprints are forever preserved along this rock and roll walk of fame located at 7425 Sunset Boulevard in front of The Guitar Center superstore.

4 – October 24, 2008: Debbie Harry was honored with the Icon Award at Billboard's third annual Women in Music breakfast, given to a woman whose art and career have blazed trails for successive generations.

3 – Summer 2008: For Blondie's 30th anniversary of *Parallel Lines* tour, Debbie and the band played their entire 1978 hit album live in its original order at every show! In 2014, Blondie is planning a 40th anniversary tour sure to be just as phenomenal.

2 – Debbie's ongoing commitment to human rights and her involvement in benefits for AIDS, LGBT rights, cancer research, animal welfare, and humanitarian aid projects demonstrate her compassion and devotion to cultural change. She was one of the first celebrities to align herself with the fight against HIV/AIDS, and she continues to participate in charitable events including AmfAR, LifeBeat, Amnesty International, Keep A Child Alive, The American Cancer Society, Riverkeeper, The Rainforest Foundation, and The Humane Society.

1 – March 13, 2006: Blondie was inducted into the Rock and Roll Hall of Fame after their first nomination at a ceremony held at the Waldorf Astoria in New York City. A touching, heartfelt introduction speech was given by Shirley Manson of Garbage, who identifies as someone directly influenced and inspired by Debbie's work with Blondie. Two hundred fans got together and purchased a full-page ad to congratulate Blondie on their accomplishment, which ran in the March 18, 2006 special commemorative issue of *Billboard* magazine. A *Billboard* poll found Blondie to be the fan favorite among all of the 2006 inductees.

Filmography

Contributed by Barry L. Kramer

This list shows films featuring Debbie Harry. It does not include episodes of television series or music videos.

Title	Year	Notes
Deadly Hero	1976	Small cameo (uncredited). Directed by Ivan Nagy.
Blank Generation	1976	A silent film by Amos Poe and Ivan Krall that includes a live Blondie performance from 1976. Released on DVD in 2001.
The Foreigner	1978	Film by Amos Poe. Debbie was also in other Amos Poe films including "Blank Generation" and "Unmade Beds". Released on DVD in 2001.
Union City	1979	Starring role. Directed by Mark Reichert.
Roadie	1980	Blondie appear as themselves and perform "Ring of Fire" live. Stars Meat Loaf, Alice Cooper, and Art Carney. Directed by Alan Rudolph.
Unmade Beds	1980	Includes footage of Debbie Harry singing circa 1976. Directed by Amos Poe; released on DVD in 2001.
Polyester	1983	Debbie Harry and Chris Stein have writing credits for music used in this film. While Debbie does not perform any of the music, her voice in the backing vocals is recognizable (but not credited). Directed by John Waters.

Videodrome	1983	Starring role. Written and directed by David Cronenberg.
Rock And Rule	1983	Debbie has a singing voice in this animated movie, in which she, Chris Stein, and Clem Burke worked on songs (along with Cheap Trick, Earth Wind and Fire, Iggy Pop, and Lou Reed). Directed by Clive A. Smith. Planned to be released on DVD in 2005.
Forever Lulu	1986	Debbie plays Lulu (a non-speaking role). Written, produced, and directed by Amos Kollek. This film has also appeared on video under the name "Crazy Streets".
Hairspray	1987	Directed by John Waters.
Satisfaction	1988	Debbie has a small part. This film has had multiple titles; also known as "Girls of Summer" (on TV) and "Sweet Little Rock & Roller" (in Europe). Directed by Joan Freeman.
New York Stories	1989	Debbie plays a very small cameo as herself.
Tales from the Darkside: The Movie	1990	Debbie plays a sinister housewife who is told three stories by a young boy she holds captive. Directed by John Harrison. Playing a different part, Debbie also starred in the 1987 episode "The Moth" of the "Tales From the Darkside" TV series.
Mother Goose Rock 'n' Rhyme	1990	Made for TV movie in which Debbie plays The Old Woman Who Lived In A Shoe. Directed by Jeff Stein.
Intimate Stranger	1992	Starring role. Includes portions of two live songs. This film was originally titled "After Midnight" and shown at the Cannes film festival in 1991. Directed by Allan Holzman.
Body Bags	1993	Debbie plays a nurse in one segment of this made for TV movie by John Carpenter.
Dead Beat	1994	Small cameo. Film by Adam Dubov. This film was also known as "The Phony Perfector" (working title?).

Heavy	1995	Starring role. Directed by James Mangold. This film had been previously titled "Upstate Stories" but opened at the Sundance Film Festival as "Heavy" on January 17, 1995. The premiere in New York was in September, and it received an award in Cannes.
Drop Dead Rock	1995	Starring role. Also stars Adam Ant.
Sandman	1995	Deborah Harry stars in this short black and white independent film written and directed by Marco Capalbo. There was a screening of this film in New York on October 27, 1995.
Six Ways To Sunday	1997	Starring role. Directed by Adam Bernstein.
Red Lipstick	2000	Deborah Harry plays Ezmerelda the psychic. Written and directed by Alexandra King.
Downtown 81	2000	Directed by Edo Bertoglio. This film is a day in the life of the young artist Jean Michel Basquiat. Also known as "New York Beat" (1981). Also features appearances by other Blondie band members and associates.
The Fluffer	2001	Debbie has a small cameo.
All I Want	2002	Directed by Jeffrey Porter. Also known as "Try Seventeen."
Spun	2002	Directed by Jonas Akerlund.
Dueces Wild	2002	Directed by Scott Kalvert.
My Life Without Me	2003	Directed by Isabel Coixet. Debbie plays the mother of a young woman who conceals the fact she's dying of cancer.
A Good Night To Die	2003	Directed by Craig Singer.

Discography
Contributed by Barry L. Kramer

This is the complete discography of official LP and CD regular and promotional releases in the United States that featured Debbie Harry. The list is presented with the albums in chronological order (except reissues), and singles (not in chronological order) grouped following the albums (even if they were issued in a different year). Test pressings, tapes (8-track and cassette), and bootleg albums are not included in this list. Most soundtracks and various-artist compilation albums featuring previously available Blondie or Debbie Harry tracks have also been omitted from the list. However, some of them *are* included if there is a reason, such as if they published a track for the first or only time, or if they contain a track previously unavailable on CD.

Some foreign items of particular interest are mentioned in the notes.

Complete archival information, including track lists, foreign releases, and bootleg listings, is constantly being accumulated and will appear on the web site of the Debbie Harry Collector's Society at http://debbieharry.net

Key:
LP = vinyl long-playing album.
CD = compact disc (album or CD single).
PD = picture disc.

7" = 7" single, no picture sleeve.
7"PS = 7" single with picture sleeve.
12" = 12" single, no picture sleeve.
12"PS = 12" single with picture sleeve.
wlp = white label promo. Typically a 7"; often with a different B-side than the regular issue.

Artist	Title	Desc.	Label	Catalog #	Year	Notes
The Wind in the Willows	**The Wind in the Willows**	LP	Capitol	SKAO-2956	1968	Original release with gatefold cover including lyrics.
The Wind in the Willows	**The Wind in the Willows**	LP	Capitol	CAP-2274	1979	Reissued with printing on the front cover "featuring Debbie Harry". This also became available on CD in the U.K. in 1993 and was reissued in 2000
The Wind in the Willows	Moments Spent	7"	Capitol	P 2274	1968?	A regular issue (yellow and orange label with black printing) and a promo issue (yellow label with black printing "promotion record" and "not for sale") exist. b/w "Uptown Girl".
The Wind in the Willows	**The Capitol Disc Jockey Album**	LP	Capitol	SPRO-4583	1968	Promo LP from July 1968 featuring Wind in the Willows tracks.

Artist	Title	Desc.	Label	Catalog #	Year	Notes
Blondie	**Blondie**	LP	Private Stock	PS-2023	1976	Regular issue. One pressing has printing "Blondie" and the stock numbers only above the horizontal line on the label. An alternate pressing also has track information for the first three songs above the line.
Blondie	**Blondie**	LP	Private Stock	PS-2023	1976	Two white label promo versions exist with a sticker and promo label. Alternate pressing has differing label printing analogous to regular issue. A test pressing from Specialty Records Corporation also exists, dated December 9, 1976.
Blondie	**Blondie**	LP	Chrysalis	CHR1165	1976	Original Chrysalis issue.
Blondie	**Blondie**	LP	Chrysalis	PV 41165		Chrysalis discount reissue (same record as original pressing).
Blondie	**Blondie**	CD	Chrysalis	VK-41165		Original Chrysalis issue of the CD.
Blondie	**Blondie**	CD	Chrysalis	F2 21165	1990?	Chrysalis reissue of the CD.

Artist	Title	Desc.	Label	Catalog #	Year	Notes
Blondie	**Blondie**	CD	Chrysalis	72435-33596-2-1	2001	Chrysalis/Capitol remastered reissue with 5 bonus tracks. An advance promo exists showing the release date.
Blondie	X Offender / In The Sun	7"	Private Stock	PS 45,097	1976	There were three pressings of this single that can only be distinguished by careful examination of the inscriptions in the vinyl. First pressing was 1976 June 07; it contains an additional number (pvt 1231 mbw). Third pressing is labeled PVT 1231-M.
Blondie	X Offender	7"	Private Stock	PS 45,097	1976	Labeled as a promo; has an additional number (pvt 1351 bw). Contains stereo and mono versions on opposite sides. Three pressings exist with slightly different label printing.
Blondie	In The Flesh	7"	Private Stock	PVT 1329 SP	1976	b/w "Man Overboard"
Blondie	In The Flesh	7"	Private Stock	PSR 45,141	1976	b/w "Man Overboard" (alternate pressing).

Artist	Title	Desc.	Label	Catalog #	Year	Notes
Blondie	In The Flesh	7"	Private Stock	PSR 45,141	1976	Labeled as a promo. Contains stereo and mono versions on opposite sides. Four different versions exist, each with slightly different label printing and secondary catalog number.
Blondie	**Plastic Letters**	LP	Chrysalis	CHR 1166	1977	Original pressing has a green label on LP. The second pressing has the same catalog number but a blue and white label on the record.
Blondie	**Plastic Letters**	LP	Chrysalis	PV 41166		Discount reissue; has the same record as the second pressing of CHR1166.
Blondie	**Plastic Letters**	CD	Chrysalis	VK-41166		First CD release.
Blondie	**Plastic Letters**	CD	Chrysalis	F2-21166	1990?	CD reissue.
Blondie	**Plastic Letters**	CD	Chrysalis	72435-33598-2-9	2001	Chrysalis/Capitol remastered reissue with 4 bonus tracks. An advance promo exists showing the release date.
Blondie	Denis	7"	Chrysalis	CHS2220	1977	b/w "I'm On E"

Artist	Title	Desc.	Label	Catalog #	Year	Notes
Blondie	Denis	7" wlp	Chrysalis	CHS2220	1977	White label promo with printed sleeve; contains mono and stereo versions.
Blondie	**Parallel Lines**	LP	Chrysalis	CHE 1192	1978	LP included lyrics insert and contained the 5:50 version of "Heart of Glass" (unavailable on any U.S. CD of Parallel Lines until 2001). An alternate pressing exists with the 3:54 version). A test pressing from Columbia Record Productions also exists, dated August 28, 1978.
Blondie	**Parallel Lines**	PD	Chrysalis	CHP5001	1978	Two versions exist: one with a clear border and one with a black border.
Blondie	**Parallel Lines**	LP	MFSL	MFSL1-050	1978	Mobile Fidelity Sound Lab "Original Master Recording" with orange stripe across top.

Artist	Title	Desc.	Label	Catalog #	Year	Notes
Blondie	**Parallel Lines**	CD	Chrysalis	VK-41192	1985	This CD has a different version of "Heart of Glass" than the original LP. This is mislabeled on the packaging. Also released by BMG (D-101778), Columbia House, and RCA music clubs in multiple formats.
Blondie	**Parallel Lines**	CD	Chrysalis	F221192	1985	This is a reissue with an edited version of "Heart of Glass" (3:54).
Blondie	**Parallel Lines**	CD	Chrysalis	72435-33599-2-8	2001	Chrysalis/Capitol remastered reissue with 4 bonus live tracks. An advance promo exists showing the release date. Also released by BMG (D-1412683) music club.
Blondie	**Parallel Lines**	CD		GZS-1062		DCC gold disc includes original version of Heart of Glass as bonus track.
Blondie	Hanging On The Telephone	7"	Chrysalis	CHE-2266	1978	Record is made in USA. Export single with small center hole.
Blondie	Hanging On The Telephone	7"PS	Chrysalis	CHS2271	1978	b/w Fade Away And Radiate.

Artist	Title	Desc.	Label	Catalog #	Year	Notes
Blondie	Hanging On The Telephone	7"PS wlp	Chrysalis	CHS2271	1978	White label promo; contains mono and stereo versions.
Blondie	Heart Of Glass	7"PS	Chrysalis	CHS2295	1979	b/w 11:59
Blondie	Heart Of Glass	7"PS	Chrysalis	CHS2295	1979	Pressed in clear vinyl.
Blondie	Heart Of Glass	7"	Chrysalis	CHE-2275	1979	U.S. record - an export single with small center hole. b/w Rifle Range.
Blondie	Heart of Glass	7"PS wlp	Chrysalis	CHS2295	1979	Promo; contains mono and stereo versions.
Blondie	Heart Of Glass	7"	Chrysalis	VS8 42944		Chrysalis Classic b/w Hanging On The Telephone
Blondie	Heart Of Glass	12"	Chrysalis	CDS-2275	1978	Record features a photo of DH on the label in die cut art sleeve.
Blondie	I'm Gonna Love You Too	7"	Chrysalis	CHS2251	1978	b/w Just Go Away.
Blondie	I'm Gonna Love You Too	7" wlp	Chrysalis	CHS2251	1978	Promo with printed sleeve; contains mono and stereo versions.
Blondie	One Way or Another	7"	Chrysalis	CHS2336	1979	b/w Just Go Away
Blondie	One Way or Another	7" wlp	Chrysalis	CHS2336	1979	White label promo; contains mono and stereo versions.

Artist	Title	Desc.	Label	Catalog #	Year	Notes
Blondie	One Way Or Another	12"	Chrysalis	CHS 10 PDJ	1979	Promo with die cut art sleeve and sticker.
Blondie	One Way Or Another	7"	Chrysalis	VS8 42945	1979	Chrysalis Classic b/w Dreaming
Blondie	One Way Or Another	7"	EMI	COL-6091		"Back To Back Hit Series" issue b/w Dreaming
Blondie	Picture This	7"	Chrysalis	CHS-2242	1978	U.S. record - an export issue with small center hole. Time on A side says 2:63
Blondie	**Eat To The Beat**	LP	Chrysalis	CHE 1225	1979	Original Chrysalis issue.
Blondie	**Eat To The Beat**	LP	Chrysalis	R133997	1979	RCA music club issue.
Blondie	**Eat To The Beat**	LP	Chrysalis	PV4 1225		Discount reissue; has the same record as the second pressing of CHR1166.
Blondie	**Eat To The Beat**	CD	Chrysalis	VK-41225		Original Chrysalis issue of the CD.
Blondie	**Eat To The Beat**	CD	Chrysalis	F2 21225		
Blondie	**Eat To The Beat**	CD	Chrysalis	72435-33597-2-0	2001	Chrysalis/Capitol remastered reissue with 4 bonus live tracks. An advance promo exists showing the release date.

Artist	Title	Desc.	Label	Catalog #	Year	Notes
Blondie	Atomic	7"PS	Chrysalis	CHS2410	1980	b/w Die Young Stay Pretty
Blondie	Atomic	7"PS wlp	Chrysalis	CHS2410	1980	White label promo; contains mono and stereo versions.
Blondie	Atomic	12"	Chrysalis	CHS19-PDJ	1980	This is a one-sided test pressing which was not released in the U.S.
Blondie	Dreaming	7"	Chrysalis	CHS2379	1979	b/w Living In The Real World
Blondie	Dreaming	7" wlp	Chrysalis	CHS2379	1979	Promo with printed sleeve; contains mono and stereo versions.
Blondie	Dreaming	12"	Chrysalis	CHS14-PDJ	1979	Promo label, no PS.
Blondie	The Hardest Part	7"PS	Chrysalis	CHS2408	1979	b/w Sound-A-Sleep
Blondie	The Hardest Part	7"PS wlp	Chrysalis	CHS2408	1979	Promo; contains mono and stereo versions.
Blondie	**Autoamerican**	LP	Chrysalis	CHE 1290	1980	
Blondie	**Autoamerican**	LP	Chrysalis	PV-41290		Discount reissue; has the same record as original release.
Blondie	**Autoamerican**	LP	Chrysalis	R133996		RCA music club issue.
Blondie	**Autoamerican**	CD	Chrysalis	VK-41290		Original Chrysalis issue of the CD.

Artist	Title	Desc.	Label	Catalog #	Year	Notes
Blondie	**Autoamer-ican**	CD	Chrysalis	F2 21290		
Blondie	**Autoamer-ican**	CD	Chrysalis	72435-33595-2-2	2001	Chrysalis/Capitol remastered reissue with 3 bonus tracks. An advance promo exists showing the release date.
Blondie	Rapture	7"PS	Chrysalis	CHS 2485	1980	b/w Walk Like Me
Blondie	Rapture	7" wlp	Chrysalis	CHS 2485	1980	Promo contains long and short versions.
Blondie	Rapture	7"	Chrysalis/ ERG	S7-18303		B/w One Way Or Another. Labeled "for jukeboxes only." Plain white sleeve.
Blondie	Rapture	12"	Chrysalis	CHS25-PDJ	1980	Promo with Chrysalis art sleeve and sticker and picture label. Contains long and short versions.
Blondie	The Tide Is High	7"PS	Chrysalis	CHS2465	1980	b/w Suzy & Jeffrey
Blondie	The Tide is High	7"PS wlp	Chrysalis	CHS2465	1980	White label promo; contains mono and stereo versions.

Artist	Title	Desc.	Label	Catalog #	Year	Notes
Blondie	The Tide is High	7"	Chrysalis	VS8 42698		b/w "Rapture". Two versions exist: one has the blue and white Chrysalis label; the other is a Chrysalis Classic.
Blondie	The Tide is High	7"	EMI	COL-6115		"Back To Back Hit Series" issue b/w Heart of Glass
soundtrack	**Roadie**	2LP	Warner Bros.	2HS 3441	1980	Original soundtrack features Blondie performing "Ring of Fire" live.
soundtrack	**Roadie**	LP	Warner Bros.	WB861	1980	Promo version is only one LP.
soundtrack	**American Gigolo**	LP	Polydor	PD-1-6259	1980	Original soundtrack album contains extended version of "Call Me Two pressings exist with slightly different label printing.
soundtrack	**American Gigolo**	LP	Polydor	813 632 1-Y-1	1980	Labeled "Previously released as PD-1-6259"; this record has a "sound savers" specially priced sticker.
soundtrack	**American Gigolo**	LP	Polydor	R151961	1980	RCA music club issue.
soundtrack	**American Gigolo**	CD	Polydor	0422813632 21	2001	Previously available on CD only in other countries.

Artist	Title	Desc.	Label	Catalog #	Year	Notes
Blondie	Call Me	12"	Polydor	PRO 124	1980	White label promo b/w Night Drive
Blondie	Call Me	7"PS	Chrysalis	CHS2414	1980	Regular issue with Richard Gere on PS. Note: "Call Me" was not associated with a regular Blondie album.
Blondie	Call Me	7"PS	Chrysalis	CHS2414	1980	Second pressing with Debbie Harry on the PS.
Blondie	Call Me	7"PS wlp	Chrysalis	CHS2414	1980	White label promo with Richard Gere on PS; contains mono and stereo versions.
Blondie	Call Me	7"	Chrysalis	VS8 42946	1980	Chrysalis Classic. There are two versions distinguishable by the size and color of the Chrysalis logo printed on the record label. b/w Atomic.
Blondie	Call Me	7"	EMI	COL-6073		"Back To Back Hit Series" issue b/w Rapture
Blondie	Llamame	12"	Salsoul	SG341	1980	This is the Spanish version of "Call Me".
Blondie	Llamame	12"	Salsoul	SG341 DJ	1980	Promo. Art sleeve (not a PS).
Blondie	Llamame	12"	Caytronics	CY-1219	1980	No PS.

Artist	Title	Desc.	Label	Catalog #	Year	Notes
Blondie	Llamame	7"	Caytronics	CY8-19		Promo ("D.J. copy not for sale").
Blondie	**Supergroups In Concert**	3LP	ABC	SGC105	1980	Produced for the ABC Radio Network by Pat Griffith and Kevin Kalunian of Griffith Kalunian Productions. 3LP set (live in London) with cue sheet, running time 99:50. Very rare promo.
	The Robert W. Morgan Special of the Week	LP	Watermark Inc.	SWS-802-12	1980	Promo. Air date 1980 June 21-22.
Blondie	**At Home With Debbie Harry & Chris Stein**	LP	Chrysalis	CHS24PDJ	1981	Promo includes insert sheets with printed questions corresponding to the answers recorded on the record.
Jimmy Destri	**Heart On A Wall**	LP	Chrysalis	CHR1368	1981	Debbie Harry - backing vocals. Promo versions are gold stamped on the jacket.
Debbie Harry	**Koo Koo**	LP	Chrysalis	CHR 1347	1981	
Debbie Harry	**Koo Koo**	LP	Chrysalis	PV-41347		Discount reissue.

Artist	Title	Desc.	Label	Catalog #	Year	Notes
Debbie Harry	**Koo Koo**	CD	Razor & Tie	7930182184 -2	1998	Not released on CD in the U.S. until 1998. The album was available earlier in Australia and later in the U.K.
Debbie Harry	Backfired	7"PS	Chrysalis	CHS2526	1981	b/w Military Rap
Debbie Harry	Backfired	7"PS wlp	Chrysalis	CHS2526	1981	White label promo; contains long and short versions.
Debbie Harry	Backfired	12"PS	Chrysalis	CDS-2547	1981	
Debbie Harry	Backfired	12"	Chrysalis	CHS33-PDJ	1981	Promo.
Debbie Harry	Chrome	12"	Chrysalis	CHS32-PDJ	1981	Promo in a generic printed sleeve with sticker (no PS). b/w Under Arrest.
Debbie Harry	The Jam Was Moving	7"PS	Chrysalis	CHS2554	1981	b/w Inner City Spillover
Debbie Harry	The Jam Was Moving	7"PS wlp	Chrysalis	CHS2554	1981	White label promo. Double A-sided.
Blondie	**A Conversation With Deborah Harry & Chris Stein**	3LP	DIR Broadcasting	CB-1	1981	Promo.
	The Robert Klein Radio Show	2LP	A Froben Production	RKRS-24	1980	"The best of the Robert Klein radio show" promo. Air date 1981 April 05. Plain white sleeve.

Artist	Title	Desc.	Label	Catalog #	Year	Notes
Blondie	**The Best of Blondie**	LP	Chrysalis	CHR 1337	1981	Original release.
Blondie	**The Best of Blondie**	LP	Chrysalis	FV 41337		This appears to be an identical reissue of CHR 1337 with paper labels printed with the new number placed over the old number.
Blondie	**The Best of Blondie**	LP	Chrysalis	R153320		RCA music club issue.
Blondie	**The Best of Blondie**	CD	Chrysalis	VK-41337	1984	
Blondie	**The Best of Blondie**	CD	Chrysalis	F2 21337		
Blondie	**The Hunter**	LP	Chrysalis	CHR 1384	1982	
Blondie	**The Hunter**	LP	Chrysalis	PV 41384		Discount reissue.
Blondie	**The Hunter**	LP	Chrysalis	R104733		RCA music club issue.
Blondie	**The Hunter**	CD	Chrysalis	VK-41384		
Blondie	**The Hunter**	CD	Chrysalis	72435-33670-2-2	2001	Chrysalis/Capitol remastered reissue with one bonus track. An advance promo exists showing the release date.
Blondie	Island of Lost Souls	7"PS	Chrysalis	CHS2603	1982	

Artist	Title	Desc.	Label	Catalog #	Year	Notes
Blondie	Island of Lost Souls	7"PS wlp	Chrysalis	CHS2603DJ	1982	White label promo. Double A-sided.
Blondie	Island of Lost Souls	12"	Chrysalis	CHS 40 PDJ	1982	Promo.
Blondie	War Child	12"	Chrysalis	CHS 39 PDJ	1982	Promo.
soundtrack	**Videodrome**	LP	Varese Sarabande	STV 81173	1982	Reverse side of jacket contains photos of Debbie as Nicki Brand.
soundtrack	**Scarface**	LP	MCA	MCA 6126	1983	Original soundtrack contains "Rush, Rush".
Debbie Harry	Rush, Rush	7"	Chrysalis	VS4-42745	1983	Note: "Rush, Rush" was not associated with a regular album.
Debbie Harry	Rush Rush	7"PS wlp	Chrysalis	VS4 42745	1983	Promo.
Debbie Harry	Rush, Rush	12"PS	Chrysalis	4V9-42741	1983	Regular issue.
Debbie Harry	Rush, Rush	12"PS	Chrysalis	4V9-42741	1983	Gold stamped promo.
soundtrack	**Krush Groove**	LP	Warner Bros.	9 25295-1	1985	Original soundtrack contains "Feel The Spin".

Artist	Title	Desc.	Label	Catalog #	Year	Notes
Debbie Harry	Feel The Spin	12"PS	Geffen	0-20391	1985	"Feel The Spin" was not associated with a regular album. Has an art cover - not really a picture sleeve (but not just a jacket). Also in promo version (gold stamped on the jacket).
Debbie Harry	**Rockbird**	LP	Geffen	GHS 24123	1986	This LP was issued with four different cover colors, all with the same catalog number.
Debbie Harry	**Rockbird**	LP	Geffen	GHS 24123	1986	Promo copies are gold stamped regular issue.
Debbie Harry	**Rockbird**	CD	Geffen	9 24123-2	1986	
Debbie Harry	French Kissin	7"PS	Geffen	7-28546	1986	
Debbie Harry	French Kissin	7"PS	Geffen	7-28546	1986	Promo label.
Debbie Harry	French Kissin	12"PS	Geffen	0-20575	1986	
Debbie Harry	French Kissin	12"PS	Geffen	PRO-A-2594	1986	Promo labeled (record and PS) with blue-green picture sleeve containing dance mix.

Artist	Title	Desc.	Label	Catalog #	Year	Notes
Debbie Harry	In Love With Love	7"PS	Geffen	7-28476	1986	Regular issue contains London Mix Edit and "Secret Life".
Debbie Harry	In Love With Love	7"PS	Geffen	7-28476	1986	Promo label; contains London Mix Edit and identical labeling on both sides. Note: this mix was released with the second "I Can See Clearly" CD single in England.
Debbie Harry	In Love With Love	12"PS	Geffen	0-20654	1986	Includes 3 remixes.
Debbie Harry	In Love With Love	12"PS	Geffen	0-20654	1986	Promo version, just a gold stamped copy of the regular issue.
Debbie Harry	In Love With Love	12"PS	Geffen	0-20687	1986	
Ramones	Halfway To Sanity	CD	Sire	9 25641-2	1987	Debbie Harry featured on vocals for one track ("Go Lil Camaro Go").
Ramones	Halfway To Sanity	LP	Sire	9 25641-1	1987	Debbie Harry featured on vocals for one track ("Go Lil Camaro Go").
soundtrack	Hairspray	CD	MCA	MCAD-6228	1988	Debbie has one uncredited line inserted into Rachel Sweet's "Hairspray": "Can't you see? I'm spraying my hair!"

Artist	Title	Desc.	Label	Catalog #	Year	Notes
soundtrack	**Married to the Mob**	LP	Reprise	1-25763	1988	Contains "Liar, Liar" performed by Debbie Harry.
soundtrack	**Married to the Mob**	CD	Reprise	9 25763-2	1988	
Debbie Harry	Liar, Liar	CD	Reprise	PRO-CD-3206	1988	CD single with 1 track. Promo: just a CD - no insert.
Debbie Harry	Liar, Liar	7"PS	Reprise	7-27792	1988	"Liar, Liar" was not associated with a regular album. b/w "Queen of Voudou".
Debbie Harry	Liar, Liar	7"	Reprise	7-27792	1988	Promo version b/w "Liar, Liar".
Debbie Harry	Liar, Liar	7"	Reprise	7-27792-A	1988	Promo.
soundtrack	**A Nightmare on Elm Street 4**	LP	Chrysalis	OV 41673	1988	Typo in label - reads "Rip Her To Sheds"
Debbie Harry / Blondie	**Once More Into The Bleach**	2LP	Chrysalis	V2X 41658	1988	This is a remix album (a 2LP gatefold).
Debbie Harry / Blondie	**Once More Into The Bleach**	2LP	Chrysalis	F1 21658	1988	Reissued with new catalog number sticker and lower price.
Debbie Harry / Blondie	**Once More Into The Bleach**	CD	Chrysalis	VK 41658	1988	
Blondie	Denis '88	7"PS	Chrysalis	VS4-43328	1988	Remix.

Artist	Title	Desc.	Label	Catalog #	Year	Notes
various artists	**Like A Girl, I Want You To Keep Coming**	LP	Rough Trade	GPS 040	1989	Giorno Poetry Systems Records.
various artists	**Like A Girl, I Want You To Keep Coming**	CD	Rough Trade	GPS 040 CD	1989	Includes "Invocation To Papa Legba".
Dee Dee King	**Standing In The Spotlight**	LP	Sire	9 25884	1989	
Dee Dee King	**Standing In The Spotlight**	CD	Sire	9 25884-2	1989	Debbie Harry - backing vocals.
Thompson Twins	**Big Trash**	LP			1989	Includes "Queen of the USA" (telephone vocals by Deborah Harry).
Thompson Twins	**Big Trash**	CD	Red Eye / Warner Bros.	W2 25921	1989	
various artists	Spirit Of The Forest	12"PS	Virgin	7 96551-0	1989	
various artists	Spirit Of The Forest	7"PS	Virgin	VS 1191	1989	
various artists	Spirit Of The Forest	CD	Virgin	PRCD2795	1989	1-track CD single.
Deborah Harry	**Def, Dumb, & Blonde**	LP	Sire	9 25938-1	1989	Promo copies are gold stamped regular issue.
Deborah Harry	**Def, Dumb, & Blonde**	CD	Sire	9 25938-2	1989	This CD contains the standard leaflet.

Artist	Title	Desc.	Label	Catalog #	Year	Notes
Deborah Harry	**Def, Dumb, & Blonde**	CD	Sire	9 25938-2	1989	This CD contains a "holographic" title only insert (no leaflet).
Deborah Harry	I Want That Man	7"PS	Sire	22816	1989	
Deborah Harry	I Want That Man	7"PS	Sire	22816	1989	Promo label. Some or all promos had jukebox strips (stickers in the PS).
Deborah Harry	I Want That Man	CD	Sire	PRO-CD-3680	1989	Promo CD single picture disc with graphics on the disc but no insert.
Deborah Harry	I Want That Man	12"PS	Sire	9 21322-0	1989	
Deborah Harry	I Want That Man	12"PS	Sire	9-21322	1989	Promo version: stamped sleeve with sticker.
Deborah Harry	Sweet And Low	CD	Sire	9 21446-2	1989	CD single with 4 tracks.
Deborah Harry	Sweet And Low	CD	Sire	9 21492-2	1989	CD single with 6 tracks.
Deborah Harry	Sweet And Low	12"PS	Sire	0-21446	1989	
Deborah Harry	Sweet And Low	12"PS	Sire	0-21446	1989	Promo version: stamped sleeve with sticker.
Deborah Harry	Sweet And Low	12"PS	Sire	0-21492	1989	

Artist	Title	Desc.	Label	Catalog #	Year	Notes
Deborah Harry	Sweet And Low	12"PS	Sire	0-21492	1989	Promo version: stamped sleeve with sticker.
various artists	**Sounds by Light**	CD	Warner Bros.	PRO-CD-3623	1989	Promo CD contains "Invocation To Papa Legba" by Deborah Harry (different mix than GPS 040).
various artists	**Just Say Da (Volume IV of Just Say Yes)**	CD	Sire	9 26240-2	1990	Contains "Maybe For Sure (Tunguska Event 7" Mix)" by Debbie Harry.
various artists	**Red Hot + Blue**	CD	Chrysalis	F2 21799	1990	This benefit album, a tribute to Cole Porter, features Debbie's duet with Iggy Pop, "Well Did You Evah". This was released as a single in England, but not in the U.S.
soundtrack	**Prelude to a Kiss**	CD	RCA	RCA 07863 66076 2	1992	Deborah Harry performs the main title and "Prelude to a Kiss"
soundtrack	Prelude to a Kiss	CD	RCA Milan	RDJ 62324 2	1992	Promotional CD single.
various artists	**Get Out**	CD	Sire/Reprise	PRO-CD-5435	1992	Promotional CD issued with "Out" magazine charter subscriptions; includes "I Want That Man" Remix/Edit, same as the 12".

Artist	Title	Desc.	Label	Catalog #	Year	Notes
various artists	**Cash Cow**	CD	Giorno Poetry Systems	ESD 80712	1993	Alternate catalog number: GPS 044. Features Debbie Harry on "Moroccan Rock (Pipe Of Pain)".
various artists	**Heck On Wheels Volume 3**	CD	Warner/ Reprise	PRO CD 6457	1993	Promo CD includes "Communion" by Deborah Harry.
Deborah Harry	**Debravation**	CD	Sire	9 45303-2	1993	U.S. CD contains two bonus tracks not present in most other countries.
Deborah Harry	**Debravation**	LP	Sire		1993	
Deborah Harry	I Can See Clearly	CD	Sire/ Reprise	9 41000-2	1993	CD single with 7 tracks.
Deborah Harry	I Can See Clearly	CD	Sire/ Reprise	PRO CD 6336	1993	CD single with 2 tracks. Promo cover and CD design, containing single version and album version.
Deborah Harry	I Can See Clearly	12"PS	Sire/ Reprise	9 41000 0	1993	
Blondie	**Blonde and Beyond**	CD	Chrysalis/ ERG	F2 21990	1993	Blondie compilation of rarities and unreleased material. Also contains the original version of "Heart of Glass" released on the Parallel Lines LP in 1978.

Artist	Title	Desc.	Label	Catalog #	Year	Notes
Die Haut	**Head On**	CD	Triple X Records	51148-2	1993	Includes "Don't Cross My Mind" (vocals by Debbie Harry).
various artists	**DIY Blank Generation: The New York Scene**	CD	Rhino	R2 71175	1993	Includes "X Offender" and "In The Flesh". This version of "X Offender" is <u>not</u> the original single version. It and "In The Flesh" are identical to the album versions.
various artists	**Brace Yourself! A Tribute to Otis Blackwell**	CD	Shanachie	5702	1994	Features Deborah Harry singing "Don't Be Cruel".
Jazz Passengers	**In Love**	CD	High Street	72902 10328 2	1994	Includes "Dog In Sand" (vocals by Deborah Harry).
Blondie	**The Platinum Collection**	2CD	Chrysalis	F2 31100	1994	Compilation of singles and early Blondie demos.
Blondie	**The Platinum Collection**	LP	Chrysalis	F2 31100	1994	
Blondie	Rapture	CD	Chrysalis	F2 58277	1994	CD single with 8 tracks. Contains remixes of "Rapture" and the soundtrack version of "Call Me".
Blondie	Rapture	2x12" PS	Chrysalis/ EMI	VV 58277	1994	One PS containing two records with "Rapture" remixes.

Artist	Title	Desc.	Label	Catalog #	Year	Notes
Blondie	Rapture	2x12"	Chrysalis/ EMI	SPRO 58277	1994	K-Klass and Guru "Rapture" mixes; two records in a single white sleeve with a b&w sticker.
Blondie	**Remixed Remade Remodeled**	CD	Chrysalis/ EMI	F2 32748	1995	This is a remix album.
Blondie	Atomic	CD	Chrysalis/ EMI	7243 8 58340 2 8	1995	CD single with 8 tracks.
Blondie	Atomic	7"		S7-18396	1995	CEMA jukebox single
Blondie	Atomic	2x12" PS	Chrysalis/ EMI	VV58340	1995	One PS containing two records with "Atomic" remixes.
Blondie	Heart Of Glass	CD	Chrysalis/ EMI		1995	CD single.
Blondie	Heart Of Glass	2x12" PS	Chrysalis/ EMI	VV 58387	1995	One PS containing two records with nine "Heart of Glass" remixes.
Blondie	Union City Blue	CD	Chrysalis/ EMI	F2 58474	1995	CD single with 7 tracks. Contains remixes of "Union City Blue" and a live version of "I Feel Love" from 1980.
Blondie	Union City Blue	2x12" PS	Chrysalis/ EMI	VV 58474	1995	One PS containing two records with 6 "Union City Blue" remixes and a "One Way or Another" remix.

Artist	Title	Desc.	Label	Catalog #	Year	Notes
Los Fabulosos Cadillacs	**Rey Azucar**	CD	SDI (Sony Discos Inc.)	CDZ-81596 2-478664	1995	Includes "Strawberry Fields For Ever" (sic) - vocals by Deborah Harry.
various artists	**Sedated in the Eighties (No. 4)**	CD	The Right Stuff (EMI)	T2-34661	1995	Features Blondie performing "Hanging on the Telephone" live (previously unreleased).
soundtrack	**Virtuosity**	CD	Radioactive	RARD-11295	1995	Soundtrack features "No Talking Just Head" performed by The Heads featuring Deborah Harry.
The Heads	**No Talking Just Head**	CD	MCA		1996	Includes "No Talking Just Head".
The Jazz Passengers	**Individually Twisted**	CD	32 Records	32007	1996	Featuring Deborah Harry.
Blondie / Pat Benatar	**Back To Back Hits**	CD	Capitol / CEMA special Markets	S21-18969	1996	Compilation includes five singles from Blondie and five from Pat Benatar. Reissued in 2001 (HYR2-3125) with a different cover.
Blondie	**Essential Blondie Picture This Live**	CD	Chrysalis/ EMI-Capitol	72438-21440-2-1	1997	Labeled as "limited edition"; 15 live tracks.
various artists	**We Will Fall: The Iggy Pop Tribute**	CD	Royalty Records	RTY106	1997	Features Adolph's Dog performing "Ordinary Bummer".

Artist	Title	Desc.	Label	Catalog #	Year	Notes
Groove Thing	**This Is No Time...**	CD	Eightball/ Lightyear	54195-2	1997	Includes "Command & Obey" featuring Debbie Harry.
Groove Thing	Command & Obey	12"PS	Eightball	54201-1	1997	Art sleeve, not quite a picture sleeve.
Groove Thing	Command & Obey	12"	Eightball	EB-134	1999	1999 remixes – 3 tracks.
Deborah Harry & Robert Jacks	Der Einziger Weg ("The Only Way")	CD	Eco-Disaster Music	ECM CD004	1998	4-track CD containing "Love Theme from Texas Chainsaw Massacre: The Next Generation" (4 versions)
Blondie	**No Exit**	CD	Beyond	BYJC-78003-2	1998	Mainly black CD is printed "for promotional use only" and has early artwork.
Blondie	Maria	CD	Beyond	BYDJ-78040	1998	2-track promo CD single, predominantly black.
Los Fabulosos Cadillacs	**20 Grandes Exitos**	CD	Sony		1998	This collection features Deborah Harry doing guest vocals on "Strawberry Fields Forever".
Blondie	**The Best Of Blondie**	CD	EMI	15384	1998	3CD boxed set containing 36 tracks.

Artist	Title	Desc.	Label	Catalog #	Year	Notes
Blondie	**Ten Best of Blondie**	CD	EMI	72434-98056-2-0	1999	"The Best of Blondie" – 10 track compilation; part of EMI's "Ten Best Series."
Luscious Jackson	**Electric Honey**	CD	EMI	7243-49-60842-9	1999	"Fantastic Fabulous" features Deborah Harry vocals.
Blondie	**No Exit**	CD	Beyond	63985-78003-2	1999	Blue and white CD is printed "for promotional use only" and has final artwork.
Blondie	**No Exit**	CD	Beyond	63985-78003-2	1999	First pressing (released 23 Feb) includes 3 live tracks, listed only on sticker on the outer wrapping. Second pressing has same catalog number, but doesn't include the live tracks. The Japanese version (BVCP-21037) contains an extra studio track ("Hot Shot").
Blondie featuring Loud Allstars	No Exit	12"	Loud	RDAB-65699-1	1999	Promo 12" in a Loud sleeve with a red Blondie sticker (contains 6 tracks).
Blondie	Maria	12"	Logic / Beyond / BMG	74321-78040-1	1999	Released 1999 March 16, in a Logic sleeve with a Blondie sticker.

Artist	Title	Desc.	Label	Catalog #	Year	Notes
Blondie	Maria	12"	Logic	LGSP-78040-1	1999	"Maria Dubs" white label promo contains two remixes: "Ether Dub", "White Trash Dub".
Blondie	Maria	CD	Logic / Beyond / BMG	74321-78040-2	1999	Contains Maria (Soul Solution Full Remix), Maria (Talvin Singh Remix), Maria (Talvin Singh Rhythmic Remix Edit), and album version. Released 1999 March 23.
Blondie	Maria	CD		38-E810245867 C13		Test pressing contains Maria (Alternate Rock Mix), Maria (Alternate Rock Mix Edit).
Blondie	Screaming Skin	CD	Beyond/ BMG	BYDJ-78051		Promo contains Screaming Skin (Radio Edit) and album version.
Blondie	Nothing Is Real But The Girl	CD	Beyond/ BMG	BYDJ-78042		Promo contains Nothing Is Real But The Girl (Radio Remix), Nothing Is Real But The Girl (Radio Remix with alternate intro)
soundtrack	**Six Ways To Sunday**	CD	Will Records	WIL 33661	1999	Includes classic "Sunday Girl", new "More More More", and Debbie has a short speaking part in "Sex Ed".

Artist	Title	Desc.	Label	Catalog #	Year	Notes
Soundtrack	**200 Cigarettes**	CD	Mercury	314 538 738-2	1999	Includes classic "In the Flesh" and new Blondie Medley (Rapture / Maria / No Exit the AllStar Rock Remix).
Blondie	**Blondie Live**	CD	Beyond	63985-78066-2	1999	Live recording of the 23 Feb 1999 Town Hall (New York City) show. Released 23 Nov 99. This recording was released internationally with a slightly different title: **Livid**
Blondie	**Blondie Live**	CD	Eagle		2004	2004 re-release.
Andy Summers	**Peggy's Blue Skylight**	CD	BMG		2000	Debbie Harry performs "Weird Nightmare" on this collection of Charles Mingus songs.
Blondie	**Blondie Is The Name Of A Band**	CD	Phantom		2000	10 tracks from the 1978 live recording of the German TV rock show "Musikladen".
Roy Nathanson	**Fire at Keaton's Bar & Grill**	CD	Six Degrees Records	657036-10242-2	2000	Features Deborah Harry vocals on the track "Cups".
Kiki & Herb	**Do You Hear What We Hear**	CD			2000	Debbie Harry is special guest on two tracks.

Artist	Title	Desc.	Label	Catalog #	Year	Notes
Blondie	**The Curse Of Blondie**	CD	Sanctuary	06076-84666-2	2004	Both the regular and the promo versions contain the "Good Boys" video.
Blondie	**The Curse Of Blondie**	CD/ DVD	Silverline		2004	A "Dual Disc": audio CD on one side, DVD with 5.1 channel audio on the other. Released 2004 Nov 02.
Blondie	Good Boys	CD	Sanctuary	SANDJ-85595-2		5-track promo CD with black and white artwork and CD. In the U.S., this single was not released on CD to the general market.
Blondie	Good Boys	CD	Sanctuary	SANDJ-85600-2		2-track promo CD.
Blondie	Good Boys	CD	Sanctuary	SANDJ-85615-2		5-track promo CD.
Blondie	Good Boys	CD	Sanctuary			3-track promo CD with "Blow-Up" mixes.
Blondie	Good Boys	12"	Sanctuary	SANDJ-85595-1		33rpm 12" promo with 4 mixes.
Blondie	**Live By Request**	CD	Sanctuary		2004	Includes 4 bonus tracks from A&E's Live By Request not shown during the show's May 7 live broadcast from the John Jay College Theater in NYC. Also available on DVD.

Artist	Title	Desc.	Label	Catalog #	Year	Notes
Blondie	**The Curse Of Blondie**	CD	Sanctuary	06076-84666-2	2004	Both the regular and the promo versions contain the "Good Boys" video.
Blondie	**The Curse Of Blondie**	CD/DVD	Silverline		2004	A "Dual Disc": audio CD on one side, DVD with 5.1 channel audio on the other. Released 2004 Nov 02.
Blondie	Good Boys	CD	Sanctuary	SANDJ-85595-2		5-track promo CD with black and white artwork and CD. In the U.S., this single was not released on CD to the general market.
Blondie	Good Boys	CD	Sanctuary	SANDJ-85600-2		2-track promo CD.
Blondie	Good Boys	CD	Sanctuary	SANDJ-85615-2		5-track promo CD.
Blondie	Good Boys	CD	Sanctuary			3-track promo CD with "Blow-Up" mixes.
Blondie	Good Boys	12"	Sanctuary	SANDJ-85595-1		33rpm 12" promo with 4 mixes.
Blondie	**Live By Request**	CD	Sanctuary		2004	Includes 4 bonus tracks from A&E's Live By Request not shown during the show's May 7 live broadcast from the John Jay College Theater in NYC. Also available on DVD.

Artist	Title	Desc.	Label	Catalog #	Year	Notes
Blondie	**Singles Box**	CD	EMI	5487392	2004	Boxed set of 15 CDs that correspond to all of the original Chrysalis U.K. singles including the original artwork.
Blondie	**3 Pack**	CD	Capitol	72435-78692-2-5	2004	3CD boxed set containing the 2001 re-releases of Parallel Lines, Eat To The Beat, and Autoamerican.
Blondie & The Doors	The Rapture Riders	CD	EMI	094634755023	2005	Remix of Blondie single "Rapture" with The Doors "Riders on the Storm"
Blondie	**Greatest Hits: Sight & Sound**	CD	EMI	0946 3 45054 2 0	2005	Two-disc compilation album of music and video
Blondie	**Greatest Hits: Sight & Sound**	CD	Capitol	0946 3 47218 2-0	2006	
Blondie & The Doors	The Rapture Riders		Capitol	094636283227	2006	
Blondie	**Live in Toronto**	CD	Movieplay	MPG 74082	2006	Recorded in concert August 18, 1982 at Canadian National Expo ("Tracks Across America" Tour)
Moby	New York, New York	CD	Mute	12Mute371	2006	Moby single featuring Deborah Harry
Deborah Harry	**Necessary Evil**	CD	Eleven Seven Music	150	2007	Harry's fifth solo album

Artist	Title	Desc.	Label	Catalog #	Year	Notes
Deborah Harry	Two Times Blue	CD	Eleven Seven Music	158	2007	Single release from Necessary Evil
Deborah Harry	Two Times Blue	12"	Eleven Seven Music	159	2007	
Deborah Harry	Fit Right In	CD	Tenth Street Entertainment	n/a	2008	Non-album single
Blondie	**Platinum**	CD	EMI	5-09992-13347-2-6	2008	12-track compilation album released in Europe and Canada
Blondie	**Singles Collection: 1977–1982**	CD	EMI/ Chrysalis	5099996803721	2009	Revised and edited 2CD jewel case version of the previous 2004 15CD singles box set.
Blondie	**Blondie at the BBC**	CD, LP, DVD	Chrysalis	5099964215822	2010	BBC recordings – *Top of the Pops, Old Grey Whistle Test* etc – from 1978–79
Blondie	**Blondie at the BBC**	CD, LP	EMI	6421582	2010	
Blondie	**Panic of Girls**	CD, LP	Future Publishing	CRP/05/06/11	2011	Ninth studio album
Blondie	What I Heard	CD	Five Seven Music	n/a	2011	Two-track promo CD, single from Panic of Girls
Blondie	Mother	Digital download	Five Seven Music	54576427	2011	Single from Panic of Girls
Blondie	**Parallel Lines/Plastic Letters**	CD	EMI/ Chrysalis	50999 0952492 7	2011	2CD compilation

Internet Resources
Contributed by Louis A Bustamante

Deborah Harry and Blondie web resources

Name	URL
Official Blondie Web Site	http://www.blondie.net
Official Blondie Fan Forum	http://www.blondiemusic.com
Debbie Harry Collector's Society	http://www.debbieharry.net
Deborah Harry Home Page	http://www.deborahharry.com
The Complete Blondie Discography	http://www.recmod.com/
The Blondie Review	http://www.geocities.com/blondiereview/index.html
Union City	http://www.unioncity.force9.co.uk/
Picture This (UK Fanzine)	http://homepage.ntlworld.com/blondie2000/
Blondie Retro Fan Club	http://blondie_retrofanclub.tripod.com/
Blondie At CBGB's	http://www.cbgb.com/shrine/shriners/blondie.htm
From Punk To The Present Book	http://www.blondiebook.com/
Rip Her To Shreds	http://www.rip-her-to-shreds.com/
Rob Roth/Click + Drag	http://www.clicknyc.com/
Mick Rock Photos	http://www.mickrock.com/
Bob Gruen Photos	http://www.bobgruen.com/files/blondie.html
Grateful Joe Photos	http://www.gratefuljoe.com/debbie.html
John Sibby Photos	http://www.gratefuljoe.com/concerts/sibbygallery/johnsibby.html
Platinum Blondie (French)	http://www.platinumblondie.com/
Pretty Baby (Japanese)	http://page.freett.com/sundaygirl/
Modern Culture	http://www.bway.net/~modcult/ (Roberta Bayley Images) rbimages.html
Goodie Magazine	http://www.goodie.org/
TV Party	http://www.tvparty.org/

Contributors' Biographies

Joey Arias is, according to Deborah Harry, 'a real classic' New York performer, singer and drag artist. His favorite Blondie song is 'Hanging on the Telephone'.

John Bartlett is the New York designer behind his own men's and women's collections. His favorite Blondie song is 'Sunday Girl'.

Roberta Bayley is a great chronicler of the punk rock movement. Her pictures are included in the photography book Blank Generation *and she is the co-author of* Patti Smith: A Biography *with Victor Bockris. Bayley also worked as the door person at CBGB's and ran Blondie's US fan club in the late 70s.*

Adam Bernstein is the director of the 1998 feature film Six Ways to Sunday, *which stars Deborah Harry.*

Rodney Bingenheimer is an infamous Los Angeles DJ, a nightlife impresario and even a recording artist. His single 'Little GTO' features The Brunettes, an alias for Blondie. You can still catch Bingenheimer late nights on radio station KROQ. His favorite Blondie songs are 'Pretty Baby', 'In The Sun' and 'T-Bird'.

Victor Bockris is a prolific biographer whose work includes books about Muhammed Ali, Keith Richards, Andy Warhol, Lou Reed, William Burroughs, The Velvet Underground, John Cale, Patti Smith and of course, Blondie. He is also the author of New York City Babylon, *a book of his collected essays. He is the inspiration for the Blondie Song 'Victor'.*

Boone, Brian & Terence are Blondie fanatics and producers of the Manhattan cable access TV show, The Boone Show. *Brian (aka The Dope) is also the centerpiece of the New York band The Dopes.*

Lady Bunny is the founder and organizer of the outdoor music festival of peace, love and wigs, Wigstock, *which is held annually in New York during Labor Day weekend. The Lady's favorite Blondie song is 'Denis'.*

Paul Burston is the long-time Gay London editor at Time Out London *and contributes to publications including* The Sunday Times, *the* Guardian *and the* Independent. *Burston is also the author of the book* Queens' Country *and the Marc Almond biography,* Gutter Heart.

Louis A Bustamante is an artist and musician living in Phoenix, Arizona. He is webmaster of the Official Blondie Web Site and has run the DHBIS (Deborah Harry & Blondie Internet Service) fan club for over ten years. He collaborated with the band Swivek on a single titled 'Debbie Doesn't', and has remixed Blondie's 'Union City Blue' under the pseudonym 'Jammin' Hot'. He also runs his own site, Tiki Lab (www.tikilab.com). He fell in love with Blondie in 1978 at 12 years old and never looked back.

David Byrne, *primarily known as the musician who co-founded the group Talking Heads, has also been involved in many other projects including work with Brian Eno, Twyla Tharp, Robert Wilson, Jonathan Demme and Bernardo Bertolucci. In 1989 he began solo recordings including Rei Momo (1989), the self-titled David Byrne (1994), Look into the Eyeball (2001) and Love this Giant (2012). Byrne has his own label, Luka Bop, and is also involved with photography and design.*

John Cantwell *is a Deborah Harry superfan and has her signature tattooed on his right arm. He is also a member of the Los Angeles based comedy troupe The Nellie Olsens.*

Robert Christgau *joined the* Village Voice *in 1974 and was music editor until 2006. He is the author of the book* Grown Up All Wrong *and the husband of Carola Dibbell.*

Bob Colacello *is a special correspondent for* Vanity Fair *magazine and was the editor of Andy Warhol's* Interview *magazine from 1971 to 1983. He is also the author of the book* Holy Terror.

Sarah Conley *was the creative life-force behind the Deborah Harry fanzine,* Underground Girl.

David Cronenberg *is the twisted but brilliant mind behind such extremely creepy films as* Scanners, Dead Ringers, The Fly *and* Crash. *His 1982 cult classic,* Videodrome, *was Deborah Harry's major motion picture debut.*

Carola Dibbell *is a New York based writer and the author of the novel,* Girl Talk. *Her essay 'Inside Was Us: Women and Punk' appears in* Trouble Girls: The Rolling Stone Book of Women in Rock. *She is also the wife of Robert Christgau.*

Jancee Dunn, *who is currently a contributing editor to* O, The Oprah Magazine, *made her name with her work for* Rolling Stone *magazine, which appeared from 1989 to 2003. She was also a VJ on MTV's alternative network, M2. Her favorite Blondie song is 'Dreaming'.*

Vincent Fremont *worked with Andy Warhol from 1969 until his death in 1987. He was the producer of Warhol's various televisions projects and is currently the exclusive agent to Warhol's drawings, paintings and sculptures, as well as the head of his own New York based company, Fremont Enterprises.*

David LaChapelle *is a New York photographer whose images of celebrities including Madonna, Leonardo DiCaprio, Elton John, Jim Carrey, the Smashing Pumpkins and Deborah Harry have appeared in such magazines as* Details, Interview, Vanity Fair, Rolling Stone *and* Detour. *Some of his best work is captured in his best-selling book,* LaChapelle Land.

Pleasant Gehman *has been living in and writing about the LA rock scene since 1975 in publications including her own punk fanzine* Lobotomy, Slash, New York Rocker *and* LAWeekly. *Formerly a member of the band The Screaming Sirens, she is a poet (Senorits Sin, Princess Hollywood), screenwriter (The Running Kind), and burlesque dancer.*

H. R. Giger *won an Academy Award in 1979 for his Production Design on the movie* Alien *and his eponymous museum opened in 1998 in Gruyères, Switzerland. He did the artwork for Deborah Harry's Koo Koo album and subsequently collaborated with Harry on two music videos – 'Backfired' and 'Now You Know I Know'.*

Miss Guy *is the lead singer of the New York band the Toilet Boys, DJ at the club SqueezeBox and a sometime make-up artist who has worked with Deborah Harry. His favorite Deborah Harry album cover is* Rockbird.

Maja Hanson, *daughter of artist Duane Hanson, grew up in South Florida influenced by her father's art and the local aesthetic of loud prints and tacky kitsch. Hanson attended the Rhode Island School of Design, and started her own collection of sexy women's wear called Maja, in 1995. Hanson likes to blast her* Best of Blondie *CD while designing in her studio.*

Ashley Heath *was Senior Editor and Fashion Director of* The Face *for many years, and cofounded* POP *magazine with Katie Grand in 2000. Heath is a self-confessed 'massive' Blondie fan, and his favorite Blondie song is 'Susie & Jeffrey'. He also strongly believes that* Autoamerican, *his favorite Blondie album, should be critically re-evaluated.*

Sam Hill *is the lead singer of the British Blondie cover band Once More Into The Bleach.*

John Holmstrom *is the New York based publisher of High Times and the founding editor of* Punk *magazine. His favourite Blondie song is 'I'm on E'.*

Joan Jett *was the lead singer of the pioneering all-girl punk bank The Runaways. As a solo artist, her 1981 album* I Love Rock 'n' Roll *produced a number one single by the same name.*

Theresa Kereakes *was the photographer for the punk fanzine Lobotomy and is now a film and TV producer in New York. Her favorite Blondie album is the one most strongly tied to her memories of her LA punk youth –* Plastic Letters.

Paul Klein *was the lead singer and founder of Deborah Harry's first band, the Wind in the Willows. He is now the owner and president of an international business advisory firm in St Louis, Missouri and has one son in rock 'n' roll – Eric (aka Belvy K) of the punk bands 7 Seconds and Libertine. One of his favorite Deborah Harry songs is the one he maintains was her first: the Willow's 'Buried Treasure'.*

Theo Kogan, *of Theo & The Skyscrapers, was the lead singer of the New York band The Lunachicks and a back-up singer on the Blondie album* No Exit. *The Lunachicks did a wicked punk rock cover version of 'Heart of Glass'.*

Barry L. Kramer *is the founder and president of the Debbie Harry Collector's Society and the owner and technical administrator of the Official Blondie Web Site (www.Blondie.net). He is recognized as the primary archivist of information and materials related to Deborah Harry and Blondie, and likes to play Parallel Lines, look into the clear night sky and think about how much we've been touched by their presence, dear.*

Peter Leeds *was Blondie's first manager, from 1977 when the band released its first album –* Blondie *on Private Stock Records – until 1979 when 'Heart of Glass' was Blondie's first number one single in the US.*

Kurt Loder *is the New York-based author of the Tina Turner autobiography,* I, Tina *and a series of essays collected in* Bat Chain Puller: Rock 'n' Roll in the Age of Celebrity. *A former senior editor at Rolling Stone, he is an MTV News anchor in the US. One of his favorite Blondie songs is 'Fan Mail', and he was upset to find that it was not included on* The Platinum Collection.

Chris Makos, *photographer, was Andy Warhol's best friend and documented thousands of public and private moments with the artist. He currently lives in New York and his work is the subject of two photography books,* White Trash *and* Makos.

James Mangold *is the film maker who reinvented Deborah Harry in* Heavy. *His other films include the critically acclaimed* Copland, Girl Interrupted, Walk the Line *and* The Wolverine.

Shirley Manson is the magnificent Scottish lead singer of the pop band Garbage.

Evelyn McDonnell is assistant professor of journalism and new media at Loyola Marymount University. The author of Queens of Noise: the Real Story of the Runaways and Army of She: Icelandic, Iconoclastic, Irrepressible Bjork, she co-edited the anthology Rock She Wrote: Women Write About Rock, Pop, and Rap with Ann Powers and the anthology Stars Don't Stand Still in the Sky with Karen Kelly, and co-wrote the official book about the Jonathan Larson musical RENT with Kathy Silberger. She is also the former music editor at the Village Voice and former editor of the desisted 'zine, Resister. Her favorite Blondie song is 'Dreaming'.

Patrick McMullan is a New York based photographer who contributes regularly to national and regional magazines including New York, Bazaar, Vanity Fair, Manhattan File and Ocean Drive. He also curates the 'Page Five' column in Interview magazine and is an important fixture at every hip soiree. His favorite Blondie song is 'Call Me'.

Mark Mothersbaugh is a founding member of the Akron, Ohio new wave band DEVO. He runs his own company Mutato Muzika in Los Angeles, which produces music for films, television and national advertising campaigns. All of the DEVO guys work with him. He collaborates frequently with the film maker Wes Anderson, and also wrote the music for The Rugrats Movie, which included a cover version of Blondie's 'One Way or Another'.

Michael Musto is a New York based author who used to write the fabulous weekly column La Dolce Musto for the Village Voice. Ask him what his favorite Blondie song is, and he'll tell you that it's whatever is au courant.

Roy Nathanson, lead horn blower of the Jazz Passengers and onetime member of the Beat noir jazz art ensemble, the Lounge Lizards, likes the irreverent Blondie song 'Rip Her To Shreds'.

Glenn O'Brien, a long-time downtown denizen and friend of Chris Stein and Deborah Harry (his cohorts on Glenn O'Brien's TV Party), continues to write extensively about Blondie and Deborah Harry. O'Brien was the editor and art director of Interview magazine in the 70s and penned the influential 'Beat' music column. Formerly a columnist for both Paper and Details magazines, O'Brien is currently The Style Guy for GQ and was editor of Madonna's book SEX.

Lucy O'Brien is the author of She Bop: The Definitive History of Women in Rock, Pop and Soul, and the biographies Madonna: Like an Icon, Annie Lennox and Dusty, about the late, great Dusty Springfield. She has contributed to publications including the Guardian, Cosmopolitan, Spare Rib, New Statesman and The Face, and also works in film television and radio.

Gail O'Hara has written for many publications and was formerly the music editor at Time Out New York.

Todd Oldham is a New York based designer with namesake retail stores in New York, Los Angeles, Miami and Tokyo. His favorite Blondie album cover is Plastic Letters.

Alyson Palmer is the vocalist and bassist of the New York-based band BETTY. Her favorite Blondie album is No Exit. For more info about BETTY, see their website www.helloBETTY.com.

Tina Paul is a New York based photographer best know for documenting the downtown nightlife culture. One of her favorite Blondie songs is 'You Look God In Blue'.

Lisa Robinson is a maverick music writer and the co-founder of the seminal 70s New York music magazine, Rock Scene. In the 70s she was also an editor at Hit Parader and Creem and a contributor to Rolling Stone. A former member of the nominating commitee of the Rock and Roll

Hall of Fame, she is now a columnist for Vanity Fair *magazine. Her book* There Goes Gravity: A Life in Rock and Roll *will be published in 2014.*

Rob Roth, *media master, cyberguru, glamnerd and artist is the designer of the Blondie album* No Exit *and the No Exit tour stage show. One of his favorite Blondie songs is 'Victor'.*

RuPaul *is an LA-based performer who currently hosts the reality television show,* RuPaul's Drag Race. *His favorite Deborah Harry video is 'Sweet and Low' and his favorite song is a tie between 'Dreaming' and Harry's duet with Kermit the Frog of 'The Rainbow Connection'.*

Kate Schellenbach *is the drummer for New York based band Luscious Jackson. Her favorite Blondie album is* Parallel Lines. *Deborah Harry sings on the song 'Fantastic Fabulous' on the Luscious Jackson album* Electric Honey.

Michael Schmidt *is an Emmy-nominated fashion designer who has worked with Cher, Tina Turner, Bon Jovi and the woman he says he'd 'take a bullet for', Deborah Harry. He was also the promoter of the New York queer rock 'n' roll club, SqueezeBox.*

Fred Schneider/B-52's *is a member of the inspired New Wave band, the B-52s. Their 1998 album* Time Capsule *contains a song inspired by Deborah Harry called 'Debbie'. His favorite Blondie song is 'Attack of the Giant Ants'.*

Bob Sellstedt *was a fan of Blondie's in the late 70s/early 80s who began making customized, one of a kind Deborah Harry dolls after (sob!) Blondie broke-up. There are only twenty-five of the dolls in total and Deborah Harry has two of them.*

Chris Stein *is the co-founder of the band Blondie and Deborah Harry's best friend.*

Mim Udovitch *is a New York based writer and feminist critic.*

ChiChi Valenti and Johnny Dynell *are the great minds behind the New York club Mother and its most famous love child, the legendary Jackie 60.*

John Waters *is the film maker behind cult classics such as* Polyester, Female Trouble, Desperate Living, *and the children's film he made by accident,* Hairspray, *which co-stars Deborah Harry.*

Brooke Webster *was the owner and promoter of the New York live music party, FraggleRock and the bar Meow Mix and its Los Angeles spin-off, Meow Mix West. Her favorite Blondie song is 'Die Young, Stay Pretty'.*